GUIDE TO CAPE COD

Help Us Keep This Guide Up to Date

Every effort has been made by the author and editors to make this guide as accurate and useful as possible. However, many things can change after a guide is published–establishments close, phone numbers change, facilities come under new management, and so on.

We would love to hear from you concerning your experiences with this guide and how you feel it could be improved and be kept up-to-date. While we may not be able to respond to all comments and suggestions, we'll take them to heart, and we'll also make certain to share them with the author. Please send your comments and suggestions to the following address:

The Globe Pequot Press
Reader Response/Editorial Department
P.O. Box 480
Guilford, CT 06437

Or you may e-mail us at:

editorial@globe-pequot.com

Thanks for your input, and happy travels!

GUIDE TO

Cape Cod

EVERYTHING YOU NEED TO KNOW TO ENJOY ONE OF NEW ENGLAND'S PERFECT VACATION DESTINATIONS

Fifth Edition

by Jerry Morris

The Globe Pequot Press

Guilford, Connecticut

The prices and rates listed in this guidebook were confirmed to be accurate at press time. We recommend, however, that you call establishments before traveling in order to get the most up-to-date information.

Copyright © 1992, 1995, 1998, 2000 by The Globe Pequot Press
Copyright © 1988 by Frederick Pratson

Cover photo: Jane Booth Vollers
Cover, text, and map design: Nancy Freeborn / Freeborn Design
Interior photos: Courtesy of Cape Cod Chamber of Commerce.
Recipes: p. 11: courtesy Wedgewood Inn, Yarmouth; p. 161: courtesy Belfry Inn, Sandwich; p. 198: courtesy Whalewalk Inn, Eastham.

Library of Congress Cataloging-in-Publication Data
Morris, Jerry.
    Guide to Cape Cod : everything you need to know to enjoy one of New England's perfect vacation destinations / by Jerry Morris.—5th ed.
        p. cm.
    Rev. ed. of: Guide to Cape Cod / Frederick Pratson. 4th ed. 1998.
    Includes index.
    ISBN 0-7627-0647-3
        1. Cape Cod (Mass.)—Guidebooks. I. Pratson, Frederick John. Guide to Cape Cod. II. Title.

F72.C3 M69 2000
917.44'920444—dc21

                                                                        00-028438

Manufactured in the United States of America
Fifth Edition/First Printing

CONTENTS

Life on Cape Cod

Visiting Cape Cod

Activities and Attractions

Guide to Towns, Accommodations, and Dining

Cape Cod

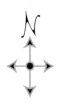

Provincetown

Truro

Wellfleet

Eastham

Orleans

Brewster

Bourne Sandwich

Yarmouth

Dennis

Barnstable

Harwich

Chatham

Mashpee

Falmouth

CHAPTER ONE

Life on Cape Cod

"The Cape"—A Personal View

To many of us who live along the northeastern seaboard of the
United States, the sobriquet "the Cape" means only one vacation
place—Cape Cod in Massachusetts. The Cape, however, is also a
favorite or much-desired vacation destination for travelers from every
other state in the Union, from the provinces of Canada, and from
many other countries.

On this fishhook-shaped peninsula jutting out into the Atlantic are
some of the best beaches and warmest waters in the East. That's the
main reason why so many come frequently to the Cape. But swimming,
sunbathing, and sailing are just part of the Cape's allure. Aesthetics is
another. Here are some of the prettiest villages in all of North America,
arranged one after the other from the Cape Cod Canal all the way to
land's end at Provincetown. The cedar-shingled Cape Cod house, with
roses blooming along slats of white picket fence, is emblematic of the
Cape. This charming style has been replicated in towns all across the
United States and Canada

Although the Cape has a rustic-nostalgic ambience, it also offers
everything for a super vacation: top-quality inns, B&Bs, hotels, resorts,
and motels; outstanding restaurants serving every manner of cuisine
from freshly caught seafood to extraordinary continental meals; leading stars and budding talents performing at playhouses, nightclubs,
bistros, and coffeehouses; every kind of shopping from budget-busting
boutiques and intriguing antiques shops to flea markets; arts-and-
crafts galleries galore; golf, sailboarding, surfing, tennis, bike touring,
seaside-trail hikes, horseback riding, nature walks, deep-sea fishing,

diving, triathlons, marathons, college baseball, and so on; summer camps, writers' and artists' workshops, and courses in just about every aspect of music, the visual arts, and dance; historic homes, fascinating museums, cruises, and whale-watching trips; and still more.

First and foremost, Cape Cod is a family vacation land. In fact, many visitors first came here on family vacations and have been returning ever since; many plan to retire or to begin new, more personally satisfying careers here. The Cape is a romantic place. Here people meet, get married, and honeymoon. Here couples come to renew themselves during priceless moments strolling on a deserted beach or sitting before a blazing hearth. The Cape is where singles, regardless of sexual preference, can experience joy, peace, inspiration, and tolerance. And the Cape is where senior citizens can discover sights, smells, tastes, and solid values reminding them of times that, in these parts, have never gone out of style. There's a special world on the Cape for everyone: the owner of a Rolls-Royce and a Hinckley yacht, the scientist, the intellectual, the artist, the factory worker, the farmer, the computer programmer, and the young of every shape, color, and musical orientation.

The Cape also holds its primacy as an ideal place because most vacationers know that on this once hostile landscape Puritan Pilgrims, English-speaking colonists seeking religious freedom, not only settled but persisted and prospered. Here, as part of Plymouth Colony, the American spirit of democracy was first planted, took root, sprouted, and blossomed all over the continent. The nostalgia for the early days of this country is retained on Cape Cod, and people from all over the world come here to bask in this spirit of freedom, rugged individualism, and self-reliance.

Profile of Cape Cod

A Capsule View of Cape Cod

Cape Cod is a sandy peninsula extending from the east coast of Massachusetts into the Atlantic Ocean. It is in the shape of a fishhook or, for some, of an arm bent at the elbow and forming a fist at land's end. Cape Cod is about 70 miles long, from the town of Bourne in the west to Provincetown in the northeast corner, and from 1 to 20 miles wide. Within the bowl formed by its north and west coasts and the east coast of mainland Massachusetts is Cape Cod Bay. Cape Cod's north and east coasts, at the forearm and fist of the peninsula, are on the open Atlantic Ocean. Most of its south coast is on Nantucket Sound, a body of water between Cape Cod and the Massachusetts islands of Nantucket and Martha's Vineyard.

The village of Woods Hole lies at Cape Cod's southwestern tip. The Elizabeth Islands, strung out to the southwest from Woods Hole, also belong to Massachusetts. Cape Cod's west/southwestern coast is on Buzzards Bay. The Cape Cod Canal at the west/northwest end is, by popular tradition, considered the beginning of Cape Cod, although a portion of the town of Bourne and a small section of the town of Sandwich are on the mainland of Massachusetts, on the west bank of the canal. Most visitors, however, consider themselves to be officially on Cape Cod once they cross the canal over the Bourne or Sagamore bridges. The islands of Martha's Vineyard and Nantucket are not part of Cape Cod, although year-round ferry access to them is available from the villages of Woods Hole and Hyannis. There is also seasonal ferry access to Martha's Vineyard Island from New Bedford. The Elizabeth Islands, a group of sixteen small islands, are privately owned, except for the island and village of Cuttyhunk, which are accessible by year-round public ferry from the city of New Bedford.

Cape Cod itself is divided into three regions comprising fifteen towns and a number of villages: the Upper Cape, composed of the towns of Bourne, Falmouth, Sandwich, and Mashpee; the Mid-Cape, with the towns of Barnstable, Yarmouth, Dennis, Brewster, Harwich, and Chatham; and the Lower Cape, with its towns of Orleans, Eastham, Wellfleet, Truro, and Provincetown. All Cape Cod towns are on the seacoast and have beaches, village harbors, and other water-related attractions and conveniences. The village of Hyannis is the commercial, retailing, transportation, and tourism center of Cape Cod. Massachusetts Military Reservation is located within the widest portion of the Upper Cape in Bourne and Sandwich.

The Upper and Mid-Cape regions have the highest year-round populations on the peninsula. The towns of the Lower Cape are less populated but rapidly growing nevertheless. In fact, Cape Cod is one of the fastest-growing areas of Massachusetts. The current year-round population is close to 210,000. The working part of this population is employed in tourism, retail services, fishing, education, and scientific research. Many people are retired from various professions and occupations. During the summer season all Cape Cod towns double or even triple their population with the influx of vacation-home owners and tourists. Except at the business centers of towns and villages, there is plenty of room on Cape Cod for people to spread out and discover their special place of peace and enjoyment.

A Blessed Landscape

Cape Cod was created by the great glaciers that spread over much of what is now Canada and the northern United States. The last of these incredible ice sheets covered Cape Cod and the islands of Martha's Vineyard and Nantucket about 25,000 years ago. Approximately 9,000 years closer to our time, the leading edge of the last of these glaciers melted and receded north, revealing massive deposits of rock and soil that had collected on bedrock. These geological collecting points gave Cape Cod its distinctive fishhook shape and formed the Elizabeth Islands and the islands of Martha's Vineyard and Nantucket. The glacier acted first like a bulldozer, pushing material forward as it advanced, then like a squeegee blade, pulling over and smoothing this debris as it melted back. In geological terms, the forward motion of the glacier built a moraine, the high-ridged spine of the Cape. The retreat formed outwash plains, the extensive flat area along the south coast of the Cape.

When you drive on the Mid-Cape Highway, Route 6, heading east toward Hyannis, you move along this high spine or moraine. Here on high ground you can see the landscape dropping off into a broad, level plain. The glacier also gouged out the many ponds and kettle holes that pockmark most of Cape Cod. Initially these large holes in the ground were filled with melted glacier ice water. They have been replenished ever since with freshwater from rain and underground streams and now provide excellent fishing, boating, and swimming. Through the millenniums the surrounding sea itself has helped to shape Cape Cod's unique configuration. The sea has added shoreline and taken it away; it has created elongated sandbars and covered over others; and it has opened channels and closed others, such as Chatham.

Today's Cape Cod landscape is a composite of many beautiful facets: some of the most magnificent sand dunes and high sand cliffs on the Atlantic coast of North America; long stretches of sand beaches; extensive salt marshes; many estuaries, ponds, kettle holes, bays, streams, rivers, harbors, islands, herring runs, inlets, and peninsulas; and thick woodlands, productive farmlands, and world-famous cranberry bogs. While pitch pines and scrub oaks are two of Cape Cod's dominant flora, the peninsula is also replete with stately elms, maples, and beeches. The flora here is gorgeous and fragrant—rosa ragusa (beach rose), bayberry, heather, holly, honeysuckle, rhododendrons, tiger lilies, and lilacs. There are peach and apple orchards, too, as well as gardens abundant in diverse flowers, vegetables, and fruits.

White-tailed deer still roam the diminishing woodlands of Cape Cod. Ospreys, Canada geese, terns, swallows, swans, sparrow hawks, red-winged blackbirds, herons, owls, and a host of other species make Cape Cod their home or stop-off point for a respite while on their annual migratory flights. Horseshoe and fiddler crabs, oysters, quahogs, razor clams, mussels, scallops, periwinkles, and whelks live and reproduce in abundance within the bays and inlets. Out at sea, within sight of shore, are lobsters, swordfish, striped bass, squid, bluefish, sharks (even the great white ones), and the venerable cod. But the crux of this complex and interconnected ecology is the surrounding sea, along with four distinct seasons and the ever-changing weather. The sea surrounds the Cape, and it is never too distant from wherever one is. The sea is moody, unpredictable, fickle. It can be inspirational one day, threatening the next.

Millennia of Human Habitation

No one knows for sure when humans first settled on Cape Cod. There are, however, native people living here today whose lineage on the Cape extends back to when the last Ice Age glacier retreated north and the land once again became acceptable to human habitation, a span of thousands of years. These native people, living together in tribes or clans, were called by many different tribal names. They organized themselves into a broader confederation, or alliance, of tribes that extended far beyond Cape Cod. This alliance was, and still is, known by the name Wampanoag, very much a group of independent states within a nation of self-governing peoples. The Wampanoag nation, in turn, was related to many other nations of native peoples by virtue of a common language, known as Algonquin. They inhabited much of what is now the eastern United States and Canada.

Because of the relatively mild climate and favorable soil conditions, the native people of Cape Cod were highly productive farmers in addition to being hunters and fishermen. Their communal way of life and the distinct culture they developed—arts, music, oral history, and religion—suited them well enough to allow them to live in harmony with nature for millennia. They placed high value on personal courage, integrity, and friendship, both among themselves and that extended to strangers coming into their midst. They saw themselves not as possessors of the land, but as its trustees. The land was to be used to serve their needs and to be venerated as a blessing from God.

Once the European presence took hold, however, the civilization of the native people on the Cape, as elsewhere on the continent, quickly weakened and faded. The insatiable desire for land on the part of the newcomers, often accompanied by greed and always by legal documents and the force of arms, destroyed the ancient concept of trusteeship and replaced it with absolute ownership according to foreign law. In addition, the colonists brought with them various diseases for which the native population had no immunity nor methods of cure. Their population was decimated. Once-thriving villages became silent and devoid of life. Outraged, in one final attempt to drive out the Europeans, the Wampanoags went to war under the leadership of the charismatic Metacomet, also known as King Philip, son of the great chief Massasoit, who welcomed and protected the first Pilgrims and who helped them to survive. King Philip's War lasted about a year and resulted in slaughter on both sides and ultimate defeat for the native people in 1676, fifty-six years after the landing of the Pilgrims at the place they called Plymouth.

Since that time the native population of Cape Cod has diminished until some believed it had disappeared altogether. Not quite. In Mashpee, for example, it is an important part of the population, as it is at Gay Head on Martha's Vineyard Island. The Wampanoags continue to decide contemporary issues affecting their destiny through their tribal councils. Their annual Mashpee Powwow brings together native peoples from all over the United States and Canada for the purpose of sharing and taking sustenance from their ancient culture.

There is speculation, though no firm evidence, that the first Europeans to sail along the coasts of Cape Cod were Vikings from Scandinavia. There is some credibility to this supposition because the Vikings had established a settlement on the northern tip of the island of Newfoundland at what is now L'Anse-aux-Meadows. After traversing the North Atlantic in their longboats and making settlement on Newfoundland, it is entirely plausible for them to have explored the coasts of North America. The mystery is why these intrepid explorers did not establish a Viking town in this more congenial climate.

Between A.D. 1500 and 1600 a number of European explorers—notably Portugal's Miguel Corte Real, England's Bartholomew Gosnold, and France's Samuel de Champlain—sailed along Cape Cod's shores. In addition, fishing vessels from Europe, their identity largely unknown to history, came into the area in search of valuable cod. It was not until 1620, however, that English Puritans ("Saints," they called themselves) under the leadership of William Bradford and William Brewster, diverted from their goal of establishing a colony in Virginia either by circumstance or the hand of God, made their first landfall in the New World on Cape Cod at Provincetown. They had their first encounter, actually an armed conflict, with the Cape's native people on the beach at Eastham. Continuing across Cape Cod Bay on the Mayflower, these Pilgrims stepped ashore on terrain that was to support one of the first permanent English settlements in North America.

Once Plymouth, their "New Jerusalem," was established and secured, shiploads of additional settlers arrived. Some of these "new-

WHAT'S IN A NAME?

Would you go visit Pallavisino? That's the early name for Cape Cod. Long before the Pilgrims arrived at Provincetown, Europeans were exploring the area. It was in 1524 that Giovanni da Verrazano saw what he described as an arm-shaped piece of land and named it for an Italian general, Pallavisino.

Then in 1602 Bartholomew Gosnold, looking for a passage to Asia, as well as sassafras, which was believed to be a cure for syphilis, renamed this land Cape Cod.

Gosnold's observations only encouraged Europeans to visit. He reported on the huge quantities of cod to be found, and that, unlike Newfoundland, these fish were found in much shallower water and close to shore.

comers" found Plymouth crowded and much of its worthwhile land already taken or selling at too high a price, not unlike today. They moved on to new lands, such as those of Cape Cod. These lands were bought for a pittance or stolen from the native people by a mind-set that considered itself superior and predestined by the Pilgrim's deity to bring civilization to a hostile wilderness and prosperity to themselves. These "deals" were sealed on parchment, backed by courts, and enforced by the militia.

With extensive English settlement of Cape Cod gaining momentum ten years after the first Pilgrim landing, the peninsula was amalgamated into Plymouth Colony. Sandwich, Barnstable, Eastham, and Yarmouth became the Cape's first towns. For thirty-seven years Plymouth Colony was administered by a governor residing in the town of Plymouth. In 1657, however, Eastham's Thomas Prence became governor, and the colony's political power now flowed from Cape Cod for several decades. What limited self-governance Plymouth Colony enjoyed was short-lived. King James II attempted to reclaim full and total sovereignty of the American colonies through agents such as Sir Edmund Andros, who was thwarted in carrying out this purpose by the crafty Yankees. The ascension to the throne of William of Orange quieted the restive colonials for a while; but soon after, Plymouth Colony as such ceased to exist. Plymouth, Massachusetts, Maine, and Nova Scotia colonies were combined into one colony, or province, by royal decree in 1691. The period from 1676 to 1763 saw Cape Cod men fighting in King Philip's War, the so-called French and Indian War, and the British campaigns to wrest control of Canada from the French.

Although Cape Codders considered themselves loyal subjects of the Crown, they did not take too kindly to being forced by it and Parliament to swallow without protest laws and administrative inconveniences that they considered oppressive and degrading to free men and women. When the Declaration of Independence was proclaimed in 1776, therefore, Cape Codders could be found on both sides—patriots and loyalists. As the bitterness of the conflict grew in intensity, Cape Cod loyalists left their homes and journeyed with others sharing their sympathies north to Canada to begin life anew, while the patriots fought for their liberty under General Washington and his officers. Both the patriots and the loyalists expressed their courage and resolve despite their doing so from different points of view. Years later, when passions had cooled somewhat and tolerance was no longer viewed as treason, some Cape loyalists returned to their hometowns, where they resumed life without acquiescence to a foreign king.

No great, epic battles were fought on Cape Cod to rival those at Bunker Hill, Saratoga, Bennington, and Yorktown. In 1779, however, a force of British troops attempted to land at Falmouth. They were sent scurrying back to their ship by local men wielding loaded cannon, primed muskets, and honed cutlasses. During the War for Independence and the War of 1812, Cape Cod towns suffered hardships due to British blockades. Cape Codders were prevented from sailing out of their own harbors to fish and to transport their wares. And when captured at sea, some were impressed into manning British ships, often under cruel conditions. When British blockade ships ran low on supplies, it was common practice to send their sailors ashore to take what was needed out of town larders and storehouses, frequently without payment and much to the distress of Cape Codders.

When the wars with Great Britain finally came to an end and both countries entered a sustained period of peace that developed into the closest of friendships, the history of Cape Cod became focused on economics—commercial enterprises and occupations that would provide a decent living and, for the extra diligent, a profit. Right from the beginning, in the early seventeenth century, the Atlantic cod fishery was the big moneymaker and reason for settlement. Being almost completely surrounded by the sea and possessing many fine harbors, usually ice-free in the winter, Cape Cod was a perfect launching pad from which to go out onto the deep waters. A number of Cape Codders fished as far north as the Grand Banks. Some eventually settled in towns and villages throughout the Canadian Maritime provinces and imparted to their culture a bit of Cape Cod. Along with the fishery came the development of such allied industries as sail making and boatbuilding.

Whaling also began early on Cape Cod. The first settlers found whales that had for no explicable reason beached themselves, as they continue to do so today. From the blubber the settlers rendered oil, which was used in candle making, as a fuel for lamps, as a lubricant, and for a wide variety of other useful purposes. As the demand for whale oil and other products increased, Cape Codders built stouter boats and went after the whales with a frenzy and an eye to good profits. In time the center of the whaling industry shifted from Cape Cod to Nantucket Island and to New Bedford, but also in time it faded away in all these places due to the large-scale commercialization of fossil fuels.

One important benefit from whaling was that it brought a new person to Cape Cod—the Cape Verdean. During long whaling voyages, typically lasting several years, it was not unusual for discontented, lonely seamen to jump ship, leaving the vessel's master shorthanded.

The Cape Verde Islands, a Portuguese colony located off the west coast of Africa, were a major resupply point for Yankee whalers. Here the whaling masters were also able to recruit Cape Verdean men to replenish their crews. When the ships came back to their Cape Cod, Nantucket, Martha's Vineyard, and New Bedford ports, many of these Cape Verdean seamen, finding themselves stranded on American shores, elected to stay rather than return to their native islands. As a result, the Cape Verdean presence on Cape Cod and in southeastern Massachusetts has existed since the nineteenth century. These industrious people came from one of the most arid archipelagos on earth, yet on Cape Cod they became some of the best vegetable and fruit farmers.

In addition to the industries of whaling and fishing, Cape Codders built speedy packet boats, which became the quickest method of moving goods and people from port to port along the coast of New England. Cape Codders also became actively involved in the international maritime trade, with some making sizable fortunes in their journeys throughout the world. Cape Cod's prosperity from these daring ventures can be seen in the gorgeous homes and estates built by sea captains and land-based merchant investors. They bought the best available lifestyle at the time from the immense profits they earned. Agriculture also contributed to the Cape's economy. Dairy and small crop farms supplied the needs of the local people. The American cranberry-growing and -processing industries began in this region. Cranberry production continues to be an important moneymaker for Cape Codders. The bogs are familiar features on the Upper and Mid-Cape landscapes. They are at their most beautiful in autumn, when the berries, floated on top of water, form acres of brilliant red carpet against deep greens of surrounding woodland and below an ultramarine blue sky. To see this juxtaposition of colors is a memorable visual experience.

Although playing a vital role in the forming of America, Cape Cod became kind of a somnolent backwater of the country as other regions pushed, bullied, and built themselves into prominence. Until the advent of large-scale tourism, Cape Cod essentially remained a place of small towns and villages where the Yankee ethos of self-reliance, hard work, religion, neighborliness, thrift, patience, and prudence was dominant. Deception and fraud existed, of course, but to a lesser degree than they did wherever life moved along at a more frenetic pace.

In a very real sense those frenzies, pressures, and stresses that plagued Americans in other parts of the country were responsible for the resurgence of Cape Cod. Because Cape Cod retained the attractive-

CRANBERRY TREAT

Long associated with Thanksgiving and turkey, the cranberry is finding its way into many a treat. On the back roads of the Cape you can
still find cranberry bogs, and in Harwich there is an annual Cranberry Harvest Festival in October. But at the Wedgewood Inn in
Yarmouth you can treat yourself to some of Gerrie Graham's delicious Cranberry Fruit-Nut Bread.

To make it, take 2 cups all-purpose sifted flour, 1 cup sugar, 1½
teaspoons double-acting baking powder, ½ teaspoon baking soda, 1
teaspoon salt, ¼ cup shortening, ¾ cup orange juice, 1 egg well
beaten, ½ cup chopped nuts (a generous cup), and 2 cups fresh cranberries, chopped.

Sift together the flour, sugar, baking powder, baking soda, and
salt. Cut in shortening until mixture resembles coarse cornmeal.
Combine orange juice with the well-beaten egg. Pour orange-egg mixture all at once into dry ingredients, mixing just enough to dampen.
Carefully fold in chopped nuts and cranberries. Spoon into greased
loaf pan (9 x 5 x 3 inch). Spread corners and sides slightly higher than
center. Bake in moderate oven, 350° Fahrenheit, about an hour until
crust is golden brown and inserted tooth-pick comes out clean.
Remove from pan, cool, store overnight for easy slicing. The bread
freezes well.

It's also a treat to stay at Gerrie and Milt Graham's Wedgewood
Inn, a majestic-looking home built in 1812 for a maritime attorney.
Opened as an inn in 1983, the structure has been refurbished, and a
Carriage House out back offers more modern rooms, along with an
impressive common room. Breakfasts are in the main house along
Route 6A.

ness and the values of America's past in addition to the allures of a
gentle climate and seashore, the movers and shakers of this country
discovered that they could renew both their spirits and bodies here.
Cape Cod became synonymous with relaxation, with letting the
wounds heal and the cobwebs fall away; with enjoying friends without
many of the stifling, formal conventions of urban society; and experiencing the magnificent natural environment of the Cape. Cape Cod
took on a new luster and became even more fashionable when John F.

Kennedy was elected president of the United States and the family compound in Hyannisport became the Summer White House in the early 1960s.

Also attracted to Cape Cod during the summer were artists, writers, actors, philosophers, and scientists. The creative people and the intellectuals came not only to lounge on the beach or in hammocks while sipping gin and tonics but to produce ideas of substantial value. Some of America's greatest talents received inspiration for their work on the Cape. The scientist Louis Agassiz and the playwright Eugene O'Neill are but two of many such individuals. With both the affluent and the intellectual giving an enthusiastic imprimatur to summertime on the Cape, others of more modest bank accounts and/or abilities discovered this peninsula to be their most favorite vacation place as well. Cape Cod became accessible to the general public with the building of better highways and widespread automobile ownership. With more people coming onto the Cape, more places of accommodation, restaurants, attractions, entertainment, gift shops, and diversions were developed to serve their needs.

Along with the transformation of Cape Cod into a popular vacation spot, another phenomenon took hold. As people fell in love with the natural and human environment of the Cape during the summer, many decided that *this* was the place to spend their retirement years.

This phenomenon has not abated. Each year retirees settle in by the thousands, and the permanent population of the Cape continues to grow, as do the various kinds of businesses and professions that serve their needs. In addition to the retirees, the young and middle-aged, representing a wide range of professions, crafts, and occupations, have moved onto the Cape. There is also an increasing population of top-level business executives who reside year-round on the Cape but who commute to offices in Boston and New York City. The real estate and land-development businesses have enjoyed an upward curve in sales and prices thanks to this influx. That rose-festooned Cape Cod cottage in Chatham that cost $20,000 a couple of decades ago now goes for up to $1 million. Those who bought low and held on have surely profited.

In the not-too-distant past, Cape Codders were a relatively homogeneous breed in terms of ethnicity, religion, attitudes, and family longevity on this peninsula. They were the overwhelming majority, and their culture dominated. The typical Cape Codder was a Republican Protestant who made a living at a small entrepreneurial operation. Today's Cape Codders are far more diverse. Their ancestry is Portuguese, Greek, Quebec-French, Polish, Italian, Finnish, Irish, African, and Asian. Residents today are Roman Catholic, Jewish, Mormon, Baptist, Episcopalian, Methodist, Lutheran, Congregational, and Greek Orthodox. The majority of Cape Codders now tend to vote Democratic rather than Republican. The Cape Cod ethos has changed so radically that the region now includes one of the country's largest gay communities (at Provincetown), enclaves of multimillion-dollar homes such as those at Oyster Harbors, and some of the finest scientific minds in the world doing oceanographic and biological research at Woods Hole. Cape Cod's villages of the past are gone, but their glowing nostalgia and lovely appearances remain. The pace of living is faster now, and the roads can get as crowded, slow moving, and grid-locked as in any urban area. Yet one can find places throughout the Cape that are isolated, where there are only the sounds of wind and sea, and where beaches seem to extend forever.

The Four Seasons of Cape Cod

Cape Cod is a favorite vacation destination in all four seasons of the year. Holiday weekends throughout the year draw large numbers of visitors. For example, many people have made it their tradition to spend the Thanksgiving and Christmas holidays on the Cape because its early American atmosphere creates the perfect setting and mood.

The holiday weekends of Memorial Day, Fourth of July, Labor Day, and Columbus Day are peak periods within peak periods. Because of the relatively mild climate in fall, winter, and spring, Cape Cod has become well known for offering year-round golf, an unexpected treat for those who consider New England woefully frigid.

The summer season begins in mid-May and concludes around mid-September, with July and August being the peak months. At the height of summer, temperatures seldom rise above 80° Fahrenheit, although as in 1999's heat wave many did give thought to installing air conditioning. The Cape has a generous share of perfect beach weather—bright skies, fluffy clouds, warm water, and comfortable temperatures. There are also "pea-soup" foggy days, however, when figures on the beach become ghostly apparitions in the mist. While it's foggy along the coast, though, it's usually oppressively hot, hazy, and humid well inland. Ocean water for swimming is warmest from August to the end of September. Every kind of leisure-time activity takes place on the Cape during the summer—swimming, boating, surfing, golf, tennis, baseball, beachcombing, biking, hiking, picnics, fishing, and so on. People come to the Cape to relax, to be themselves, and to shed many of the hangups and formalities that beset them back home.

Unless you are going to some swank affairs, comfortable, casual clothing is all you need to bring—shorts, cotton sweaters, sports jackets, light dresses, bathing suits, and some foul-weather gear (rain jacket and hat). The best restaurants on the Cape like to see men come in wearing jackets, but ties are optional; light-fabric skirts, dresses, or pants are right for women. Most places of business will not allow you in their establishments without shoes and a shirt.

Autumn on Cape Cod is perhaps its most prized time. The weather is usually mild. The water is still warm enough for swimming. The atmosphere is usually crystal clear and invigorating. The sky and the ocean are rich shades of blue. The flora of the Cape becomes a feast for the eyes in its array of reds, yellows, and oranges. There are fewer people on the Cape, and you thus have more elbowroom and less competition for tables at favorite restaurants. The golf links are at their best and so is the sailing. Most hotels, inns, and motels lower their prices considerably, and there are sales and bargains everywhere. If you liked the Cape in summer, you'll adore it in autumn. The Thanksgiving holiday has special meaning on the Cape because the very first one in America was celebrated at Provincetown. Although the Pilgrims had their first Thanksgiving feast in nearby Plymouth, the first prayers of thanksgiving were offered by them in 1620 at Provincetown before they landed at Plymouth. What could be better than enjoying your Thanksgiving Day feast at an old Cape Cod inn with all the trimmings, both in terms of food and heritage?

It used to be the perception among outsiders that winter was the Cape's somnolent time, when things and people went into hibernation. While it is true that much of nature goes to sleep in winter, however, this season has traditionally been a highly productive time for the year-round residents of Cape Cod. There are enough social, cultural, civic, sporting, and educational events going on every day to exhaust even the most energetic individual.

If you've ever wanted to walk for miles on a beach totally empty of humans, this is the time to come to the Cape. The clarity of light dur-

CHANGE

I have witnessed the end of an era. My house overlooks a wonderful marsh in South Chatham that for years had a 300-foot towering radio antenna and numerous poles hung with wires. These served as the main communications center for ships at sea. The radio station, WCC (Wireless Cape Cod), was a direct descendant of the Marconi Wireless Station, which pioneered transatlantic communication from Wellfleet.

From that station news of the *Titanic* disaster first reached the United States. Later WCC would help with the first polar expeditions, provide weather information to Charles Lindbergh on his transatlantic flight, even handled the last communications with Amelia Earhart before she disappeared on her round-the-world flight.

The Chatham station ended operations in 1997, its work taken over by satellites. In a generous move, MCI, the last owners of the station, sold its multimillion-acre land holding in South and North Chatham to the town for a mere $900,000, the cost of removing the antenna and transmitting station.

Now the town owns Forest Beach, and the marsh that backs up to it. Only a couple of poles remain, nesting homes to ospreys.

A bit of this communications history can be viewed in Orleans at the French Transatlantic Cable Station Museum, a humble-looking building from which a cable once ran across the ocean floor linking Europe and North America.

ing the winter months is superb. If you need to get away from the stress of your job, the Cape in winter will help renew you. Enough fine places of accommodation and restaurants are open to take care of your needs. Just bring warm clothes and a camera to capture those beautiful facets of Cape Cod that are denied to those who just come here in summer.

"Fickle" is the word that best describes spring on Cape Cod. Sometimes spring comes early, sometimes late. The only thing you can count on from a Cape Cod spring is its unpredictability. In April many of the places of accommodation and restaurants that closed up for the winter begin reopening. Along with migratory birds, tourists and residents who spend the winter months in Florida begin arriving with the sprouting of crocuses and tulips. You see more people on the golf links and more boats going into the water. In a very real sense mid-May is the start of Cape Cod's "new year," when year-round folks smile a bit more and anticipate the crazy, frenetic season when the narrow peninsula once again welcomes visitors from every state in the Union, every province of Canada, and scores of countries around the globe.

Living, Retiring, and Working on Cape Cod

It is inevitable. People come to Cape Cod, fall in love with the place, then make plans to move and live there permanently. The population on Cape Cod continues to grow and has produced advantages: a greater variety, quantity, and quality of services; a more diverse, affluent, and better-educated population; increased commercial and business activities and opportunities; improved schools and medical facilities; and a broader selection of cultural activities. The disadvantages include higher real estate prices, a labor shortage, an increasing demand on town services (water, roads, sewage, police, fire, etc.), and traffic congestion.

The Cape is especially attractive to retirees. The winter climate is relatively mild, and the lifestyle is very comfortable, though not inexpensive. You'll find most of the services you need on the Cape—doctors, dentists, lawyers, and stockbrokers. There are all kinds of educational and cultural programs in which to participate. Every Cape Cod town has agencies and organizations that serve the needs of retired people. Many local businesses have jobs for retirees, and there are countless opportunities for volunteering.

Cape Cod for Canadian and British Visitors

International visitors have been arriving on Cape Cod in greater numbers in recent years. Canadians, of course, have been arriving for years, as there are strong ties between Canada and Cape Cod. Many towns in the Canadian Atlantic Provinces (Nova Scotia, Prince Edward Island, and New Brunswick, in particular) were settled by Cape Cod families especially before and during the American Revolution, when those loyal to the crown sought refuge from the independence-minded colonists.

There are other ties that bind. During the nineteenth and twentieth centuries, thousands of French-Canadians (Quebeçois) settled in New England mill towns and factory cities. Some of their American-born progeny established businesses on Cape Cod or came to work here in many different professions and occupations. The same can be said for thousands of English-speaking Canadians who also came to work in New England, known to them as "The Boston States."

If you are interested in your family's genealogy, local historical societies will help you trace your roots on Cape Cod. Today it is quite common to see cars bearing license plates from most of the Canadian provinces. Many businesses catering to tourists fly the Canadian maple-leaf flag alongside the Stars and Stripes. The number of Canadian visitors is directly tied to the value of the Canadian dollar versus the American. In 1999, when the Canadian dollar was at an all-time low, few Canadians ventured south to Cape Cod or New England

More and more people from Great Britain are coming to Cape Cod for vacations. British accents are heard in every town and village. Although Cape Codders were ardent revolutionaries and builders of the United States, strong Anglophilia has always existed on this hook-shaped peninsula, perhaps more so today than before. The Union Jack is a common sight; a scenic highway commemorates the "Old King," Charles II; there is an inn named after Queen Anne; there are towns named after their counterparts in England; steak and kidney pie, fish and chips, and Bass Ale are on the menus at a number of eateries.

More recently, other international visitors have discovered the Cape. A frequently heard language is that of German. WE SPEAK GERMAN is a sign that can be found outside many an inn. Irish and Jamaican accents can also be heard at businesses that cater to tourists. Many Irish and Jamaican students have work permits that allow them to work on Cape Cod from May through October.

CHAPTER TWO

Visiting Cape Cod

Easy to Reach, Enjoy

Cape Cod is very easy to reach. A car is still the best means of transportation, though. Even though there is bus service between some areas of the Cape, the best way to discover all the Cape offers is to have the freedom of your own wheels.

Those who do travel by other means of transportation will find rental vehicles available in the larger towns of Cape Cod as well as airports in Boston and Providence, Rhode Island. The drive from either city to the Cape bridges is less than ninety minutes. The Cape is also included in many package tours sold through travel agents or found in travel sections of newspapers and magazines. While a package tour can eliminate the need to look for accommodations, meals, or activities, a guide such as this will help not only in choosing a package tour by comparing what is offered on the tour and what is available on Cape Cod, but also in choosing activities or dining when on your own from the tour.

For those who need to arrive on Cape Cod without a car, there are good alternatives. Hyannis, the Cape's hub, has good air service from Boston, Providence, New York, and elsewhere. Excellent bus service is available from Boston and Providence. Amtrak, at present, offers only connecting bus service to the Cape.

Boat service is available during the summer from downtown Boston to Provincetown, making a day trip or longer stay on the Cape very easy. Even those just visiting "America's hometown," Plymouth, will find seasonal daily boat service to Provincetown.

The question for most visitors is where to go on Cape Cod. There really is no wrong choice, and once on the Cape visiting other areas is easy. Sandwich and Falmouth are the first towns over the bridges. Falmouth has miles of sandy beaches and is the gateway to Martha's Vineyard. Sandwich is the oldest town on the Cape, as well as one of its prettiest. It has beaches with sand dunes, and the best museum on the Cape—Heritage Plantation, with wonderful gardens, lots of Americana, and a great auto museum within a replica of a Shaker barn.

Hyannis is the commercial center of the Cape, with huge shopping centers including a mall with all the name stores. The largest year-round resorts and motels are here. It is the home of the Kennedys, the air center of the Cape, and the ferry and plane connection to Martha's Vineyard and Nantucket. It is also a good hub, as no point on Cape Cod is more than an hour's drive from Hyannis. In summer, especially on a rainy day, it can be very congested with visitors.

Yarmouth, just next door, can be equally congested in summer, especially along Route 28 on the south side. But that stretch also offers some of the best accommodations—at reasonable prices—attrac-

FROM COD TO DOGFISH

"Chatham, a quaint drinking village with a fishing problem" reads the bumper sticker. While most will see this as a bit of humor, there's a bit of sadness to it as well. For Chatham, as well as other Cape Cod fishing villages, does have a fishing problem.

The cod, so important to New England and Maritime Canada, is dwindling in supply. Measures to limit fishing cod are being taken, putting fishermen up and down the coast out of business.

The cod has been so important to the economy of Massachusetts that it is the official state fish. A large cod sculpture has hung for more than a hundred years over the House of Representatives at the State House in Boston. While fishermen still leave from the Chatham Fishing Pier, you may more than likely see dogfish, rather than cod, in their catch.

The dogfish, once scorned, has become a fish in demand. A spiny miniature shark, the dogfish is popular in Europe, where it is served as fish and chips. It's also popular in Asia, where it is used for shark fin soup. The belly flaps of the fish are used to make fish jerky, and its brains are used in cancer research.

tions, and restaurants. On the Cape Cod Bay side along Route 6A, Yarmouth takes on an entirely different look, with the images one expects of the Cape.

Provincetown, at the very tip of Cape Cod, has its own flavor. Provincetown is unique: It's where the Pilgrims first landed, it has been both a colorful fishing village and an artists' colony, it has sand dunes and the National Seashore, and it offers a lively and accepting gay scene. However, whichever town you choose to stay in on Cape Cod, you'll find places to satisfy all your vacation needs.

A friend, for example, has been vacationing for the last twenty years at the very same cottage colony just steps from Dennis along Cape Cod Bay. I have chosen Chatham, at the "elbow" of the Cape, to live. It has all the Cape experiences—sandy beaches, a lighthouse, a picturesque village with great shops, classic inns, fishing, nature preserves, and great dining. When we first looked for a house, a real estate agent tried to lure us to Orleans—"It's always sunny here when Chatham is foggy." We found there is some truth to that, but Chatham's ambience, as well as the view from our house, is one I wouldn't trade for anywhere else on the Cape.

Getting the Most Value Out of Your Cape Vacation

The information provided in this guide has been structured so that it is easy to use and quick to get to when you need to know something fast. For example, two of the most important areas of concern for travelers are where to stay and where to eat. Recommendations of accommodations and restaurants are listed immediately after a description of each town. Categories such as beaches, entertainment, and sports activities, however, have separate listings that reveal at a glance the full range of options available to you on Cape Cod. The index at the end of the book is also a quick, convenient locator of information. Specific dollars-and-cents information is not given in this guide because it is probable that such figures will not be accurate by the time you read this book. The most direct way to know what it will cost is to contact the places of accommodation and other businesses listed in these pages. Addresses and telephone numbers, as well as Web sites or e-mail addresses, have been provided herein for that purpose.

Practical Information

TELEPHONE AREA CODE

All Cape Cod towns are area code 508.

SEAT BELTS

It is the law in Massachusetts that drivers and passengers wear seat belts. It is a secondary offense: If you are stopped for a traffic violation and are not wearing a seat belt, you will be fined.

MOTORCYCLE HELMETS

It is Massachusetts law, enforced by fines, that all persons driving/riding motorcycles wear safety helmets.

LIQUOR PURCHASE & USE

It is the law in Massachusetts that persons purchasing liquor in retail outlets, lounges, taverns, restaurants, and the like must be at least twenty-one years of age. If there is doubt about your age, you will be asked to supply legal proof. Massachusetts has strict laws regarding the legal drinking age and imposes penalties on both the purchaser and the seller. The laws are also severe for driving under the influence of drugs or alcohol.

BANKING

Cape Cod banks are open daily generally from 9:00 A.M. to 3:00 P.M., and many branches have extended weekday hours and hours on Saturday. The larger Boston banks have branches on the Cape. As of this writing, BankBoston and Fleet Bank have merged. The new Fleet Boston Bank is maintaining all locations of the former BankBoston and selling the Fleet locations to banks on Cape Cod from outside Massachusetts. Supermarkets, such as Stop & Shop, have bank branches in their stores that are open into the evening and on Saturday and Sunday. A tip: If you need cash and do not want to pay ATM fees, use your ATM bank card to purchase food in a supermarket and ask for cash back. Be sure to check before going through the checkout line to be sure the supermarket accepts your card, and what the limit on cash is. ATM machines can be found throughout Cape Cod in banks, stand-alone sites, supermarkets, and some gas stations and convenience stores.

CREDIT CARDS OR CASH

Visa, MasterCard, and their international equivalents are widely accepted throughout Cape Cod. American Express is also accepted at many establishments. Diners Club, Carte Blanche, and Discover cards are accepted but not as widely as the other three. Some stores, places of accommodation, and restaurants, however, do business on a "cash only" (including traveler's checks) basis. When in doubt, ask before you purchase.

BUSINESS HOURS

Business hours on Cape Cod typically run from 8:30 or 9:00 A.M. to 4:30 or 5:00 P.M. Retail stores are open from 9:30 or 10:00 A.M. to 6:00 P.M. Malls and stores catering to visitors stay open to 9:30 P.M., sometimes later. All are open Sundays from 10:00 A.M. to at least 6:00 P.M. There are also some supermarkets and convenience stores that operate twenty-four hours a day every day.

RELIGIOUS SERVICES

Most religious groups have churches, temples, or meeting houses on Cape Cod, and visitors are welcome to attend.

TIPPING

For a restaurant bill, excluding the state tax, 15 to 20 percent is appropriate; for chambermaids, two to three dollars per night is fine. Leave tips for students working in various establishments.

RENTAL CARS

Hertz, Avis, Enterprise, Budget, Thrifty, and National provide rental services in large communities such as Falmouth, Hyannis, Chatham, Dennis, Harwich, Orleans, Brewster, and Provincetown.

SEASONS

Although the period from mid-June to mid-September is still the most popular time, Cape Cod has become a four-season getaway. Fall, especially with foliage and harvest festivals, as well as lower prices, is attracting more visitors to the Cape. Visitors in winter and spring will find a quieter, more relaxing time, ideal for discovering a cozy inn, walking the beaches, or even playing golf. There are good shopping, dining, accommodations, and activities available all year.

WEATHER

Average temperatures (in degrees Fahrenheit)

	High	Low		High	Low		High	Low
January	40	25	May	62	48	September	70	56
February	41	26	June	71	56	October	59	47
March	42	28	July	78	63	Nivember	49	37
April	53	40	August	76	61	December	40	26

Average rainfall (in inches by month)

May	3.2	July	3.0	September	2.8
June	2.9	August	3.5	October	3.3

For the latest weather information, call 771–5522.

Accommodations

The system for determining the cost of accommodations used in this guide is as follows: under $60 = inexpensive; $60 to $120 = moderate; $120 and up = expensive. Keep in mind that Cape Cod is a resort area in a higher priced region of the country and is priced accordingly.

High-season for most places of accommodation on the Cape is approximately from mid-June to mid-September, although a number of them advertise a lower "off-season" until the beginning of July and do so again after Labor Day. July and August are the busiest months. Advance reservations at the best inns, resorts, motels, and B&Bs are essential during those months, although you may still be able to find a room during the busy period. Many establishments require a deposit in advance and/or major credit card information.

During high-season almost every place of accommodation charges top rates. When making reservations, be sure to ask about packages that can provide lower rates and extra services, meal discounts, and various amenities as incentives: AARP and autoclub discounts, special rates for children, and meal plans.

If you have difficulty finding accommodations, call the local chamber of commerce information office, which maintains a list of available lodging. This can be particularly helpful during holiday periods.

Cottages and homes close to beaches are available for rent throughout Cape Cod during the summer season. The cost of renting a fully furnished home with a water view at peak season can range from $1,000 to more than $2,000 a week. Homes available during the months of May, June, September, and October can rent for less. There is also a large selection of more modest homes and cottages that rent from $350 to $1,000 per week, with lower rates in off-season. Most rentals are arranged through real estate agencies located in the various towns and villages on Cape Cod.

The Cape Cod Chamber of Commerce will be happy to supply you with information about accommodations on the Cape. Contact the chamber at (888) 332-2732 or 862-0700, by fax at 362-3698, or on the Internet at www.capecodchamber.org. For bed-and-breakfast accommodations, write Bed & Breakfast Cape Cod, P.O. Box 1312C, Orleans, 02360, or call (800) 541-6226.

Pets are being welcomed at more and more lodging places on the Cape. Do check before arriving at the door. Also, pets are not welcome at most beaches, and may have restrictions placed on them by the National Park Service and at other attractions. Veterinarians can be found throughout the Cape.

Dining

The restaurants listed in this guide have been selected on the basis of the quality of their food, service, and reputation. Prices are rated on the basis of dinner for two; the cost of drinks, wine, tips, and taxes is not factored in. A restaurant is rated *Inexpensive* if a meal for two totals less than $25, *Moderate* if it costs between $25 and $50, and *Expensive* if it costs more than $50.

You can save money by taking advantage of lower cost "early-bird specials" offered by many Cape Cod restaurants. These specials are usually served for an hour starting around 4:00 P.M. or when the restaurant first opens for dinner. If you are traveling with children, be sure to ask for special kids' menus; they feature appealing dishes that usually cost less than those on the regular menu.

Advance reservations are a must at many Cape Cod restaurants, particularly during the months of July and August, as the Cape's best restaurants are booked even in the off-season. There are also many popular places that accept guests only on a first come-first served basis. To avoid long lines at these restaurants, arrive early.

A few places don't accept credit cards, and others take only certain ones. American Express, Visa, and MasterCard and their international equivalents are most commonly accepted on the Cape.

FAVORITE MEAL

Breakfast is my favorite meal. To my delight, the Cape serves up some great reasons for getting up in the morning. Two of the best spots are Jack's Outback in Yarmouth along Route 6A and Larry's PX on Route 28 in Chatham.

Jack's is off the highway, down a drive behind some 6A shops (look for the small sign on 6A). It's unconventional and legendary, a help-yourself kind of place that serves only breakfast and lunch. Note the hand-lettered signs that tell you not only what's on the menu, but also the rules about ordering on your own, getting your own coffee and utensils, cleaning up, and, of course, paying.

Larry's PX is another place where the locals meet. It opens at 5:30 A.M. to serve fishermen. Later carpenters, electricians, and other faithfuls take over the counter stools and booths.

Larry's dates from 1955, and it looks it. Nothing fancy—Formica counters, wooden booths, a few tables. But the food is good and the service friendly. As a connoisseur of home fries, I give Larry's one up.

You'll find almost every kind of cuisine on Cape Cod—continental, North American, ethnic, and exotic. Fresh seafood reigns on the menus of most Cape Cod dining places—New England lobster, oysters, clams, quahogs, swordfish, halibut, Boston scrod, mako shark, and bluefish.

Attractions

Admission to attractions in this guide are designated by these self-explanatory terms: *Admission Charged, Free,* or *Donation Accepted.* Many attractions charging admission offer lower rates for senior citizens, children, and groups.

Cape Cod is well endowed with museums, historic homes and buildings, special collections, libraries, rides and cruises, and amusements.

Information Centers

Information on individual Chambers of Commerce is listed under the towns in which they are located. Information centers are also a good place to stop to learn about local events, get directions, and find last-minute accommodations, beaches, and publications that include discount coupons to attractions, dining, activities, and more.

Major information centers on the Cape and along routes to Cape Cod are:

Cape Cod Chamber of Commerce
Junction of Routes 6 and 132 in Hyannis; open year-round
(888) 332-2732 or 862-0700; www.capecodchamber.org

Information Booth at Sagamore Rotary
Open daily from Memorial Day to Columbus Day
888-2438

Cape Cod National Seashore Headquarters
Marconi Station in South Wellfleet, off Route 6
349-3785

Division of Tourism
Massachusetts Department of Commerce and Development
100 Cambridge Street
Boston, MA 02202
(617) 973-8500 or (800) 227-MASS

For the convenience of travelers using Route 3 southbound from Boston, there is a Tourism Information Center, 746-1152, located in Plymouth at a rest-and-picnic plaza with easy access on and off this primary road from the Boston area to the Cape.

For those traveling on I-495 there is a large information center with rest rooms and picnic tables shortly after the highway becomes Route 25. I-495 ends in the Wareham area and becomes Route 25, which takes visitors over the Bourne Bridge. The center is easy to reach by those taking I-190 from Providence. I-190 connects with I-495. 759-3814

Just after exit 6 on the Mid-Cape Highway, Route 6, there is a rest area with an information center. 362-9796

Most Cape Cod towns have information centers. Addresses and telephone numbers are included in the town information section of this book.

Web Sites

The Cape Cod Times offers a Web site with information on the Cape, the weather, events, traffic, news, jobs and more: www.capecodonline.com

Cape Cod: www.capecodvisit.com

Restaurant menus: www.capecodmenus.com

Bourne: www.canalreg@capecod.org

Brewster: www.capecodtravel.com/brewster

Chatham: www.chathamcapecod.org

Dennis: www.dennischamber.com

Eastham: www.easthamchamber.com

Falmouth: www.falmouth-capecod.com

Harwich: www.harwichcc.com

Hyannis: www.hyannischamber.com

Mashpee: www.mashpeechamber.com

Orleans: www.capecod-orleans.com

Provincetown: www.ptownchamber.com

Sandwich: www.canalreg@capecod.org

Truro: www.virtualcapecod.com/chambers/truro.html

Wellfleet: www.capecod.net/wellfleetcc

Yarmouth: www.yarmouthcapecod.com

Publications

The following publications are excellent sources of information about what's happening on Cape Cod throughout the year:

The Cape Cod Times, daily and Sunday newspaper; 319 Main Street, Hyannis, MA 02601, 775-1200

Cape Cod Life, magazine; 4 Barlows Landing Road, Pocasset, MA 02559, 564-4466

The following books will also be helpful in touring and appreciating Cape Cod:

Cape Cod: Gardens and Houses, Catherine Fallin, published by Simon & Schuster

Short Bike Rides in Cape Cod, Nantucket, & Martha's Vineyard, Edwin Muller and Jane Griffith, published by The Globe Pequot Press

Traces of Thoreau: A Cape Cod Journey, Stephen Mulleney, published by Northeastern University Press

Cape Cod, Henry David Thoreau; *The Outermost House,* Henry Beston; the two great classics about the peninsula

Traveling to and around the Cape

By Car

Most visitors to Cape Cod come by car, recreational vehicle, van, or truck. Before the superhighway was built, the ride from Boston to Hyannis could take from four to seven hours, depending on traffic. You came not for the day, as is the case now for many, but to stay for several days or for the entire summer season. Today, the trip can be done in two hours or less, except on weekends and holidays, when it seems as if the entire world is clogging the road to the Cape.

Highways connect Cape Cod to everywhere in the country and to the provinces of Canada. If you are traveling from southern Connecticut, New York City, New Jersey, southern Pennsylvania, Delaware, Maryland, Washington, D.C., Virginia, and points south and west, take the interstate highways to I-95 North. Continue on I-95 to Providence, Rhode Island. At Providence the highway divides: I-95 continues north to Boston; I-195 heads east to Cape Cod while passing through the historic cities of Fall River and New Bedford in Massachusetts. There are signs along the way, so you won't get lost, as well as plenty of restaurants, motels, and gas stations, at locations off the highway. At the town of East Wareham, I-195 connects with I-495 and

then state Route 25, which takes you to the Cape Cod Canal and the Bourne and Sagamore bridges crossing over to the Cape.

If you're coming from the north or northwest via I-495, I-95, I-93, and U.S. Route 1, get onto State Highway 3 South, which will take you all the way to the Sagamore Bridge at the Cape Cod Canal. Another alternative, if coming from the west and northwest, is to take I-495 South to 25 to the Cape Cod Canal at the Bourne and Sagamore bridges.

Bourne Bridge, at the southwest end of the canal, and Sagamore Bridge, at its northeast end, are the only two land accesses onto the Cape. Bourne Bridge connects with Route 28, which goes along Buzzards Bay and the southern coast of Cape Cod to Orleans. Sagamore Bridge connects with the Mid-Cape Highway, Route 6, which is the Cape's fast road all the way from the canal to Provincetown. Route 6 is a divided, four-lane highway from the canal to Dennis, at which point it becomes a two-laner; it broadens in stretches from Orleans to Provincetown. Roads parallel the canal and connect Routes 28, 6, and also 6A, which is the scenic highway along the north coast of the Cape.

Get a detailed road map of New England at a local gas station or bookshop or from an auto club (AAA, etc.); or buy the inexpensive Rand McNally *Road Atlas*, which comes in handy wherever you travel in North America.

Hyannis is located approximately in the center of Cape Cod. It is 245 miles from New York City, 331 miles from Philadelphia, 470 miles from Washington, D.C., 355 miles from Montreal, 622 miles from Toronto, 483 miles from Ottawa, 468 from Quebec City, 77 miles from Boston, and 77 miles from Providence.

RENTAL CARS

With locations at the airport, on the Cape, or the islands:

Alamo Rent A Car, 800-327-9633

Avis, 800-331-1212

Bargain Rent-a-Car, 771-1298

Budget, 800-527-0700

Enterprise, 800-325-8007

Hertz, 800-654-3131

National, 800-CAR RENT

Rent a Wreck, 771-9667 or 888-486-1470

Sears, 790-1480

Thrifty, 800-367-2277

Trek Rent A Car, 771-2459

By Air

Regularly scheduled air service, some seasonal, to Cape Cod and the islands is available from Boston, New York, Providence, and New Bedford (Martha's Vineyard and Nantucket only).
Most air service is to Hyannis. From Boston, Cape Air offers service to Provincetown.
Airlines offering service are:

Cape Air (771-6944 or 800-352-0714) serves Hyannis, Martha's Vineyard, Nantucket, Provincetown, Boston, New Bedford, and Providence.

Nantucket Airlines (228-6234 or 800-635-8787) serves Hyannis, Martha's Vineyard, Nantucket, Provincetown, Boston, New Bedford, and Providence.

Continental Connection (800-523-FARE) serves Hyannis, Nantucket, and LaGuardia in New York.

US Airways Express (800-428-4322) serves Hyannis, Martha's Vineyard, Boston, and New York.

Island Airlines (228-7575, 775-6606, or 800-248-7779) serves Nantucket and Hyannis.

Ocean Wings Commuter (228-3692 or 800-295-5842) serves Hyannis and Nantucket.

AIRPORTS
Commercial and private flights:
Barnstable Municipal Airport, 775-2020
Provincetown Municipal Airport, 487-0241

PRIVATE FLIGHTS
Cape Cod Airport in Marston Mills, 428-8732
Chatham Municipal Airport, 945-9000
Falmouth Airport, 548-9617

By Bus

Plymouth & Brockton (771-6191; www.p-b.com) serves Hyannis, Provincetown, Plymouth, and Boston including Logan Airport.
Bonanza (775-5524 or 800-556-3815; www.bonanzabus.com/index. htm) serves Falmouth, Hyannis, Providence, Boston, and New York City.

ON CAPE COD

Cape Cod Regional Transit Authority (385-8326 or 800-352-7155; www.allcapecod.com/ccrta). Vehicles have bike racks.

Service is offered in Falmouth and to Woods Hole on the Woods Hole Shuttle (WHOOSH) generally between May 29 and Labor Day. For ticket information, call 548-8500 or (800) 526-8532.

Also offered are SeaLine service between Hyannis and Falmouth, The Village between Hyannis and Barnstable Harbor, and The H2O Line between Hyannis and Orleans. All connections are at the Plymouth & Brockton bus terminal in Hyannis.

Travel is also offered between Hyannis and Provincetown by Plymouth & Brockton.

Cape Cod Trolley has service between Falmouth (548-8500 or 800-526-8532) and Mashpee; in the Hyannis (362-5230 or 800-449-6647) area, with service to the ferry dock from the bus terminal; in Yarmouth, leaving from the Hyannis bus terminal; and in Dennis (398-3568 or 800-243-9920), with connecting service from the H2O line.

The Provincetown Summer Shuttle (432-3400) offers seasonal service in town and to the beach.

SHUTTLE SERVICE

For those driving to Cape Cod in summer to take the ferry to the islands, free parking is available at Cape Cod Community College on Route 132 at exit 6 off Route 6. Free shuttle service is provided to the Ocean Street dock and downtown Hyannis.

BUS SERVICE ON THE ISLANDS

Martha's Vineyard Transit Authority (627-7448; www.vineyardtransit.com)

Martha's Vineyard Island Transport (693-1589; www.vineyardinfo.com/islandtransport)

Nantucket Regional Transit Authority (228-7025; www.nantucket.net/trans/nrta)

By Boat

Bay State Cruises (487-9284 or 617-457-1428) offers service between Boston and Provincetown. A choice of fast or regular ferry service is offered.

Cape Cod Cruises (800-242-2469) offers service between Plymouth and Provincetown.

Yankee Fleet (800-942-5464; www.yankeefleet.com) has service between Gloucester (on Boston's North Shore) and Provincetown.

TO THE ISLANDS

The Steamship Authority (477-8600; www.islandferry.com) has year-round service for vehicles and passengers between Hyannis and Nantucket and Falmouth and Martha's Vineyard. High-speed ferry service is also offered to Nantucket from Hyannis, cutting the two-hour trip in half. Advance reservations (the earlier the better, as the ferry is often sold out of vehicle space) are required for automobile transportation to Martha's Vineyard. For day-of-sailing reservations Friday through Monday from May through Labor Day, call 477-7447.

Hy-Line Cruises (778-2600 or 888-778-1132; www.hy-linecruises.com) has seasonal passenger-only service from Hyannis to both Nantucket and Martha's Vineyard. High-speed ferry service to Nantucket is also offered.

Hy-Line Cruises (Oak Bluffs, 693-0112; Nantucket, 228-3949) also offers seasonal inter-island service between Martha's Vineyard and Nantucket.

Island Queen (548-4800; www.islandqueen.com) has seasonal service between Falmouth and Martha's Vineyard.

Freedom Cruise Line (432-8999; www.capecod.net/freedom) offers seasonal service between Harwich Port and Nantucket.

Sea Comm Transport (295-1448) offers service between Onset and Martha's Vineyard.

Cape Island Express Lines (997-1688) has service between New Bedford and Vineyard Haven, and New Bedford and Cuttyhunk (992-1432).

By Rail

There is connecting bus service from Amtrak (800–USA RAIL; www.amtrak.com) stations in Boston and Providence.

On Cape Cod, the Cape Cod Central Railroad (771-3800 or 888-797-RAIL; www.capetrain.com) offers scenic rides and excursion trips to bike and walking paths.

Biking

For bike paths and routes, see "Best Bike Trails" in the Activities and Attractions section. Also check with information centers on Cape Cod, or call the Bicycle Coalition of Massachusetts at (617) 491-7433 (www.massbike.org).

Walking

For suggested walks, see "Best Cape Walks" in the Activities and Attractions section. Or call the Cape Cod Pathways at 362-3828 (www.capecodcommission.org.walk).

Access to the Cape

Because the canal separates the peninsula from the Massachusetts mainland, Cape Cod is virtually an island. There are only two accesses for cars, buses, and trucks: Sagamore Bridge on the north end and Bourne Bridge at the south. Highways parallel both sides of the canal and provide access to both bridges—Route 3 on the Cape Cod side and Route 6 on the mainland side. A third bridge, in the Bourne area, provides a crossover for trains.

The Cape's primary highways are Route 6 and Route 28. Route 6 is also called the Mid-Cape Highway. It runs the entire length of the Cape from the Sagamore Bridge all the way to Provincetown. From the Sagamore Bridge to Dennis, Route 6 is a four-lane, divided expressway providing easy access to towns along the way. It's the fast-track road to Hyannis, Orleans, and Provincetown. From Dennis to Provincetown the road narrows to two lanes. This section can be dangerous, so be careful when passing and put on your headlights for safety. Route 28 goes from the Bourne Bridge, along the Cape's southern coast, to Orleans. The section from Bourne to Falmouth is a four-lane, divided expressway, with access to Otis Air Force Base and Camp Edwards at the Otis rotary. At Falmouth it becomes a narrow, two-lane road going through the various towns along this coast. Route 28 is Cape Cod's busiest highway, and, during the summer season, you should expect heavy, slow traffic everywhere.

Alternate routes 6A and 28A are the Cape's main scenic highways. Route 28A from the Otis rotary to Falmouth is a lovely drive through villages on the southwest coast. Route 6A from Sandwich to Provincetown, called "The Old King's Highway," is considered by most travelers the best road for experiencing the true essence of Cape Cod. It is largely devoid of the concentrated commercialization that exists on Route 28. The Cape's principal north/south roads are Route 130 from Sandwich to Mashpee, Route 149 from West Barnstable to Cotuit, Route 132 from Barnstable to Hyannis, Route 134 from Dennis to Yarmouth, Route 124 from Brewster to Harwich, Route 137 from Brewster to Chatham, and Route 39 from Harwich to Orleans.

The popularity of Cape Cod has made driving here, to put it mildly, terrible. If you can cope with the heavy traffic in some areas, however, Cape Cod will be a rewarding vacation place. Cape traffic is heaviest from mid-May to mid-October. Route 28 is very busy throughout the year. Getting onto the Cape, expect traffic backups starting Friday afternoon and continuing through Saturday afternoon. Getting off the Cape, expect delays starting after lunch on Sunday and continuing well into the evening. Allow for extended hours beyond these periods during long holiday weekends. Try to avoid peak traffic periods by coming and going at other times during the day or night. During the summer season, expect congestion just about everywhere.

For traffic information on the radio (seasonal), listen to WBZ (AM1030), WCRB (FM 102.5), WPLM (FM 99.1) in Boston; on the Cape, WQRC (FM 99.9), with report throughout the day; or WXTK (FM 95.1), WCOD (FM 106.1), WPXC (FM 103), WRZE (FM 96.3), or WCIB (FM 102).

On the Internet: www.smartraveler.com or www.capecodusa.com.

If you are biking Cape Cod, use designated bike trails, which will take you just about anywhere on the peninsula (see "Best Bike Trails"). Whenever possible, avoid roads with heavy traffic and keep well to the side. There is no biking on Route 6, the Mid-Cape Highway. Biking has become such a popular activity that the probability of riders and motor vehicles colliding on busy roads is quite high, and accidents do happen. Most secondary roads are safe for bikers and offer inspiring scenery and fewer hazards. Watch out for pedestrians while riding in villages. Common sense and basic safety procedures will make biking on Cape Cod fun.

Health and Safety

Cape Cod can do wonders for your body and soul, provided you stay healthy and avoid accidents. The towns of Cape Cod and the Cape Cod National Seashore do everything they can to provide visitors with a hazard-free environment, but some risks cannot be absolutely eliminated. The following health and safety tips are provided to bring you back home happy and relaxed.

When hiking in woods, on the beach, or in marsh or shrub areas, check yourself, companions, children, and pets for ticks on clothing and hair. Lyme disease is spread by deer ticks, so if you are bitten and experience flulike symptoms, see a doctor immediately. If you are allergic to insect bites, obtain medical help right away. Also while hiking, be careful not to expose skin to poison ivy, which is one of the more common, less desirable plants.

When on the beach, avoid prolonged exposure to the sun. Sunscreens should be used for extended periods on the beach and water. Be sure you buy one strong enough to provide both protection and a tan. Invest in better sunglasses that protect your eyes from damaging ultraviolet and infrared light. A good sun hat is also advised. Don't swim beyond the ability of lifeguards to rescue you. The waters at some beaches, during tidal and weather changes and high-wave periods, have powerful, deadly undercurrents that are difficult to handle by even the strongest swimmers. Swim in calm, shallow areas and always keep children under close supervision. Also, be wary of sharp obstacles hidden in the water.

When walking to and from the beach, wear sandals or shoes that protect your feet from the broiling sand and hidden pieces of sharp debris. Don't dig large holes in the sand; they can be hazardous to you and others. Do not climb up and down the high cliffs along Cape Cod National Seashore. They are composed of loose sand and clay materials that crumble easily and can cause a crippling fall. Be aware of tidal changes when hiking out on narrow peninsulas jutting into the sea. A high tide can cover low areas and strand you for several hours. Although storms along the coasts are very dramatic to observe, do not watch them from places where you can be swept into the sea by the wind or struck by falling power lines and tree branches.

Emergencies

For emergencies requiring local police, fire service, or ambulance service, dial 911.

For general information, call 877-227-3263, or check out the Web site at www.capecodhealth.org.

HOSPITALS

Falmouth:

Falmouth Hospital, 548-5300, Ter Heun Drive, off Route 28; twenty-four-hour emergency care

Hyannis:

Cape Cod Hospital, 771-1800, 27 Park Street; twenty-four-hour emergency care

CLINICS

Bourne:

Bourne Health Care, 340 Main Street, 759-5731

Bourne Medical Associates, 170 Clay Pond Road, 759-7117

Chatham:

Chatham Medical Associates, 945-0187, 78 Crowell Road

Falmouth:

Falmouth Walk-In Medical Center, 540-6790, Route 28

Harwich:

Long Pond Medical Center, 432-4100, 525 Long Pond Drive

Hyannis:

Health Stop, 771-7520, K-Mart Plaza, Route 132

Mid-Cape Medical Center, 771-4092, Route 28

Mashpee:

Mashpee Family Medicine, 800 Falmouth Road, 477-4282

Orleans:

Orleans Medical Center Walk-In, 255-9577, Route 6A

Provincetown:

Provincetown Medical Group, 487-3505, 16 Shank Painter Road

Outer Cape Health Services, Harry Kemp Way, 487-9395

Sandwich:

Falmouth Hospital Urgent Care Center, Route 130, 833-4950

John H. Lewis Medical Center, Route 130, 888-0770

South Dennis:

Cape Cod Medical Center, 394-7113, Route 134

Wellfleet:

A.I.M. Clinic, 349-3131, Route 6

Yarmouth:

Yarmouth Medical Center, 23-G White's Path, 760-2054

PHARMACIES

Almost every town has one or more pharmacies. Some are closed on Sunday. Check the Yellow Pages of the local phone directory for the one nearest you and its times of operation. The Prescription Center in Falmouth, for example, has a twenty-four-hour emergency hotline, 540-2410, for prescription drugs and oxygen. *Travel tip:* Always carry prescriptions for essential drugs that cannot be legally dispensed without them. Some CVS pharmacies stay open until midnight in summer.

Listed Below Are Additional Agencies that Provide Emergency Assistance:

Emergency, anywhere on Cape Cod: 911

U.S. COAST GUARD:
Cape Cod Canal: 888-0335
Chatham: 945-0164
Provincetown: 487-0070
Woods Hole: 548-5151

STATE POLICE:
Bourne: 759-4488
South Yarmouth: 398-2323

CAPE COD AIDS COUNCIL:
Hyannis: 778-5111

SUICIDE PREVENTION - THE SAMARITANS:
(800) 893-9900

POISON HOTLINE:
(800) 682-9211

ALCOHOLICS ANONYMOUS:
(800) 637-6237

BATTERED WOMEN:
(800) 439-6507

MISSING CHILDREN'S HOTLINE:
(800) 843-5678

PARENTAL STRESS HOTLINE:
(800) 632-8188

For People with Disabilities

Most lodging, restaurants, and other services are accessible to the disabled. The Cape Cod Disability Access Directory can be found at information centers throughout Cape Cod. The guide lists sources of information, and access guide to theaters, beaches, ATM, and other services and attractions.

Surf chairs for access to beaches are available at many beaches in Falmouth, Barnstable, and Harwich, and a few in Chatham, Eastham, Orleans, Provincetown, and Dennis. To reserve chairs in Bourne, call 866-2580; Falmouth, 548-8623; Mashpee, 457-0495; Sandwich, 888-0525; and Brewster, 896-2737.

For more information contact the Cape Cod disability councils in Barnstable, 790-6305; Bourne, 759-0650; Brewster, 896-2737; Chatham, 945-5168; Dennis, 394-8300; Eastham, 240-5900; Falmouth, 548-7611; Harwich, 430-7513; Mashpee, 539-1500; Orleans, 255-2133; Provincetown, 487-7003; Sandwich, 888-4910; Truro, 349-3635; Wellfleet, 349-0300; and Yarmouth, 398-2231. Or check out the Web site at www.capecod.net/ccdad/.

Handcycles, large tricycles powered by hands, arms, and. upper body, are available for rent at the Cape Cod Rail Trail in Brewster. Call 896-8200.

Traveling to Martha's Vineyard, Nantucket, and Plymouth

While this guide concentrates exclusively on Cape Cod, information on three easy-to-do destinations off the Cape is included, as many visitors do not feel a visit to Cape Cod is complete without at least seeing Martha's Vineyard and Nantucket islands and Plymouth, "America's hometown." Each can be done as a day visit and with little preparation. Each area offers tourist information that is easily available.

Cape Cod, Nantucket, and Martha's Vineyard, as well as Plymouth, are each distinct and separate worlds, and each one is deserving of its own special focus and treatment.

Access to the islands is by ferry or flights from Hyannis, and Plymouth is just an hour by car. Because of limited ferry space and difficulty in getting vehicle reservations, the islands are best seen on foot and without cars. Vehicles are not needed to tour the islands, and parking is available near all ferry terminals. For viewing out-island areas, transportation from bikes and mopeds to rental cars and organized tours can be easily arranged on the islands.

Martha's Vineyard

Martha's Vineyard is an island just forty-five minutes from the Falmouth area. It offers good biking, history, beaches, architecture, and celebrities.

Ferries arrive at either Oak Bluffs or Vineyard Haven, from where it is easy to arrange sightseeing (a two-hour bus tour is available when the ferry lands), rent bikes or other vehicles, or just wander on your own.

Oak Bluffs is known for its "gingerbread" cottages, homes of early visitors who gathered for Methodist camp meetings in the 1800s. Today at the "camp" site is the Tabernacle, one of the largest wrought-iron structures in the world and scene of island concerts and other events. The Flying Horse Carousel, which dates from 1876, is fun for everyone.

Vineyard Haven, the main ferry port and the island's second oldest town, offers William Street, lined with homes on the National Register and museums to explore.

Martha's Vineyard is also much larger than Nantucket (20 by 10 miles, vs. Nantucket's 14 by 3.5 miles); Vineyard Haven to Gay Head is 18 miles, a bike ride only for the hardy. While distant, a visit to see the

150-foot-high, color-streaked clay cliffs of Gay Head is well worth it, as are visits to the island's other towns from Edgartown to Chilmark.

Excellent dining and accommodations are available on the island.

For more information, contact the Martha's Vineyard Chamber of Commerce, Box 1698, Beach Road, Vineyard Haven, 02568, 693–0085, or on the Web at www.mvy.com.

There are events throughout the year on the island, although most are still centered around the spring to fall season. In December, Christmas celebrations take place in Vineyard Haven and Edgartown the first of the month.

Nantucket

Nantucket is an island 22 miles off the coast of Cape Cod, a distance that adds to its otherworld flavor. Once the whaling capital of the world, Nantucket gained prominence from Herman Melville's *Moby Dick*. Reminders of what Melville saw on his visit to the island can still be found in the island's lavish captains' mansions and museums.

In Nantucket town, where the ferry lands, one can explore the quaint shops (Macy's had its beginnings here), walk on cobblestone streets, and tour whaling museums and classic houses. There is shuttle bus service to Jetties, Siasconset, Madaket, and Surfside beaches. Bikes and mopeds can be rented, and there are Jeep tours of out-of-the-way places for bird-watching or fishing.

Nantucket has a bountiful range of accommodations from classic inns to bed-and-breakfasts; a wide range of dining is also available.

For more information, contact the Nantucket Chamber of Commerce, 15 Main Street, Nantucket, 02554, 228–1700, or on the Web at www.nantucketchamber.org.

Nantucket is festive from spring to winter. In April, it celebrates the daffodil with a colorful weekend festival; in June, there is Harborfest; in October, Cranberry Harvest weekend; and in December, the delightful Christmas stroll at the beginning of the month.

Two excellent guides to the islands are *Guide to Martha's Vineyard* and *Guide to Nantucket*, both authored by Polly Burroughs, a longtime resident of Martha's Vineyard. These guides are available at your bookstore or from The Globe Pequot Press, P.O. Box 480, Guilford, CT 06437.

Plymouth

Plymouth is an easy drive of no more than an hour from most points on Cape Cod. Take Route 6 to the Sagamore Bridge and continue on to Route 3 to Plymouth.

Plymouth bills itself as "America's Hometown." Provincetown, on Cape Cod, is where the Pilgrims first landed in 1620, and there are other Pilgrim sites on the Cape, such as First Encounter Beach in Eastham. However, Plymouth lives up to its "hometown" claim because it is indeed the place where the Pilgrims, after much hardship, succeeded in founding the first permanent settlement in America.

Visitors should tour Plimoth Plantation, 746-1622, a re-creation of the Pilgrim village of 1630. The plantation is open daily, April through November, and admission is charged. Visitors can also tour the *Mayflower II*, a full-scale reproduction of the vessel the Pilgrims sailed from England. (A combination admission to the village and the *Mayflower II* is available.)

Also to see: the famous Plymouth Rock the Pilgrims stepped ashore on; Pilgrim artifacts in Pilgrim Hall Museum; Plymouth National Wax Museum (746-6468), which features dramatic scenes of the Pilgrim adventure in the New World, open daily March through December, admission charged; the impressive statue of sachem Massasoit, which has become a rallying point for today's Native Americans; Mayflower Society House; Pilgrim Maiden statue; Pilgrim Monument; Brewster Gardens; and Pilgrim Mother statue. Also here are some of the oldest homes in America, including the 1640 Richard Sparrow House, the 1666 Jabez Howland House, Coles Hill Pilgrim burial ground, and the 1809 Antiquarian House.

Along the waterfront is Cranberry World, a free museum dedicated to teaching you more than you ever wanted to know about this famous berry.

There are dining facilities at Plimoth Plantation and many restaurants along the Plymouth waterfront and nearby. Accommodations are also available in the historic area.

For more information, contact The Plymouth County Development Council, P.O. Box 1520, Pembroke, 02359; (800) 231-1620.

CHAPTER THREE

Activities and Attractions

Outdoors

Public Beaches

One of the main reasons why so many people come to the Cape is its
superb beaches. Although extensive areas of beachfront are privately
owned, there are still many public beaches, which welcome the short-
stay or seasonal visitor. The open, ocean-side beaches of the Cape Cod
National Seashore, for example, extend for nearly 40 miles in a
north/south direction along the Lower Cape.

If there is a problem regarding Cape Cod beaches at the height of
the summer season, it is parking your vehicle. Parking lots at the popular beaches fill up fast from mid-July to Labor Day. Before and after
this period, though, there isn't much of a parking crunch. Parking lots
at the main Cape Cod National Seashore beaches are large and can
usually handle most of the cars of those wanting to come in. Between
Memorial Day weekend and Labor Day, most town-managed beaches
charge a parking fee, as do managed beaches of the Cape Cod National
Seashore. There is no fee for using beach parking lots in the off-season.
If you plan on staying at a Cape location for an extended time (a week,
month, or the season), most towns will sell you a permit that allows
you to park daily at beach lots. The cost of the permit saves you money
over having to pay on a day-to-day basis and allows you to use most
town beaches.

A number of the larger beaches, both in the towns and along the
Cape Cod National Seashore, have rest room and other facilities. All
beaches prohibit overnight parking, however, except in some instances,

in the case of surf fishermen, who must obtain a special permit. Open beach fires are also banned, except by permit, but you may use a grill or stove in specially designated picnic areas. The operation of over-sand vehicles on beaches is regulated by laws, and permits are required for their use in designated areas. Most permits may be obtained at town offices or at Cape Cod National Seashore visitors centers. A number of hotels/motels and resorts have their own private beaches, and you should consider this feature when selecting a place to stay. Many accommodations also have freshwater swimming pools, whirlpools, and saunas on their premises.

When you are using the beaches, dispose of your trash in barrels set aside for this purpose. Don't leave broken glass on the beach, even when it's not your own. Don't pull up or pick beach grass, flowers, shrubbery, and other flora, as this vegetation helps to protect the beach from wind erosion, which is a major problem on the Cape. Always keep a close watch on young children in the water. Don't swim beyond a lifeguard's ability to rescue you in an emergency. Avoid getting caught in strong riptides and undercurrents. Surfers and sailboarders may not use lifeguard-protected beaches at the same time as swimmers. Check with officials for regulations and areas open to you on the beach you want to use (see the following section for more information on surfing and sailboarding).

The warmest waters for swimming are found at beaches on Buzzards Bay, Cape Cod Bay, and Nantucket Sound. The water is coldest at beaches along the open-Atlantic side, mostly those within Cape Cod National Seashore. Nude sunbathing is not permitted at Cape Cod National Seashore beaches, and this regulation is enforced by National Park Service rangers and local police.

The following are some of the many Cape Cod beaches open to the public:

BOURNE

Monument Beach, off Shore Road on Buzzards Bay: bathhouse, rest rooms, snack bar, lifeguards, handicapped accessible, free parking

Scusset Beach, near junction of Routes 3 and 6, at Sagamore: This state-owned beach is perhaps the best in Bourne. It has showers, play area, and snack bar

FALMOUTH

Falmouth Heights Beach, off Route 28 and Grand Avenue on Nantucket Sound: lifeguards, food

Megansett Beach, in North Falmouth, off Route 28A on Buzzards Bay:
lifeguards

Menauhant Beach, in East Falmouth, off Route 28 and Central Avenue
on Nantucket Sound: rest rooms, food, lifeguards; surfers allowed
after 5:00 P.M.; handicapped accessible, with beach chairs and sandchairs

Old Silver Beach, in North Falmouth, off Route 28A and Quaker Road
on Buzzards Bay: bathhouse and snack bar; surfers allowed after
5:00 P.M.; handicapped accessible, with beach chairs and sandchairs

Surf Drive Beach, in Falmouth, off Main and Shore Streets, on Nantucket Sound: bathhouse and snack bar; surfers allowed after 5:00
P.M.; handicapped accessible, with beach chairs and sandchairs

Bristol Beach, off Route 28 in the Maravista area of Falmouth Heights
on Nantucket Sound: lifeguards, sticker parking only; handicapped
accessible

Wood Neck Beach, in the Sippewissett area off Route 28 and Palmer
Avenue on Buzzards Bay: lifeguards, sticker parking only; handicapped accessible

Stoney Beach, in Woods Hole: lifeguards, sticker parking only; handicapped accessible

Chapoquoit Beach, in West Falmouth, off Route 28A and Chapoquoit
Road on Buzzards Bay: lifeguards, sticker parking only; handicapped accessible

Trunk River, Surf Drive: no parking or services

Crew's Pond (freshwater), Goodwill Park: sanitary facilities, no parking
or other services

SANDWICH

Sandy Neck Beach, off Sandy Neck Road, East Sandwich: 6-mile sand
barrier beach with dunes

Wakeby Pond (freshwater), Ryder Conservation Area, John Ewer Road:
parking, rest rooms, lifeguards

MASHPEE

South Cape Beach, off Great Neck Road on Nantucket Sound: rest
rooms, snack bar, no pets, handicapped accessible

BARNSTABLE

Craigville Beach, off Craigville Beach Road on Nantucket Sound: lifeguards, rest rooms, very popular, paid parking area

Millway Beach, in Barnstable Harbor, off Route 6A on Cape Cod Bay: lifeguards, food, rest rooms

Sandy Neck Beach, in West Barnstable, off Route 6A and Sandy Neck Road on Cape Cod Bay: lifeguards, food, rest rooms, picnic area

HYANNIS

Kalmus Park Beach, at the end of Ocean Street on Nantucket Sound: lifeguards, rest rooms, snack bar, picnic area, volleyball

Orrin Keyes Beach, off Ocean Avenue on Nantucket Sound: lifeguards, snack bar, rest rooms

Veteran's Beach, off Ocean Street in Hyannis Harbor: lifeguards, rest rooms, playground, picnic area, volleyball

YARMOUTH

Bass River Beach, off Route 28 and South Shore Drive on Nantucket Sound: lifeguards, bathhouse, rest rooms

Parkers River Beach, off Route 28 and South Shore Drive on Nantucket Sound: lifeguards, bathhouse, food

Sea Gull Beach, in West Yarmouth, off Route 28 and South Sea Avenue on Nantucket Sound: lifeguards, food, bathhouse, rest rooms

Seaview, Parkers River, and *Thatcher beaches*, in South Yarmouth, off Route 28 and South Shore Drive on Nantucket Sound: lifeguards, rest rooms, food

DENNIS

Chapin Beach, off Route 6A and Chapin Beach Road on Cape Cod Bay

Cold Storage Road Beach, in East Dennis, off Route 6A and Cold Storage Road on Cape Cod Bay

Corporation Road Beach, off Route 6A and Corporation Beach Road on Cape Cod Bay

Sea Street, Haig's, and *Glendon beaches*, in Dennis Port, off Route 28 and Old Wharf Road on Nantucket Sound

Sea Street Beach, in East Dennis, off Route 6A and South Street on Cape Cod Bay

Scargo Lake (freshwater): Scargo Beach, off Route 6A, and Princess Beach, off Scargo Hill Road

West Dennis Beach, off Route 28 and Lighthouse Road on Nantucket Sound

BREWSTER

Flax Pond (freshwater) in Nickerson State Park: also in the park, Cliff and Little Cliff ponds, with beaches

Point of Rocks Beach, off Route 6A and Point of Rocks Road on Cape Cod Bay

Breakwater Beach, off Route 6A and Breakwater Beach Road on Cape Cod Bay: public rest rooms.

Crosby Landing Beach, off Route 6A and Crosby Landing Road on Cape Cod Bay

Ellis Landing Beach, off Route 6A and Ellis Landing Road on Cape Cod Bay

Linnell's Landing Beach, off Route 6A and Linnell's Landing Road on Cape Cod Bay: handicapped accessible

Paine's Creek Beach, off Route 6A and Paine's Creek Road on Cape Cod Bay

Robbin's Hill Beach, off Route 6A and Robbin's Hill Road on Cape Cod Bay

HARWICH

Red River Beach, in South Harwich, off Route 28 and Neel Road on Nantucket Sound

Atlantic Avenue and *Bank Street beaches*, in Harwich Port, off Route 28A on Nantucket Sound

Bank Street Beach in Harwich Port: sticker parking

Red River Beach, off Uncle Venies Road, South Harwich: parking, facilities

Sand Pond (freshwater), off Great Western Road

Hinckleys Pond, Seymour Pond (both freshwater), off Route 124 and Rail Trail

CHATHAM

Cockle Cove Beach, in South Chatham, off Route 28 and Cockle Cove Road on Nantucket Sound: rest rooms, lifeguards, food, no pets

Hardings Beach, in West Chatham, off Hardings Beach Road on Nantucket Sound: rest rooms, lifeguards, snack bar, no pets allowed

Ridgevale Beach, off Route 28, at end of Ridgevale Road: nice beach for children

Forest Beach, at end of Forest Beach Road

Oyster Pond Beach, off Route 28 near town center: rest rooms

Chatham Light Beach, just below the lighthouse: no parking, shuttle service available

ORLEANS

Nauset Beach, off Shore Road from town center, a town-managed beach within the Cape Cod National Seashore on the open Atlantic. This beach has lots of sand dunes and sandy beach expanse. There are also rest rooms, a snack bar, lifeguards, areas set aside for surfing, sailboarding, scuba diving, and recreational vehicles; handicapped accessible

Skaket Beach, off Route 6 and Namaskaket Road on Cape Cod Bay: rest rooms, lifeguards, and snack bar. A 9-foot tidal change creates mini-pools and rivulets; handicapped accessible

Rock Harbor Beach, off Route 6 and Rock Harbor Road on Cape Cod Bay: handicapped accessible

EASTHAM

Campground Beach, off Route 6 and Campground Road on Cape Cod Bay

Coast Guard Beach, off Route 6 and Doane Road: a Cape Cod National Seashore-managed beach on the open Atlantic

Cooks Brook Beach, off Route 6 and Massasoit and Steele Roads on Cape Cod Bay

First Encounter Beach, off Route 6 and Samoset Road on Cape Cod Bay

Nauset Light Beach, off Route 6 and Cable Road: a Cape Cod National Seashore-managed beach on the open Atlantic

Sunken Meadow Beach, off Route 6 and Sunken Meadow Road on Cape Cod Bay

WELLFLEET

Le Count Hollow, White Crest, Cahoon Hollow, and *Newcomb Hollow Beaches,* off Route 6 along Ocean View Drive: town-managed beaches within Cape Cod National Seashore on the open Atlantic: rest rooms, snack bar, lifeguards, no pets allowed; not handicapped accessible

Marconi Beach, off Route 6 in South Wellfleet: a Cape Cod National Seashore-managed beach on the open Atlantic, rest rooms, bathhouse, snack bar; not handicapped accessible

Duck Harbor Beach, off Route 6 and via town center and Chequesset Neck Road: a town-managed beach within Cape Cod National Seashore on Cape Cod Bay: lifeguards, not handicapped accessible

Indian Neck Beach, off Route 6 on Cape Cod Bay: rest rooms, bathhouse, lifeguards, pets on leashes allowed; not handicapped accessible

Mayo Beach, off Route 6 at Wellfleet Harbor on Cape Cod Bay: rest rooms, lifeguards, ramps for handicapped, no pets allowed

TRURO

Coast Guard Beach, off Route 6 and South Highland and Coast Guard Roads: a town-managed beach within Cape Cod National Seashore on the open Atlantic

Corn Hill Beach, off Route 6 and Castle and Corn Hill Roads on Cape Cod Bay

Fisher Beach, Route 6 and County and Fisher Roads on Cape Cod Bay

Great Hollow Beach, Route 6 and Great Hollow Road on Cape Cod Bay

Head of the Meadow Beach, off Route 6 and Head of the Meadow Road: Cape Cod National Seashore–managed beach on the open Atlantic

Longnook Beach, off Route 6 and Longnook Road: a town-managed beach within Cape Cod National Seashore on the open Atlantic

Ryder Beach, off Route 6 and Prince Valley and Ryder Beach Roads on Cape Cod Bay

Pilgrim Beach, in North Truro, off Route 6A on Cape Cod Bay

PROVINCETOWN

Herring Cove Beach, off Route 6: a Cape Cod National Seashore–managed beach on Cape Cod Bay

Race Point Beach, off Route 6 and Race Point and Province Lands Roads: a Cape Cod National Seashore–managed beach on the open Atlantic: sand dunes, lifeguards, and bathhouses

Also, a 3-mile public beach along the full length of Provincetown's harbor.

In addition to saltwater beaches, there are beaches at freshwater ponds throughout Cape Cod: Grew's Pond in Falmouth; Picture Lake in Pocasset; Wakeby Pond in South Sandwich; John's Pond in Mashpee; Lovell's and Hamblin's ponds in Marston Mills; Wequaquet Lake in Centerville; Hathaway's Pond in Barnstable; Dennis Pond in Yarmouthport; Scargo Lake in Dennis; Long Pond in South Yarmouth; Sandy Pond in West Yarmouth; Walker's Pond in West Brewster; Sheep Pond in Brewster; Long Pond in Harwich; Flax Pond at Nickerson State Park in East Brewster; School House Pond in Chatham; Pilgrim Lake in Orleans; Herring and Great ponds in Eastham; and Great, Gull, and Long ponds in Wellfleet.

Surfing and Sailboarding

Surfing and sailboarding, popular and rapidly growing sports on the waters of Cape Cod, attract thousands of enthusiasts each year. Both sports, not confined just to summer, go on throughout the year thanks to insulated wet suits.

Board-surfing waves are found at beaches along Cape Cod National Seashore—Nauset Beach in Orleans, Coast Guard and Nauset Light beaches in Eastham, and Marconi Beach in South Wellfleet. The waves here are at their best during the fall and winter. Beach regulations prohibit surfing at lifeguard-protected sections, where swimmers congregate. The Salt Pond Visitor Center of the Cape Cod National Seashore in Eastham will answer your questions about regulations, locations, and conditions. One of the best sources on Cape Cod for surfing information, competitions, lessons, board sales and rentals, wet suits, clothing, and related gear is the Cinnamon Rainbows Surf Company in Orleans (255-5832), which is open all year. Cinnamon Rainbows has two locations in town, one near the Orleans–Route 6 rotary, and the other on Beach Road. Jaspers Surf Shop (255-2662) on Route 6 in Eastham and Nauset Sports (255-4752) on Route 6 in Orleans are two other sources.

Sailboarding (windsurfing) is the booming, "in" water sport on Cape Cod. Falmouth has become the center for sailboarding on the Cape because of its beaches. Cape beaches typically prohibit the launching of sailboards at lifeguard-protected beaches until late afternoon. A section of Kalmus Beach in Hyannis is reserved for sailboarding. Check with town offices for full details. If you are new to the sport, sail only in areas where, if necessary, others can rescue you. Don't sailboard without someone on the beach watching you who has the ability to get help. For prolonged periods on and in the water, insulated wet suits are a must to prevent hypothermia, which can result in death. First-timers, don't go on the water without good instruction on how to handle and maneuver your sailboard nor without knowing effective safety and survival procedures.

Cape Cod National Seashore

(Beaches, biking and hiking trails, historic attractions, etc., are detailed under specific categories in this guide.)

Cape Cod National Seashore is open to the public all year. Nominal parking fees are charged at all beaches during the summer season (either from Memorial Day weekend or the end of June to Labor Day),

but parking is free at other times during the year. Permits are required for open fires, overnight beach parking for surf-fishing, and the use of over-sand vehicles. Permits are obtained at visitors centers. Licenses for shellfish gathering are obtained at town offices. Cape Cod National Seashore Headquarters (349-3785; www.nps.gov/caco) is located off Route 6 at the Marconi Station entrance in South Wellfleet. Headquarters is open daily from 8:00 A.M. to 4:30 P.M., Monday through Friday. Salt Pond Visitor Center (255-3421) is located off Route 6 in Eastham. It is both the largest and the first one approached by most people coming to this area of the Lower Cape. Salt Pond is open daily but closed during the months of January and February. Province Lands Visitor Center (487-1256) is located off Route 6 near the junction of Province Lands Road and Race Point Road in Provincetown. Province Lands is open daily from Easter through Thanksgiving.

During the summer season, visitors centers are in operation from 9:00 A.M. to 6:00 P.M., and a diversified program of ranger-conducted interpretive activities is available seven days a week. Special evening programs also originate at the visitors centers. Contact them for a current schedule of programs, activities, and events. Interpretive activities operate on a reduced schedule from Labor Day to Columbus Day. Cape Cod National Seashore visitors centers have rangers on hand to provide information and answer questions. They also have folders, regulations, and maps describing various aspects of the national seashore. They offer interesting audiovisual programs and displays, scenic overlooks, departure points for biking and hiking trails, ample parking lots, rest rooms, picnic areas, conveniences for the handicapped, and seashore-related books for sale.

There are lodgings, campgrounds, restaurants, and stores near the entrances of Cape Cod National Seashore located along Route 6 and in the town centers of Orleans, Eastham, Wellfleet, Truro, and Provincetown. The nearest state-operated campground is at Nickerson State Park (896-3491) on Route 6A in East Brewster.

Cape Cod National Seashore, an entity of the National Park Service, is a spectacular natural and historic preserve of more than 43,500 acres running along most of the Lower Cape. It extends in a north/south direction for 40 miles through the towns of Orleans, Eastham, Wellfleet, Truro, and Provincetown. Most of its coastline is along the open Atlantic, but there are also large sections of beach along Cape Cod Bay. The Atlantic beaches are among the finest on the entire East Coast. They include miles of wide, flat stretches, high sand-and-clay cliffs, and many acres of massive sand dunes. The Atlantic side of Cape Cod National Seashore is the leading edge of the U.S. mainland against powerful storms that blow in from the northeast. The action of tide and wind keep eating away at this shoreline, while on the other side of the peninsula, on Cape Cod Bay, land is in the process of being built up by these same forces of nature.

There is an abundance of marine life in the waters and intertidal areas of Cape Cod National Seashore—horseshoe and fiddler crabs, razor clams, quahogs, oysters, lobsters, flounder, bluefish, and whales. Within the interior of Cape Cod National Seashore are other complex and fragile ecological zones and habitats: bogs, marshes, swamps, woodland, glacial ponds (kettle holes), and tidal flats; various species of flora; fauna such as white-tailed deer, foxes, rabbits, and raccoons; and a wide variety of migratory waterfowl and land birds.

Cape Cod National Seashore also has a rich human history. In South Wellfleet, Marconi built one of his transatlantic wireless signal stations. At Orleans, one of the first underwater cables linking the United States and Europe was laid. The United States Coast Guard evolved from the lifesaving operations along this coast. Hundreds of ships were wrecked offshore, including the *Whidah*, containing millions of dollars' worth of treasure now being salvaged. On lands within what is now Cape Cod National Seashore, whaling captains had palatial homes, and one of the most impressive of all, the Captain Penniman House, is open to visitors. Along the coastal length of this national seashore are several picturesque lighthouses, beacons of hope and safety for mariners.

Within Cape Cod National Seashore there are excellent beaches for swimming, fishing, sunbathing, picnicking, hiking, exploring, and surfing. There are biking and hiking trails and special trails for motorized or horseback sand-dune riding. At Salt Pond there is a sensory trail for blind hikers. There are also special ranger-conducted day and evening interpretive programs for adults and children. Cape Cod National Seashore is one of the best values going on this vacation peninsula, and it's accessible to everyone.

Bird-Watching

On Cape Cod and the islands, more than 357 species of birds can be found at various times—that's almost half the approximately 725 species of birds found in the United States.

Among good places to bird-watch:

Monomoy Island, Chatham, 945-0594, home to twenty-nine resident bird species and stopping-off point for more than 285 species of migratory birds

Ashumet Holly And Wildlife Sanctuary, Route 151, Falmouth, 563-6390

Great Salt Marsh Conservation Area, Sandy Neck Road, Barnstable, 362-8300

Bells Neck Conservation Area, Bells Neck Road, West Harwich

Salt Pond, Route 6, Eastham

Wellfleet Bay Wildlife Sanctuary, Route 6 Wellfleet, 349-2615

Province Lands, Route 6, Provincetown

The Massachusetts Audubon Society, which operates both Wellfleet Bay Wildlife Sanctuary and Ashumet Holly and Wildlife Sanctuary, offers both bird-watching and other nature programs (seal cruises, etc.) throughout the year

The Cape Cod Museum of Natural History in Brewster, 896-3867, also offers bird- and other wildlife-watches throughout the year

A WILDERNESS

Monomoy Island lies just off Chatham. It's the only national wilderness area in southern New England and is accessible only by boat. Headquarters for this wilderness is easily reached by car on Morris Island (no relation), where you can find a trail and beach backed by cliffs, sand dunes, and salt marsh.

Monomoy is fascinating for two reasons: It is one of the best birding areas in the East, and it is a lesson on how fierce the Atlantic Ocean can be. In 1958 all this land was a part of Monomoy Point, an 8-mile barrier beach. Then a storm broke through the barrier beach, creating the island. In 1978 the northeaster that brought the Blizzard of '78 to Boston (closing the city for more than a week) hit the island with enough force to split it in two. North Monomoy is 2½ miles long, with sand dunes and salt marsh. South Monomoy is 5 miles long, with woodlands, ponds, and sandy beach.

Nearly 300 species of birds find their way here; tens of thousands of sea and shorebirds pass through the area on their annual spring and fall migrations. In winter more than 100,000 common eiders, rarely seen elsewhere, can be viewed on Monomoy. Seals are also found in abundance on the island.

In Chatham and Harwich boat trips to the island are offered. Both the Cape Cod Museum of Natural History and the Wellfleet Bay Wildlife Sanctuary offer trips with naturalists. Overnight stays in the lighthouse are also possible.

Children's Camps

Because of the unique land and sea environment, historical heritage, and ability to attract top professionals in recreation, Cape Cod camps are well known for the quality of their staffs, programs, facilities, and services. For close to seven decades, thousands of children throughout North America have enjoyed the camping experience on Cape Cod. The residential and day camps listed below are recommended for your consideration. For additional information, contact the Cape Cod Association of Children's Camps, P.O. Box 38, Brewster, 02631. (ACA indicates American Camping Association accreditation.)

Animal Friends Summer Camp, coed, day, ACA; established 1945, on Megansett Harbor in North Falmouth 563-6116; c/o Animal Rescue League of Boston, P.O. Box 265, Boston, 02117; (617) 426-9170. Hands-on programs in ocean ecology, farm animals, arts and crafts; for children six to thirteen

Camps Burgess and Hayward, YMCA boys and girls, residential, ACA; established 1928, on Spectacle Pond in Sandwich; 428-2571. Family atmosphere for children eight to fourteen; programs in athletics, archery, tennis, swimming, sailing, boating, water skiing, photography, and other skills

Cape Cod Sea Camps Monomoy/Wono, coed, residential, ACA; established 1922, on Cape Cod Bay; P.O. Box 13, Brewster, 02631, 896-3451. The oldest residential camp on Cape Cod; family atmosphere for children seven to fifteen; more than forty land- and water-based activities

Wellfleet Bay Wildlife Sanctuary Natural History Day Camp, Wellfleet, 349-2615. Half-day and full-day programs offered in summer

Camp Good News, coed, residential, ACA; established in 1935; P.O. Box 95, Forestdale, 02644, 477-9731. Christian values in a comprehensive, residential camping environment; traditional activities and skills instruction; for children eight to thirteen

The Family School Summer Camp, coed, day; established in 1983; RFD 2, Brewster, 02631, 896-6555. Comprehensive day-camp program for children from one month to fourteen years; swimming, gymnastics, arts and crafts, field and racquet sports, archery, farming, nature, dance, drama, carpentry, horseback riding, sailing, and canoeing; family values stressed

Camp Farley, 4-H, coed, residential and day; established in 1934, on Wakeby Pond in Mashpee; P.O. Box 97, Forestdale, 02644, 477-0181. Development, by 4-H philosophy, of physical and emotional strengths in campers eight to thirteen; swimming, sailing, canoeing, horseback riding, archery, arts and crafts

Camp Favorite, Girl Scout, residential, ACA; established in 1962, on Long Pond in Brewster; c/o Patriot Trails GS Council, 6 St. James Avenue, Boston, 02116, 896-3831. Major programs of sailing and biking; activities chosen, carried out, and evaluated by the individual camper with the support of adult leaders; for girls eight to seventeen

YMCA Summer Day Camps at Camp Lyndon, Sandwich and Camp 123, West Barnstable; (800) 339-YMCA

Tumble Time Gymnastics, Jonathan Bourne Drive, Pocasset, 563-1200. Summer camp classes for those five to twelve

Brewster Day Camp, 3570 Main Street, Brewster, 896-6555. Programs range from sailing and canoeing to nature, music, and archery. Swimming lessons also. For infant to thirteen-year-olds

The Academy of Performing Arts, 5 Giddiah Hill Road, Orleans, 255-5510. Music, dance, and drama. "Drop-ins" welcome

Monomoy Day Camp, coed, day, ACA; established in 1963, on Cape Cod Bay; Box 13, Brewster, 02631, 896-3451. Recreational access to salt water, a lake, and a swimming pool; sailing, swimming, archery, riflery, arts and crafts, drama, athletics, and computers; children four to fifteen

Mini Golf

Sea View Playland, Lower County Road, Dennisport, 398-9084. Eighteen-hole miniature golf, plus skee ball, games, refreshments

Bass River Sports World, 928 Route 28, South Yarmouth, 398-6070. Also baseball and softball machines, game room driving range, and rock climbing wall

Cape Escape Orleans Mini Golf, 14 Canal Road, 240-1791. Near the rotary. Eighteen-holes for the "ultimate golf adventure"

The Club House Mini Golf, Route 39, across from the Stop & Shop, East Harwich, 432-4820. A lighthouse towers over the course

Cape Cod Storyland Golf, 70 Center Street, Hyannis, 778-6553. Also bumper boats

Lightning Falls Adventure Golf, 455 West Main Street, Hyannis, 771-3194

Thunder Falls Adventure Golf, 759-1747. Behind Tanger Outlet Stores. Two eighteen-hole golf courses

Bourne Bridge Adventure Golf, 759-1747. Behind Tanger Outlet Stores. Two eighteen-hole golf courses

Putter's Paradise, Route 28, West Yarmouth, 771-7394

Holiday Hill, Route 28, Dennisport, 398-8857. Waterfalls, bumper cars, and gift shop

Thunder Mine Adventure, Route 28A, Bourne, 563-7450

Wellfleet Drive-in, Wellfleet, 349-2520

Water Wizz Water Park, Routes 6 and 28, two miles from Bourne Bridge, 295-3255

Harbor Glen Miniature Golf, Route 28, Harwich, 432-8240. Has waterfalls, adjacent restaurant

Pirate's Cove Adventure Golf, 728 Route 28, Yarmouth, 394-6200. Two eighteen-hole courses with waterfalls

Public Golf Courses

Because of its relatively mild climate during the cold-weather months, Cape Cod is New England's best area for four-seasons golf. Many public courses are open all year. Call ahead, though, to be sure the course is open. Most courses have equipment and cart rentals, pro shops, lounges, snack bars and/or restaurants, and other amenities. Because of the overwhelming number of people who come to the Cape to hit the links, you should call and reserve a tee time as far as one week in advance for some of the more popular courses.

For twenty-four-hour golf information, call (800) TEE BALL.

Ballymeade Country Club, semi-private, eighteen holes, par 72, has driving range, putting green, restaurant. 125 Falmouth Woods Road, North Falmouth, 540-4005

Bass River Golf Course, eighteen holes, par 72, has views of Bass River. 62 Highbank Road, South Yarmouth, 398-9079

Bayberry Hills Golf Course, eighteen holes, par 72, has driving range, pro shop. West Yarmouth Road, South Yarmouth, 394-9557

Bay Pointe Country Club, eighteen holes, par 70, has tennis, pool. Onset Avenue, Onset, 759-8802 or (800) 248-8463

Blue Rock Golf Course, eighteen holes, par 54, has golf school. 48 Todd Road, South Yarmouth, 398-9295

The Brookside Club, eighteen holes, par 70, has driving range, pro shop. Brigadoon Road, Bourne, 743-4653

Cape Cod Country Club, eighteen holes, par 71, very scenic. Route 151, North Falmouth, 563-9842

The Captains Golf Course, thirty-six holes, par 72, named for Brewster sea captains. 1000 Freeman's Way, Brewster, 896-1716 or 896-5100

Chatham Seaside Links, nine holes, par 34. 209 Seaview Street, Chatham, 945-4774

Chequessett Yacht & Country Club, nine holes (eighteen holes with different tees), par 70/74, has ocean views. Chequessett Neck Road, Wellfleet, 349-3704

Cotuit Highground Country Club, nine holes, par 28. Crocker Neck Road, Cotuit, 428-9863

Cranberry Valley Golf Course, eighteen holes, par 72, has driving range, putting green. Oak Street, Harwich, 430-7560

Dennis Highlands Golf Course, eighteen holes, par 71, has driving range. 825 Old Bass River Road, Dennis, 385-8347

Dennis Pines Golf Course, eighteen holes, par 72. Route 134, East Dennis, 385-8347

Falmouth Country Club, eighteen holes, par 72. 600 Carriage Shop Road, East Falmouth, 548-3211

Harwich Port Golf Club, nine holes, two par 3, two par 4. South Street, Harwich Port, 432-0250

Highland Links, nine holes/eighteen holes, different tees have ocean views, Highland Light Road, North Truro, 487-9201

Holly Ridge Golf Club, eighteen holes, par 54, has driving range, pro shop, restaurant. Harlow Road, South Sandwich, 428-5577

Hyannis Golf Club, eighteen holes, par 71, has driving range, pro shop, restaurant. Route 132, Hyannis, 362-2606

King's Way Golf Club, eighteen holes, par 59, has pro shop, restaurant. Route 6A, Yarmouthport, 362-8870

New Seabury Country Club, semiprivate, public September to May, eighteen holes, par 72. Shore Drive, New Seabury, 477-9110

Ocean Edge Resort & Golf Club, eighteen holes, par 72, has driving range, pro shop. Route 6A, Brewster, 896-5911

Olde Barnstable Fairgrounds Golf Course, eighteen holes, par 71, has driving range, pro shop. Route 149, Marston Mills, 420-1141

Paul Harney Golf Club, eighteen holes, par 59. 74 Club Valley Drive, East Falmouth, 563-3454

Pocasset Golf Club, private, eighteen holes. Club House Drive, Pocasset, 563-7171

Quashnet Valley Country Club, eighteen holes, par 72, has pro shop, restaurant. 309 Old Barnstable Road, Mashpee, 477-4412

Round Hill Country Club, eighteen holes, par 71. Round Hill Road, East Sandwich, 888-3384

Sheraton Twin Brooks Golf Course, eighteen holes, par 27. 3 West End Circle, Hyannis, 775-7775

Woodbriar Golf Club, 9 holes, par 27. 339 Gifford Street, Falmouth, 495-5500

Tennis

There are public and private tennis courts located throughout Cape Cod. In addition to the courts listed below, most resorts and many motels have private tennis courts for use by their guests. Your best bet is to call for court availability.

BARNSTABLE

Cape Cod Community College, Route 132, six hardtop courts, one backboard court

Along Route 6A, two hardtop courts

BOURNE

Bourne Memorial Community Building, two courts

Behind Town Hall, one court

Head of Bay Road, one court

Queen Seawell Park, two courts

Monument Beach, Chester Park, two courts

Back of Pocasset Fire Station, two courts

Kieth Field, Sagamore, one court

BREWSTER

Ocean Edge Resort, Route 6A, 896-9000

Bamburgh House Tennis Club, 896-5023

Brewster Fire Department, Main Street

CENTERVILLE

Near Elementary School, off Bumps Road

Cotuit Elementary School, 140 Old Oyster Road

CHATHAM

Chatham Bars Inn, four all-weather courts, lessons, pro shop, 945-0096

Queen Ann Tennis, 70 Queen Ann Road, 945-4726

Playground, Kitty's Lane, South Chatham

Chatham Playground, Depot Street

Chatham High School, six courts

DENNIS

Dennis Racquet & Swim Club, off Oxbow Way, 385-2221

Sesuit Tennis Center, three courts, Route 6A, East Dennis, 385-2200

Wixon Middle School, off Route 134

EASTHAM

Norseman Athletic Club, Route 6, 255-6370

Nauset Regional High School, five courts, charge June through Labor Day

FALMOUTH

Falmouth Sports Center, six indoor courts, three outdoor courts, 548-7433

Nautilus Motor Inn, two courts, charge

Ballymeade Country Club, ten courts, 125 Falmouth Woods Road, 540-4005

Falmouth Tennis Club, three clay, three Har-Tru, Dillingham Avenue, 548-4370

Nye Park, North Falmouth, time limits

By Fire Station, two courts, West Falmouth

Woods Hole Park, two courts, Woods Hole

Elementary School, two courts, East Falmouth. Time limits

High School, eight courts, local residents have preference

Lawrence School, two courts

HARWICH

Wychmere Harbor Tennis Club, 710 Main Street, 430-7012. Seasonal

Manning's Tennis Courts, 292 Main Street, 432-3958

Melrose Tennis Center, clay courts, 792 Main Street, 539-1446

Cape Cod Technical High School, Route 24

Brooks Park, Route 39, call for reservations, 430-7553

HYANNIS

Sheraton Hyannis Hotel & Resort, two courts, West End Circle, 775-7775

The Fitness Club, 55 Attucks Lane, 771-7734

Old Barnstable Junior High School, off South Street

Barnstable Junior High School, Route 28

MASHPEE

Mashpee Leisure Services, 16 Great Neck Road, 539-1446

Southcape Resort & Club, 477-4700

ORLEANS

Eldredge Park, Route 28 and Eldredge Parkway, charge June through August

OSTERVILLE

Off West Bay Road, two courts

PROVINCETOWN

Provincetown Tennis Club, seven courts, 286 Bradford Street, 487–9574

Provincetown High School, Motta Field, Winslow Street, students have preference

Bissell Tennis Courts, 21 Bradford Street, 487–9512

SANDWICH

Wing Elementary School, off Route 130

Oak Ridge School, off Quaker Meetinghouse Road

Forestdale School, off Route 130

TRURO

Pamet Harbor Yacht & Tennis Club, 7 Yacht Club Road, 349–3772

WELLFLEET

Oliver Tennis Courts, Route 6, 349–3330

YARMOUTH

Mid-Cape Racquet & Health Club, ten courts, 193 White's Path, 394–3511

Dennis-Yarmouth Regional High School, ten courts

Flax Pond Recreation Area, four courts

Sandy Pond Recreation Area, four courts

Running

If you're into running, there's no place like Falmouth. The annual Falmouth Road Race held each August has become world famous. Entries open and close in early May. For an entry form, send a stamped, self-addressed envelope to Falmouth Road Race, P.O. Box 732, Falmouth, 02541, or check out the Web site at www.falmouthroadrace.com.

Other Falmouth races:

Quarter Deck Five, every Friday at 5:30 P.M., starting at Town Hall

April: Seagull Six Spring Classic Race, Woods Hole; Sons of Italy Road Race, Otis Air Base

May: Coast Guard 10K Road Race, Otis Air Base; March of Dimes, Walk America by the Sea, Road Race Route; Annual Biathlon on Otis

July: Paul White Road Race, 4.81 miles, North Falmouth; Falmouth Sprint Triathlon, Surf Drive

August: Annual Falmouth Road Race; no unregistered runners allowed

September: Falmouth Main Street Mile, Falmouth Track Club

October: Cape Cod Marathon, 26.2 miles, starting at Village Green; also five-leg marathon relay

November: Falmouth-in-the-Fall Road Race, 7.1 miles, Road Race course; Chase the Turkey Trot, Falmouth Academy

Best Bike Trails

Biking has become one of the most pleasurable ways of touring Cape Cod. Biking takes you out in the open and gets you close to nature. It takes longer to go from place to place, but you see everything in more detail and with greater intimacy. Biking has become such an important leisure activity on Cape Cod that most towns and the Cape Cod National Seashore have established special bike trails, some of which are totally isolated from motorized vehicles.

The entire length of Cape Cod is crisscrossed with bike trails, The Boston/Cape Cod Bikeway is in two sections: 65 miles from Boston to Bourne on the Clair Saltonstall Memorial Bikeway; and 70 miles from Bourne to Provincetown, with a side route to Woods Hole. For a map of this bikeway, send a self-addressed, stamped envelope to C.T.P.S., 27 School Street, Boston, MA 02108. The Cape Cod Rail Trail, allowing biking, jogging, and horseback riding, is 20 miles long and extends from Route 134 in Dennis to Locust Road in Eastham. Parking is available at Nickerson State Park in Brewster, Route 124 in Harwich, and at the Salt Pond Visitors Center (Cape Cod National Seashore) in Eastham. A booklet entitled *Bikeways on Cape Cod* is free from the Cape Cod Chamber of Commerce.

Whether on a short or extended bike tour, *always keep to the right of the trail*; don't speed, and look out for other bikers, hikers, and dogs. Most bike trails have paved surfaces, but watch for slippery patches of sand. The terrain is generally flat with some hilly areas. There are several bike rental and repair shops on the Cape (a listing of rental places is provided below). The following are Cape Cod's best bike tours. If you want more information about these and other tours, get a copy of *Short Bike Rides on Cape Cod, Nantucket & the Vineyard* by Edwin Mullen and Jane Griffith, available at bookstores or from The Globe Pequot Press, P.O. Box 480, Guilford, Connecticut 06437.

Cape Cod Canal in Sandwich—6.8 miles from Bourne Bridge to Sandwich along the canal and to the Sandwich attractions of Heritage Plantation, Glass Museum, and Hoxie House

Bourne—15.5 miles from Bourne Bridge to North Falmouth through the villages of Cataumet and Pocasset

West Barnstable to Sandy Neck—4.3 miles from the Old Village Store to Sandy Neck Beach on Cape Cod Bay, one of the most extensive marsh, beach, and sand-dune areas on Cape Cod

Barnstable to Cummaquid—6.8 miles along historic Route 6A with its beautiful old homes and adjacent beaches

West Falmouth to Woods Hole on the "Shining Sea Trail"—5 miles on the trail, named in honor of Katherine Lee Bates, author of "America" ("...from sea to shining sea"); to Woods Hole with its many scientific institutions, Harvard Square atmosphere, and steamship access to the islands of Martha's Vineyard and Nantucket; also to Nobska Point with its famous lighthouse and to Quissett Harbor, one of the loveliest on the East Coast

Osterville to Centerville—7 miles through affluent Osterville and past some of the grand mansions on Cape Cod

The Cape Cod Rail Trail—19.6 miles from Brewster to the Salt Pond Visitor Center of the Cape Cod National Seashore on what was formerly the main Cape Cod railroad line

West Yarmouth to South Yarmouth—14.5 miles through sedate sections of Cape Cod and along its busiest stretch on Route 28

West Dennis to Harwich Port—eighteen miles meandering past historic homes and fine harbors on the Cape's south coast

Harwich to West Chatham—14 miles along the coast of one of Cape Cod's most prestigious towns

West Brewster to Dennis—21 miles weaving past historic homes, the Cape Cod Museum of Natural History, Sealand of Cape Cod, art galleries, and craft shops

Brewster to Nickerson State Park—8 miles through lovely scenery with several freshwater ponds; camping in Nickerson State Park

Chatham—8.5 miles along a meandering route of pretty byways and the waterways of Chatham; great for exploring a quintessential Cape Cod town

Orleans—13.2 miles from Rock Harbor on Cape Cod Bay to Nauset Beach, a part of Cape Cod National Seashore where intrepid surfboard riders take on the waves

Eastham to Coast Guard Beach—3.7 miles (one of Cape Cod National Seashore's bike trails) from Salt Pond Visitor Center to both Coast Guard and Nauset Light beaches along Ocean View Drive

South Wellfleet to Marconi Station—9.6 miles from the Massachusetts Audubon Society reservation on Cape Cod Bay to Marconi Wireless Station and Marconi Beach within Cape Cod National Seashore

South Wellfleet to LeCount Hollow—9.7 miles to Le Count Hollow, White Crest, Cahoon Hollow, and Newcomb Hollow beaches, all within Cape Cod National Seashore along Ocean View Drive, an area of high sand-clay cliffs and broad beaches

Wellfleet to Great Island—6.8 miles through Wellfleet Center and along the town harbor to the Great Island Trail's head and to Duck Harbor Beach on Cape Cod Bay, both within Cape Cod National Seashore

North Truro to The Highlands—9.8 miles within Cape Cod National Seashore from Pilgrim Lake past famous Highland Light (Cape Cod Light), Jenny Lind Tower, Head of The Meadow Beaches, and nearby massive sand dunes

Province Lands—8.75 miles (the major Cape Cod National Seashore bike trail in the Provincetown area) along Herring Cove and Race Point beaches, Beach Forest area, rolling sand dunes, and the Province Lands Visitor Center

Provincetown—8.5 miles through Cape Cod's most fascinating and colorful town via Commercial Street and then to Herring Cove and Race Point beaches within Cape Cod National Seashore

Bike Rentals

BOURNE

P&M Cycles, 759-2830, 29 Main Street, Buzzards Bay

SANDWICH

Cape Cod Bike Rentals/Sandwich Cycles, 833-2453, 40 Route 6A

FALMOUTH

Art's Bike Shop, 800-563-7379, Old Main and County Roads
Bike Zone, 540-BIKE, 278 Teaticket Highway, Route 28
Corner Cycle, 540-4195, 115 Palmer Avenue
Holiday Cycles, 540-3549, 465 Grand Avenue, Falmouth Heights

HYANNIS

Bike Zone, 775-3299, 323 Barnstable Road
Cascade Motor Lodge, 775-9717, 201 Main Street
One World Bike Rental, 771-4242, 631 Main Street

YARMOUTH

All Right Bike & Mower Shop, 790-3191, 627 Route 28
Barbara's Bike and Sports Equipment, 760-4723, Route 134
The Outdoor Shop, 394-3819, 50 Long Pond Drive
Yarmouth Bicycle & Fitness, 394-8941, 63 White's Path

BREWSTER

Rail Trail Bike Rentals, 896-8200, 302 Underpass Road
Brewster Bike Rental, 896-8149, 442 Underpass Road

HARWICH

Harwichport Bike Company, 430-0200, 431 Route 28

CHATHAM

Bert & Carol's Lawnmower and Bicycle Shop, 945-0137, 347 Route 28,
   North Chatham
Bikes & Blades, 945-7500, 195 Crowell Road

ORLEANS

Orleans Cycle, 255-9115, 26 Main Street

EASTHAM

Idle Times Bike Shop, 255-8281, Route 6

Little Capistrano Bike Shop, 255-6515, across from Salt Pond Visitors Center

TRURO

Bayside Bikes, 487-5735, 102 Shore Road

WELLFLEET

Black duck Sports Shop, 349-9801, Route 6

Idle Times Bike Shop, 349-9161, Route 6

PROVINCETOWN

Arnold's, 487-0844, 329 Commercial Street

Galeforce Bicycle Rental, 487-4849, 144 Bradford Street

Nelson's Bike Shop, 487-8849, 43 Race Point Road

Ptown Bikes, 487-8735, 42 Bradford Street

Best Cape Walks

The philosopher Henry David Thoreau was so impressed with his hike along the windswept, sea-shaped Lower Cape that he wrote a book about his trek that has since inspired thousands. Thoreau's *Cape Cod* has become a classic of American literature. To hike in any area of Cape Cod is to experience nature at its best. Hugh and Heather Sadlier have written an excellent guide to experiencing the Cape on foot. Their *Short Nature Walks: Cape Cod, Nantucket, and the Vineyard* is available at bookstores or from The Globe Pequot Press, P.O. Box 480, Guilford, Connecticut 06437. When hiking Cape Cod, be sure to wear comfortable shoes. While on trails, don't pick flowers or pull up beach grass and shrubbery. Don't litter, and watch out for poison ivy. Check clothing, hair, and pets for ticks, which can cause Lyme disease. Hikers allergic to insect bites should get immediate medical treatment if bitten.

The following short hikes are among the best on Cape Cod. Each area has easy and more strenuous trails. Some areas charge a nominal fee for parking or admission during the summer. Elderly persons and young children should be able to hike most of these areas without much strain or discomfort.

Ashumet Holly Reservation, run by the Massachusetts Audubon Society, is located off Route 151 in Falmouth and noted for its varieties of European and Oriental hollies; it was originally developed by Wilfred Wheeler. Ashumet Holly is one of Cape Cod's premier attractions. Admission is charged. Round-trip distance—1¼ miles.

Lowell Holly Reservation is a 130-acre natural preserve located between Wakeby and Mashpee ponds in the town of Mashpee, and reached via South Sandwich Road. This park of diverse plantings was owned and developed by Abbott Lawrence Lowell, a president of Harvard, who donated it to the Massachusetts Trustees of Reservations, a prominent conservation organization. Admission is charged. Round-trip distance—2 miles.

Wakeby Holly Sanctuary and Recreation Area in Mashpee has trails that take you through fine stands of high holly trees, 150-year-old beeches, tall pines, oaks, and maples. The trail goes beside a formerly productive cranberry bog. There is a nature center here and a beach on Wakeby Pond. Boating and fishing are allowed on the pond, though you need a license for freshwater angling, which can be obtained at Sandwich town offices. Access is from Route 130 to Cotuit Road. Admission is charged. Round-trip distance—2.1 miles.

The Old Briar Patch in Sandwich memorializes Thornton W. Burgess, the children's author who wrote about the adventures of Peter Rabbit, Reddy Fox, Hooty Owl, and Paddy Beaver. The Old Briar Patch Trail brings you into swampy areas and those of tall white pine. Access is from Route 6A in Sandwich to Chipman Road to Crowell Road and then into a parking area off Gully Lane. Admission is free. Round-trip distance—2 miles.

Talbot's Point Salt Marsh Wildlife Reservation in Sandwich is a peninsula of land that juts into one of the largest salt-marsh areas on Cape Cod. The trails take you through stands of red pine and beech. Access is from Route 6A and Old Colony Road. Admission is free. Round-trip distance—1½ miles.

Sandy Neck, located in West Barnstable, is a magnificent ecological composite of high, undulating sand dunes; one of the longest uncluttered beaches on Cape Cod; broad salt marshes supporting a wide variety of birds and marine life; and the ever-changing moods

A HIKE AND PADDLE ALONG THE CAPE

"A journey of a thousand miles begins with a single footstep"—or, perhaps, paddlestroke.

Al LePage has a dream; he's out to create an East Coast Trail, a pathway that would stretch from the Florida Keys all the way to the coast of Maine. LePage took the first steps—and paddled—toward this goal along the coast of Cape Cod in the summer of 1999.

"A Cape Cod hike and paddle illustrates the opportunities to be discovered along an East Coast Trail quite well," said LePage. "The Great Beach of Cape Cod, with its towering dunes, the smell of salt marsh, the quiet of a pine forest, ripples on kettle-hole ponds, is a chance to connect with nature's beauty. Glaciers and the Ice Age, the Native Americans who lived there, the *Mayflower* and the Pilgrims, whaling ships, Marconi's wireless station are all chances to connect with history. Cape Cod architecture and lighthouses, cranberry bogs, and art galleries offer a chance to connect with local culture."

Others have hiked these shores, including Henry David Thoreau. LePage's mission is to not only preserve the natural, historic, and cultural resources of the shore, but to open the shorefront to all for recreation. Much of the Cape's shorefront is private, based on laws dating to colonial times. By combining kayaking with his "walk," LePage is proving an East Coast Trail is possible. He points to the Appalachian Trail as proof of a dream becoming reality.

If you want to try this hike and paddle, read Thoreau's *Cape Cod* (the book is a staple in Cape bookstores), visit the Cape Cod National Seashore visitors center for information, or contact LePage at the National Coast Trail Association in Oregon by calling (503) 335-3876 or on the Web at www.coasttrails.org.

of Cape Cod Bay's water and sky. At Sandy Neck you can hike for hours, swim, comb the beach for cast-off odds and ends, enjoy a picnic, fish, and get a nice tan. Access is off Route 6A near the West Barnstable and Sandwich town line. Admission is charged for parking during the summer.

Yarmouth Botanic Trails take you from an herb garden into open fields, areas of pines and oaks, and past Miller's Pond. Various species of wildflowers grow along this route. Access is off Route 6A, behind

Yarmouth Post Office. Admission is charged. Round-trip distance—
1¼ miles.

John Wing Trail in Brewster allows you to explore beautiful Wing's
Island: thirty-three acres of upland and ninety acres of beach and
salt marsh on Cape Cod Bay in Brewster. Access off Route 6A, with
parking at the Cape Cod Museum of Natural History. Admission is
free. Round-trip distance—1.3 miles.

Cape Cod Museum of Natural History is in Brewster. Admission is charged
to visit the museum itself but the trails are free. North Trail
explores the salt-marsh area. Access is off Route 6A and main building of museum. Round-trip distance—¼ mile. South Trail takes you
through a marsh and into an upland area of fine, old beech trees.
Access off Route 6A, across the highway from the museum complex. Round-trip distance—¾ mile. Also, John Wing Trail offers a
walk with good birding through salt marsh to Wing Island.

Stoney Brook Mill Sites lie in Brewster, where, during the summer, you
can watch grain being milled the old-fashioned way. There's also
the tranquillity of a mill pond, a herring run, and the beauty of
diverse flowers and plantings. Access off Route 6A and Stoney
Brook Road. Admission is free. Round-trip distance—¼ mile.

The Seaside Trail in Chatham runs along the harbor and brings you to
salt marshes, dunes, saltwater inlets, and areas of beach plum and
salt-spray rose. You can comb the beach for shells and watch the
terns and gulls wheeling above. Access is off Route 28, Barn Hill
Road, and Harding's Beach Road. Admission is charged. Round-trip
distance—2 miles.

Fort Hill Trail (Cape Cod National Seashore) in Eastham takes you to a
whaling captain's house, Nauset Marsh and views of the open
Atlantic, Skiff Hill, and along the boardwalks through Red Maple
Swamp. Access off Route 6. Admission is free. Round-trip distance—1½ miles.

Buttonbush Trail (Cape Cod National Seashore) in Eastham is a special
sensory trail for the blind along which they can smell, feel, and hear
the natural environment around them. Access off Route 6, starting
from the Salt Pond Visitor Center. Admission is free. Round-trip
distance—¼ mile.

Nauset Marsh Trail (Cape Cod National Seashore) in Eastham shows you
the diverse ecological zones of this area of the Lower Cape: salt
pond, estuary, marsh, and upland woods, also the variety of birds,
small mammals, and intertidal marine life. Access is off Route 6,

starting from Salt Pond Visitors Center. Admission is free. Round-trip distance—1.2 miles.

Wellfleet Bay Wildlife Sanctuary in South Wellfleet is run by the Massachusetts Audubon Society and offers several hiking trails that explore the woodlands, marshes, and fresh- and saltwater areas adjacent to Cape Cod Bay. This is a good bird-observing area. Access off Route 6; watch for signs. Admission is charged. Round-trip distance—1½ miles.

Atlantic White Cedar Swamp Trail (Cape Cod National Seashore) lies in South Wellfleet at Marconi Station Site. The best part of this hike is the walk on a meandering boardwalk through a swamp thick with white cedars and other flora. Access off Route 6; follow signs to Marconi Station Site. Admission is free. Round-trip distance—1¼ miles.

Great Island Trail (Cape Cod National Seashore) in Wellfleet is a long hike on a peninsula that juts into Wellfleet Harbor and Cape Cod Bay. This area was used by whalers as a station complete with a tavern. It is now a place of sand dunes, beach grass, pitch pines, and magnificent views. Great Island is also a prime bird-observing area. Bring a sun hat and a canteen of water for this hike. Also watch that you don't get cut off by high tide in the lower areas toward the peninsula's end. Access off Route 6, through Wellfleet Center, and at the end of Chequesset Neck Road. Admission is free. Round-trip distance—8.4 miles.

Pilgrim Spring Trail (Cape Cod National Seashore) in North Truro takes you to salt meadows, giant sand dunes, and views of the Atlantic. In 1620 the Pilgrims refreshed themselves here with the first fresh water since leaving England. Access off Route 6; watch for signs. Admission is free. Round-trip distance—¾ mile.

Small Swamp Nature Trail (Cape Cod National Seashore) in North Truro provides a hardy walk during which you observe birds, small mammals, and indigenous flora. It goes over undulating, sandy terrain and offers views of dunes and salt meadows. Access from the Interpretive Shelter in the Pilgrim Spring area (see above) off Route 6. Admission is free. Round-trip distance—¾ mile.

Beech Forest Trail (Cape Cod National Seashore) in Provincetown is virtually at land's end on Cape Cod. It traverses sand dunes, explores a forest of beech trees, and goes around a freshwater pond. Access off Route 6 and Race Point Road in the Province Lands area. Admission is free. Round-trip distance—1 mile.

Fishing, Boating, and Shellfishing

Fishing is one of Cape Cod's most popular activities for all ages. You do not need to buy a license or pay special town fees to fish for saltwater species, which include cod, haddock, striped bass, salmon, tuna, swordfish, flounder, sea bass, ocean perch, halibut, and shark. Most Cape Cod beaches allow surf casting; however, individual towns and the Cape Cod National Seashore require surfcasters to obtain permits for overnight parking at beaches. Towns and the Cape Cod National Seashore require permits for the use of recreational vehicles on beaches. Many beaches are off limits to RVs. Freshwater fishing is regulated, and you do need a license, which can be obtained at town halls. Children under fifteen are not required to have a license. Many persons with disabilities can get freshwater fishing licenses for free. Cape Cod has lots of bait-and-tackle shops, boat-rental places, marinas, charter-fishing boats, and boat-launching sites. Most deep-sea fishing operations provide equipment, bait, snacks, drinks, and fish-cleaning services.

Cape Cod Tides

To those unfamiliar with the ways of the sea, the odd thing about high tides along the Cape Cod shoreline is that they occur at different times at different sections along the coast. For example, when it is high tide at Boston, high tide will not occur at Monument Beach at Buzzards Bay for three more hours. Conversely, when it is high tide at the Cape Cod Canal and at Truro, it is also high tide in Boston. Precise tide tables are available at most stores throughout Cape Cod and are published in the local newspapers. The timing of high and low tide is important to know when planning for boating, fishing, and shellfish gathering.

Deep-Sea Fishing Charters

Boat charters are all seasonal, running from May to October. There are two types of fishing boats—charter and party. Charter boats take up to six passengers, have licensed captain and crew, and go for bass and bluefish. Party boats can carry up to sixty passengers, furnish bait and rods, and go for bottom fish such as flounder, fluke, tautog, cod, and pollock.

In addition to the charters listed below, most major Cape Cod harbors have a number of other operators providing fishing expeditions and related services.

Trips can range from four to eight hours; many offer rental or use of rods and reels.

FALMOUTH

Falmouth Harbor Charter, 180 Scranton Avenue, 495–6900
Patriot Party Boats, Clinton Avenue at Inner Harbor, 548–2626 or
    800–734–0088

BARNSTABLE

A-1 Sportfishing Charters, Barnstable Harbor, 362–9719
A Tightlines Sport Fishing, Barnstable Marina, 790–8600
Barnstable Harbor Charter Fleet, 187 Millway, 362–3908
Blish Point Fishing Charters, 10 Hezekiah's Way, 362–2161

HYANNIS

Captain Bob's Deep Sea Fishing, Ocean Street, 778–1166
Helen H Deep Sea Fishing, 137 Pleasant, 790–0696, year-round
Hy-Line Cruises, 138 Ocean Street, 790–0696

DENNIS

Albatross Deep Sea Fishing, Sesuit Harbor, 385–3244
Bay Charters, 43 New Boston Road, 385–2936

HARWICH

Golden Eagle Deep Sea Fishing, South Harwich, 432–5611
Pauly V., Harwich Port, 430–0053
Yankee Deep Sea Fishing Parties, Saquatucket Harbor, 432–2520

BREWSTER

Brewster Flats Fishing & Outfitters, 2655 Main Street, 896–2460
Sea Witch Sport Fishing, 1709 Main Street, 896–2493

CHATHAM

Cape Cod Outdoors, 1082 Orleans Road, 945–6052
Cape Fishing Charters, 1082 Orleans Road, 945–2256
Coastline Sport Fishing, 945–4971
Monomoy Charters, 140 Kelley Lane, 945–1118
Pleasant Bay Charters, 1906 Main Street, 430–2277

ORLEANS

Capt. Cook Sport Fishing, 255–2065
Eastwind Sport Fishing Charters, 21 Oak Lane, 420–3934
Rock Harbor Charter Boat Service, Rock Harbor, 255–9757 or
    800–287– 1771

WELLFLEET

Cape Mariner Excursions, 349–6003
Naviator, Town Pier, Wellfleet, 349–6003

YARMOUTH

Drifter Sport Fishing Charters of Cape Cod, 398–2061

PROVINCETOWN

Cee Jay, MacMillan Wharf, 487–4330
Ginny G, MacMillan Wharf, 246–3656
Shady Lady, Bradford Street Extension, 487–0182

Bait-and-Tackle Shops

The following is a listing of some Cape Cod bait-and-tackle shops.
Most are open all year.
Maco's, Route 6 in Buzzards Bay, 759–9636
Red Top, Main Street in Buzzards Bay, 759–3371
Green Pond Fish'n Gear, Menauhant Road in East Falmouth, 548–2573

Canal Marine, Freezer Road in Sandwich, 888-0096
Sandwich Ship Supply, Tupper Road in Sandwich, 888-0200
The Cape Orvis Shop, Harwich, 432-4466
Nelson's Bait & Tackle, Provincetown, 487-0034
Blackbeard's Bait & Tackle, Eastham, 240-3369
Sports Port, West Main Street in Hyannis, 775-3096
Truman's, Route 132 in Hyannis, 771-3470
Bass River Bait and Tackle, Route 28 in West Dennis, 394-8666
Riverview Bait and Tackle, Route 28 in West Dennis, 394-1036
Goose Hummock Shop, Route 6A in Orleans, 255-0455
Black Duck Sports Shop, Route 6 in South Wellfleet, 349-9801
Wellfleet Marine, at the Town Pier, 349-6578
Land's End Marine, Commercial Street in Provincetown, 487-0784

Boat Rentals

The following is a listing of some boat-rental operators on Cape Cod. Among boats that can be rented at these locations are Sunfish, daysailers, jet boats, power boats, Hobie Cats, Windsurfers, and sailboats. Instruction is offered at most locations, and licenses are needed only for larger sailboats.

Maco's, Route 6 in Buzzards Bay, 759-9636
Oyster River Boatyard, Barn Hill Lane, Chatham, 945-0736
Monomoy Sail & Cycle, 275 Route 28, North Chatham, 945-8011
Cape Cod Boats, Bass River Bridge, Route 28, West Dennis, 394-9268
Cape Cod Waterway Boat Rentals, Route 28, Dennisport, 398-0080
Jack's Boat Rentals, Nickerson State Park, Route 6A, 896-8556
Adventure Water Sports, 110 School Street, Hyannis, 778-4555. Wave runners, jet skis
Aqua-Sport Jet Ski Rentals, 1 Lighthouse Inn Road, Dennis, 398-5387
Flyer's Boat Rental, 131-A Commercial Street, Provincetown, 800-750-0898. Motorboats, sailboats, wave runners, Sunfish, sea kayaks, rowboats, canoes
Wellfleet Marine Corp., Town Pier, Wellfleet, 349-2233. Sail and motorboats for harbor use
Howlin Howie's Kayak Rentals, 40 Route 28, West Dennis, 398-0060
Cape Cod Water Sports, Route 28, Harwich Port, 432-5996. Sailboats, power boats, Hobie Cats, Sunfish, canoes, surfbikes
Goose Hummock Shop, Route 6A, Orleans, 255-2620

Jack's Boat Rental, Camp Nickerson State Park, Brewster, 896–8556, also Route 6, Wellfleet, 349–9808

Small Boat Service, Wellfleet Town Pier, Wellfleet, 349–9680

Marinas

The following list offers some of the many marinas and boat-service operations on Cape Cod:

Bourne Marina, Academy Drive, Buzzards Bay, 759–2512

Coastwise Wharf Corporation, Beach Street, Vineyard Haven, 693–3854

East Marine, Falmouth Heights Road, Falmouth, 548–2704

Falmouth Harbor Marina, Falmouth Heights Road, Falmouth, 457–7000

Brewer Fiddler's Cove Marina, Fiddlers Cove Road, North Falmouth, 564–6327

Kingman Marine Incorporated, Shipyard Lane, Cataumet, 563–7136

The Marina at Green Pond, Green Harbor Road, East Falmouth, 457–9283

Red Brook Harbor Club, Shipyard Lane, Cataumet, 563–7136

Sandwich Marina, Ed Moffitt Avenue, Sandwich, 833–0808

Edwards Boat Yard, Route 28 in East Falmouth, 548–2216

Little River Boat Yard, Riverside Drive, Mashpee, 548–3511

Crosby Yacht Yard in Osterville, 428–6958

Wild Harbor Yacht Club, Wild Harbor Road, North Falmouth, 563–9492

Barnstable Marine Service, Barnstable Harbor, 362–3811

Bass River Marina, Route 28, West Dennis, 394–8341

Half Tide Marina, Frog Pond Road, Mashpee, 477–2681

Harwich Port Boat Works, Harbor Road, Harwich Port, 432–1322

Hyannis Marina, Hyannis, 775–5662

Mayfair Boat Yard & Marina, Old Mayfair Road, South Dennis, 398–3722

Millway Marina, Barnstable Harbor, Barnstable, 362–4904

Nauset Marine Marina East, Barley Neck Road, Orleans, 255–3045

Northside Marina, Sesuit Road, East Dennis, 385–3936

Outermost Harbor Marine, Seagull Road, Chatham, 945–2030

Provincetown Marina, Provincetown, 487–0571

Sea Ray Hyannis Marina, Hyannis, 775–5662

Allen Harbor Marine Service, Lower County Road in Harwich Port, 432–0353

Saquatucket Harbor Marine, Route 28 in Harwich Port, 430-7532
Chatham Yacht Basin, Barn Hill Lane in West Chatham, 945-0728
Oyster River Boatyard, off Barn Hill Road in West Chatham, 945-0736
Chatham Marina, Eliphamet's Lane in Chatham, 945-1785
Mayfair Boat Yard, Old Mayfair Road in South Dennis, 398-3722

Sailing Lessons

South East Sailing School, 115 Walnut Street, West Barnstable, 420-1144
Arey's Pond Boat Yard, Areys Lane, South Orleans, 255-0994
Flyer's Boat Rentals, 131-A Commercial Street, Provincetown, 800-750-0898
Yarmouth Recreation Department on Lewis Bay, Yarmouth, 398-2231
Cape Cod Sailing, Hyannis, 771-7918 or (800) 484-5091. Geared to adults, this program provides one- to five-day trips, living aboard
Cape Sail, Brewster, Harwich, 896-2730. Customized sailing lessons with an overnight aboard

Kayaking

Goose Hummock Outdoor Center, Route 6A, Orleans, 255-2620. Rentals and classes offered, also canoe rentals
The Paddler's Shop, Shipyard Lane, Cataumet, 563-1784. Rentals, tours.
Cape Cod Coastal Canoe & Kayak, 36 Spectacle Pond Drive, East Falmouth, 564-4051. Guided tours
Eastern Mountain Sports, 1513 Iyannough Road, Hyannis, 362-8690
Flyer's Full Service Boat Yard, 131-A Commercial Street, Provincetown, 487-0898
Off the Coast Kayak Co., 3 Freeman Street, Provincetown, 487-2692. Rentals, tours

Freshwater Fishing Places

Inland Cape Cod is speckled with many ponds and lakes offering enjoyable freshwater fishing. Trout, bass, pickerel, yellow perch, and white perch are most abundant. Freshwater fishing is permitted at the following places. For location and directions, check with local chambers of commerce or tourist information centers.

Bourne—Flax Pond and Red Brook Pond

Sandwich—Hoxie Pond, Lawrence Pond, Peters Pond, Pimlico Pond, Shawme Lake, Snake Pond, Spectacle Pond, and Triangle Pond

Mashpee—Ashumet Pond, Johns Pond, Mashpee Pond, Wakeby Pond, and Santuit Pond

Falmouth—Coonamessett Pond, Deep Pond, Grews Pond, Jenkins Pond, Mares Pond, and Siders Pond

Barnstable—Garretts Pond, Hamblin Pond, Hathaway Pond North, Long Pond Centerville, Long Pond Newtown, Lovell's Pond, Middle Pond, Mystic Lake, Shallow Pond, Shubael Pond, and Wequaquet Lake

Yarmouth—Dennis Pond, Greenough Pond, Horse Pond, Long Pond, and Big Sandy Pond

Dennis—Fresh Pond and Scargo Lake

Harwich—Bucks Pond, Eldredge Pond, Hinckley's Pond, Long Pond, Sand Pond, and Seymour Pond

Brewster—Cahoon Pond, Cliff Pond, Little Cliff Pond, Elbow Pond, Flax Pond, Griffith's Pond, Higgin's Pond, Long Pond, Lower Mill Pond, Upper Mill Pond, Seymour Pond, Sheep Pond, Slough Pond, and Walker Pond

Chatham—Goose Pond, Lovers Lake, Mill Pond, Schoolhouse Pond, and White Pond

Orleans—Baker Pond, Crystal Lake, and Pilgrim Lake

Eastham—Depot Pond, Great Pond, Herring Pond, Minister Pond

Wellfleet—Great Pond, Gull Pond, and Long Pond

Truro—Great Pond, Horseleech Pond, and Pilgrim Lake

Shellfishing

Most Cape Cod towns allow residents and nonresidents to gather shellfish—scallops, clams, oysters, and the like—for private consumption from specially designated areas and on certain days. Since shellfishing is somewhat limited and depends on conditions, it is best to check with the local town office for information. Permits are also required and are obtained at town offices. When going shellfishing, be sure to heed warnings about contamination such as the highly toxic red tide, which can cause severe sickness. Cape Cod shellfish beds have been relatively contamination-free in comparison to other areas along the New England coast. The Cape's continuing population growth and concomitant ecological changes, however, may reverse this condition in the near future unless wise action is taken by everyone concerned.

Windsurfing

Monomoy Sail & Cycle, North Chatham, 945-0811

Scuba

Aquarius Diving Center, 3239 Route 28, Buzzards Bay, 759-3483
East Coast Divers, Route 28, Hyannis, 775-1185
Sea Sports, Route 28, Hyannis, 790-1217. Also snorkeling
Cape Cod Divers, 815 Main Street, Harwich Port, 432-9035

Baseball—The Cape Cod League

If you want to see some of America's best college baseball players in action, take in the games of the Cape Cod Baseball League. They play an eight-week schedule during the summer. From out of the ranks of these players will come some of tomorrow's hottest professional stars. Local papers publish schedules and game times. Donations are accepted. Individual teams and their home fields are:

Wareham Gatemen, Clem Spillaine Field in Wareham
Falmouth Commodores, Fuller Field in Falmouth
Cotuit Kettlers, Lowell Park in Cotuit
Hyannis Mets, McKeon Field in Hyannis
Dennis-Yarmouth Red Sox, Red Wilson Field in South Yarmouth
Harwich Mariners, Whithouse Field in Harwich
Chatham A's, Veterans Field in Chatham
Orleans Cardinals, Eldredge Park in Orleans

Horseback Riding

Cape Cod riding facilities provide a wide range of services and pro-grams—riding trails, instruction from beginner to advanced jumping, day programs in riding, horse boarding, indoor riding facilities, horses for sale, tack shops, and competition sites. Not all of the following sta-bles, however, offer horse rentals for impromptu trail rides. Calling ahead is advised.

Deer Meadow Riding Stable, Route 137, East Harwich, 432-6580. Hourly trail rides offered seven days a week, in addition to a ninety-minute sunset ride; western and English saddles available

Fieldcrest Farms, 774 Palmer Avenue, Falmouth, 548–1222. Group or private English-style lessons available

Haland Stables, Route 29A, West Falmouth, 540–2522. Specializes in trail rides; English lessons are also available. Call for a trail ride appointment

Holly Hill Farm, 240 Flint Street, Marston Mills, 428–2621. Private English lessons available, expanded hours during the summer

Nelson's Riding Stable, Race Point Road, Provincetown, 487–1112. Group and private English-style lessons available

Sea Horse Farm, 34 Lynch Lane, Harwich, 430–0441. Has lighted outdoor arena, trails, and lessons

Woodsong Farm, Lund Farm Way, East Brewster, 896–5555. Group and private lessons available

If you own your own horse, you may want to ride at *Sandy Neck Beach* in West Barnstable, or at the *National Seashore Trails*. Both offer scenic rides along the beaches and dunes.

Sightseeing and Cruises

The following services provide cruises, sightseeing, or whale-watching trips:

Martha's Vineyard & Nantucket Steamship Authority, P.O. Box 284 Dept H, Woods Hole, 02543, 477–7447. Offers daily sailings to Vineyard Haven on Martha's Vineyard Island and to Nantucket. Advance reservations, essential for the transport of autos, RVs, and trucks, must be made well in advance for the summer season. Parking is available at Woods Hole and at two other locations, off Palmer Avenue and Gifford, with connecting bus service to the terminal.

Ocean Quest, Water Street, Woods Hole, 385–7656 or (800) 376–2326. Ninety-minute trips offer an introduction to oceanography from a science teacher and naturalist.

Eventide, Ocean Street Dock, Hyannis, 775–0222. Offers a variety of sails from sunset to bird-watching.

Hesperus, Ocean Street Dock, Hyannis, 790–0077. A 1937 John Alden sloop, a 50-foot wooden craft, offers three two-hour trips daily.

Island Queen, terminal located at Falmouth Harbor on Falmouth Heights Road, 548–4800. The *Island Queen* is strictly a passenger boat (bikes are allowed) offering daily sailings between Falmouth Harbor and Oak Bluffs on Martha's Vineyard Island. It is available for island tours and moonlight cruises. Motels and parking are available near the terminal. The *Island Queen* operates from late May to mid-October.

Provincetown Harbor Cruises, MacMillan Wharf, 487-4330, Provincetown. Hourly trips mid-May through mid-October.

Tiger Shark, MacMillan Wharf, Provincetown, 487-4275 or (800) 923-8773. A great family outing especially for children, who get to collect sea creatures. Four trips daily.

Bay Lady 11, 487-9308, and *Schooner Hindu*, 487-0659, MacMillan Wharf, Provincetown. Both are gaff-rigged sailing vessels. Four trips daily in season.

Hy-line Cruises, Ocean Street Dock, Pier 1 in Hyannis, 775-2600. Hy-line provides daily sailings to Nantucket and Martha's Vineyard, Hyannisport and Hyannis Harbor cruises (best view of the Kennedy compound), sunset cocktail cruises, and deep-sea fishing trips on Nantucket Sound. Operates from mid-April to the end of October.

The Schooner Freya, Northside Marina at Sesuit Harbor, Dennis, 385-4399. Offers two-hour sails on a tall ship, also sunset trips.

Water Safari's Starfish, Bass River Bridge, Route 28, Dennis, 362-5555. Ninety-minute trips along the Bass River, the Cape's largest tidal river.

South Beach Boat Excursions, Outermost Harbor Marine, Seagull Road, Chatham, 945-2030. Also seal cruises.

Chatham Water Tours, Stage Harbor Town Dock, Chatham, 432-5895. Offers harbor tours, custom cruises, and Monomoy Island tours.

Monomoy Island Ferry, Morris Island Road, Chatham, 945-5450. Also sightseeing, bird-watching, and seal tours.

Cape Cod Canal Cruises, Onset Bay Town Pier in Onset (Route 6, Onset Beach/Point Independence traffic light), 295-3883. Two- and three-hour cruises through the Cape Cod Canal from Buzzards Bay to Sandwich Basin. Also has Sunday jazz cruises, sunset cocktail cruises, and moonlight-and-music cruises. In operation from spring to autumn.

Cape Cod Duckmobiles, Hyannis, 362-1117. Former World War II amphibious vehicle provides a fun way to explore Hyannis on land and water.

...at Boat, Ocean Street Docks in Hyannis, 775-0222. The cat-...is a classic New England sailing vessel, and you can take to the ...p blue waters of Nantucket Sound on this beauty through this ...rvice. Also has moonlight cruises. Refreshments on board. Operates from mid-May to early September.

Whale-Watching

Cape Cod Whalewatch, MacMillan Wharf, Provincetown, 487-4079 or (877) 487-4079

Provincetown's Portugese Princess Whale Watch, MacMillan Wharf in Provincetown, 487-2651 or (800) 442-3188. whale-watching trips on Cape Cod Bay. Galley serves Portuguese food, cocktails, and snacks.

Dolphin Fleet of Provincetown, MacMillan Wharf in Provincetown, 349-1900 or (800) 826-9300. Whale-watching trips on Cape Cod Bay and other cruises.

Ranger V, MacMillan Wharf in Provincetown, 487-3322 or (800) 992-9333. Whale-watching trips on Cape Cod Bay. Food and drinks onboard, also a naturalist to describe the sights.

Hyannis Whale Watcher Cruises, Barnstable Harbor in Barnstable Village (off Route 6A), 362-6088 or (800) 287-0374. Whale-watching trips on Cape Cod Bay from April through October. Onboard food and beverage service.

WHALES

If you want to spot some whales, Provincetown is the place to go. Just 8 miles off the coast is Stellwagen Bank, a major feeding area for whales. Boats leaving out of Provincetown (or, alternately, Barnstable Harbor in Barnstable) reach Stellwagen faster than those from Boston or elsewhere, and you'll have more time to view the whales.\

So sure are the whale captains that you'll see these giants of the sea, that they guarantee the sightings. Forty-foot humpbacks, 70-foot-fin whales, and the endangered right whale can be spotted throughout the season, which runs from April through October.

While whale-watching is fun, Cape Codders are expressing concerns about the whales' future. A key component of the $3.7 billion Boston Harbor cleanup project is a 9.5-mile tunnel from the city that discharges more than a billion gallons of treated sewage each day into the heart of the whales' feeding grounds. Fears are that the freshwater will kill off the plankton, a part of the whales' diet.

Airplane Rides

Cape Cod Soaring Adventures, Marstons Mills Airport, Route 149 and Race Lane, Marstons Mills, 540-8081. Open all year, weather permitting.

Wille Air Tours, Provincetown Municipal Airport, 487-9989. Fifteen-minute tours in a 1930 Stinson Detroiter.

Cape Cod Flying Service, Marstons Mills Airport, Route 149 and Race Lane, Marstons Mills, 428-8732 or (888) 247-5263. Offers sightseeing tours and biplane rides. Open all year, weather permitting.

Cape Cod Flying Circus, Chatham Municipal Airport, 945-9000. Sightseeing, also biplane that can include loops.

Hyannis Air Service, Barnstable Municipal Airport, Routes 132 and 28, Hyannis, 775-8171. Sightseeing tours of up to two hours.

Dune Tours

Art's Dune Tours, at Commercial and Standish Streets, 487-1950. Jeep tours of the sand dunes in Cape Cod National Seashore. Operates from June through September.

Archery

Boones' Archery, 12 Old Lantern Lane, Harwich, 430-7900

Seal Cruises and Other Naturalist Tours

South Beach Boat Excursions, Outermost Harbor Marine, Seagull Road, Chatham, 945-2030. Also beach trips.

Chatham Water Tours, Stage Harbor Town Dock, Chatham, 432-5895. Also harbor tours, Monomoy Island tours.

International Wildlife Coalition, Hyannis, (800) 548-8704. Offers day-long trips to Nantucket and other islands, with an introduction to oceanography.

Ocean Quest, Water Street, Woods Hole, 385-7656 or (800) 376-2326. Ninety-minute trips offer an introduction to oceanography.

Monomoy Island Excursions, Route 28, Harwich Port, 430-7772. Seal and seabird cruises, island tours, sunset cruises.

Rip Ryder, Morris Island, Chatham, 945-5450. Seal cruises, Monomoy Island and South Beach ferry, bird-watching.

Outermost Harbor Marine, Morris Island Road, Chatham, 945-2030. Seal cruises, shuttles to South Beach in Chatham, and North Monomoy.

Wellfleet Bay Wildlife Sanctuary, Wellfleet, 349-2615. Trips offered throughout the year with onboard naturalists.

Cape Cod Museum of Natural History, 869 Route 6A, Brewster, 896-3867 or (800) 479-3867 in eastern Massachusetts. Also boat tours of harbors and marshes, trips to Monomoy Island.

Indoors

What To Do If It Rains

Yes, it does rain on Cape Cod, but that only means opportunities for new discoveries. One important lesson to learn is that just because it is raining where you are, it may not be raining elsewhere on the Cape. Cape Cod extends 60 miles into the North Atlantic, and quite often rain in Hyannis may also bring sun in Provincetown. Call ahead to where you want to go and ask about the weather there.

Among other ideas:

Visit a museum. The Cape has an abundance of them. Choices might be the Pilgrim Monument and Provincetown Museum; Discover Days in Dennis Port, which is just for kids; National Marine Fisheries Service Aquarium in Woods Hole; or the Cape Cod Museum of Natural History in Brewster. (See "Popular Attractions" in this section for more information.)

Shop. The Cape has become a shopper's haven with everything from nationally known chains to outlet centers. The original Christmas Tree Shop is located on Route 6A in Yarmouthport. The Cape Cod Mall in Hyannis (Route 132) is larger than ever, with all the name stores and more in indoor comfort. Antiques shops, bookstores, flea markets, and specialty shops are found throughout the Cape. (See "Shopping" and sections following it for more information.)

Discover arts and crafts. Fascinating art galleries and crafts centers make for interesting outings. Provincetown, Hyannis, and Chatham are centers for these. (See "Art Galleries" and "Crafts" for more information.)

Explore a library. Every town has an interesting one where you can check out a book by one of the Cape's many authors. The Sturgis on Route 6A is the oldest library in America. (See "Cape Cod Public Libraries" for others.)

Visit the theater. The Cape's intimate theaters have seen some of America's top stars on their stages. Many movie theaters are found here as well, most with multiple screen. (See "Entertainment" and "On Stage" for more information.)

Discover an auction. Who knows what bargains you may find? Check out the daily and weekly newspapers for announcements. (See "Antiques" for more information.)

Take off. One of the best outings to Plimoth Plantation I had with my children was on a rainy day. They loved running between the homes of this 1630 Pilgrim village. Plymouth and Plimoth Plantation are just a short drive off the Cape along Route 3. (See "Plymouth" in the Visiting Cape Cod section.)

Performing and Visual Arts

Cape Cod has long been known as the perfect place for artists, writers, musicians, dancers, craftspeople, and philosophers, all of whom come in the summer or live here year-round to find more rewarding inspiration and fewer distractions combined with a casual lifestyle. This influx of highly productive people in the arts has, over several generations, produced a rich cultural environment and outstanding institutions that express the creative spirit.

There are many opportunities for the visitor to participate in Cape Cod's cultural life. Every Cape Cod town offers a smorgasbord of cultural programs and activities throughout the year. Visitors and residents alike are encouraged to partake of whatever interests them most. The following organizations represent but a small sampling:

Cape Cod School of Art, 48 Pearl Street, Provincetown, 487-0101. Workshops for all ages in a variety of media. Programs run July through September.

Cape Cod Conservatory of Music, Art, and Dance at Beebe Woods Arts Center, Highfield Drive in Falmouth, 540-0611. A member of the National Guild of Community Schools of the Arts, the conservatory offers the broadest range of courses in the arts available on the Cape for children and adults, including musical instruments, drama, the visual arts, and dance.

The Falmouth Artists Guild, 744 Main Street in Falmouth, 540-3304. Courses in the visual arts and exhibitions.

Truro Center for the Arts at Castle Hill, Castle and Meetinghouse Roads, in Truro, 349-7511. Classes and workshops in the arts, also concerts and artists' receptions.

Woods Hole Folk Music Society, Woods Hole, 540-0320. Folk performances held first and third Sundays, October through May.

Academy Playhouse, Orleans, 255-1963. Provides year-round performances as well as classes for all ages in dance, music, and drama.

The Provincetown Art Association, 460 Commercial Street in Provincetown, 487-1750. Courses and exhibitions in the visual arts.

Entertainment

A long-standing tradition on Cape Cod is free band concerts in the town parks. These concerts, held weekly in Chatham, Buzzards Bay, Dennis, Harwich, Hyannis, Yarmouth, and Falmouth during July and August, are as eagerly awaited, enthusiastically attended, and highly regarded as performances of top stars at the Cape Cod Melody Tent. In addition, cinemas featuring current films are located in Hyannis, Falmouth, East Harwich, Wellfleet, Dennis, Provincetown, and Buzzards

Bay. Entertainment on the Cape, however, features much more than local bands and movies.

On Stage

During the summer, Cape Cod attracts many of the finest professional entertainers in the world as well as a large number of highly talented individuals hoping to become stars one day. The following list reveals where these people perform:

Cape Cod Melody Tent, Hyannis, 775-9100. The country's oldest summer theater in the round. The tent theater presents both musicals and performances by individual stars. A children's theater is held Wednesday mornings.

Cape Playhouse and Cinema, Dennis, 385-3911, cinema 385-2503. The tether is the only professional equity theater of Cape Cod and features many prominent stars. The cinema boasts the world's largest indoor mural, a heavenly fantasy by Rockwell Kent and Joe Mietziner.

The Academy of Performing Arts, 120 Main Street, Orleans, 255-1963. Offers up to fourteen major productions and a music series. Has a summer arts camp.

Opera New England of Cape Cod, 775-3858. Performs in the spring and fall at Cape Cod Community College, Route 132, Barnstable. Performances for both adults and youngsters.

Cape Cod Symphony Orchestra, 362-1111. Performs October through May. Also some pops concerts in summer in Hyannis.

Chatham Band Concerts, 945-5199. Held Friday nights in Kate Gould Park, end of June through Labor Day. A very popular and colorful performance.

Heritage Plantation in Sandwich, 888-3300. Offers a variety of musical performances from jazz to bagpipes.

The Highland Summer Theatre (548-0668), *The Highland Winter Theatre* (548-0400), and *The College Light Opera Company* (548-0668), Falmouth. Offer drama and light comedy.

Woods Hole Theatre Company, Woods Hole, 540-6524. Offers a variety of plays on a year-round basis.

Magic by the Sea, Chatham High School, Crowell Road, Chatham, 430-1305. Master magicians create amazing illusions every Tuesday evening in summer.

Harwich Junior Theater, Division Street, Harwich, 432-2002. Performances youngsters will love.

Cape Cod Melody Tent, West Main Street, Hyannis, 775-9100. Performances are held under the big tent Wednesdays at 11:00 A.M.

Cape Playhouse Children's Musical Theatre, Route 6A, Dennis, 385-3911. Famed summer playhouse has entertainment for the young set Friday mornings.

Cape Rep Theatre, Route 6A, Brewster, 896-1888. Outdoor performances of one hour shows are held usually on Tuesday and Friday.

Storytelling, 349-0103. Master storyteller Jim Wolf performs tales of old Cape Cod at the Wellfleet Methodist church (air-conditioned) three nights a week.

Monomoy Theater, Chatham, 945-1589. The Ohio University Players perform in Chatham throughout the summer.

Falmouth Town Band, Harbor Band Shell at Marina Park. Performs Thursday evenings in July and August.

Provincetown Repertory Theatre, 336 Commercial Street, Provincetown, 487-0600. Performances by an adventurous ensemble.

Provincetown Theatre Corporation, 391 Commercial Street, Provincetown, 487-8673

Barnstable Comedy Club, 3171 Route 6A, Barnstable Village, 362-6333. Since its founding in 1922, its motto has been "to produce good plays and remain amateurs." Also offers children's theater.

Back Door Bistro, at the Roadhouse, Hyannis, 775-2386. Jazz year-round.

Cape Cod Repertory Outdoor Theater, 3379 Route 6A, Brewster, 896-1888. Performances are held at an open-air theater on the former Crosby estate.

Wellfleet Drive-In, Route 6, Wellfleet, 349-7176. One of the few drive-in movie theaters left. Double features begin at dusk May through September. Play area for the kids, food stand to keep you going.

W.H.A.T., next to Town Pier, Wellfleet, 349-6835. Considered one of the top ten regional theaters.

Harwich Junior Theatre, Division Street, Harwichport, 432-2002. One of the country's top playhouses for young audiences. Also offers classes.

Chatham Drama Guild, 134 Crowell Road, Chatham, 945-0510. The show has been going on for more than sixty-five years.

Nightclubs

Cape Cod has entertaining night spots of almost every kind—places featuring rock, disco, piano, Irish, country and western, jazz, ethnic, and folk music; and places offering dining and dancing, cabaret entertainment, comedy routines, and floor shows. Because nightclub entertainment is an ever-changing feast during the summer, ask the desk person where you're staying for suggestions. A large number of Cape Cod restaurants offer live entertainment. These places are indicated in the Accommodations and Dining sections under the towns in which they are located. It's the law that last call for drinks is at 12:30 A.M., and everything has to be off the table by 1:00 A.M.

Cape Cod Public Libraries

The public libraries of Cape Cod are tranquil places for further enlightenment. Rainy days make a library an uplifting oasis. Cape libraries are important sources of information for those tracing their family roots or doing research into early American history. Most have special collections relating to the history of their local area and interesting materials (documents, works of art, etc.) that have been donated by residents. The following libraries welcome all readers, residents and visitors alike. If you wish to visit a library and take out books, call ahead for hours of operation and fees charged.

BOURNE

Johnathan Bourne Library, Sandwich Road, 759-0644

FALMOUTH

North Falmouth Public Library, Chester Street, 563-2922

West Falmouth Library, Route 28A, 548-4709

Falmouth Public Library, Main Street, 457-2555; statue of Katherine Lee
   Bates, author of the poem "America"

Woods Hole Library, Woods Hole Road, 548-8961

East Falmouth Public Library, Route 28, 548-6340

MASHPEE

Mashpee Public Library, Route 151, 539-1435; interesting materials
   relating to the history of the Wampanoag Indians

SANDWICH

Sandwich Public Library, Main Street, 888-0625; closed Sundays and
   Mondays

BARNSTABLE

Cape Cod Community College, off Route 132 in West Barnstable, 362-2132, ext. 4480; in the William Brewster Nickerson Memorial Room, the Cape's most extensive collection of books, documents, and archival materials

Hyannis Public Library, 401 Main Street, 775-2280; a large John F. Kennedy collection

Osterville Free Library, Wianno Avenue, 428-5757

Whelden Library, Route 149, 362-2262

Cotuit Public Library, Main Street, 428-8141; ship models and bound classics

Sturgis Library, on Route 6A, Barnstable Village, 362-6636; in the 1644 home of Reverend John Lothrop; considered the oldest library building in the country; an excellent collection of genealogical records and maritime-history documents and materials

Centerville Library, 585 Main Street, 790-6220

YARMOUTH

Yarmouth Library Associates, Route 6A, Yarmouthport, 362-3717

West Yarmouth Library, Route 28, 775-5206

South Yarmouth Library Associates, 312 Main Street, 760-4820

DENNIS

Dennis Memorial Library, Old Bass River Road, 385-2255

Dennis Library Department, 760-6219

BREWSTER

Brewster Ladies Library, Route 6A, 896-3913

HARWICH

Harwich Port Library, Lower County Road, 432-3320

Brooks Free Library, Main Street, Harwich, 430-7562; collection of John Rogers figurines

CHATHAM

South Chatham Library, Route 28, no phone

Eldredge Public Library, 564 Main Street, 945-5170

ORLEANS

Snow Library, Main Street, 240-3760

EASTHAM
Eastham Public Library, Samoset Road, 240-5950

WELLFLEET
Wellfleet Public Library, Main Street, 349-0310

TRURO
Cobb Memorial Library, Route 6A, 349-6895
Pilgrim Memorial Library, Route 6A, North Truro, 487-1125

PROVINCETOWN
Provincetown Public Library, 330 Commercial Street, 487-7094

Ice-Skating

Maybe not in summer, but off-season, ice-skating is a popular activity on Cape Cod.

John Gallo Ice Arena, Sandwich Road, Bourne, 759-8904

Falmouth Ice Arena, Palmer Avenue, Falmouth, 548-9083

Tony Kent Arena, Gages Way, South Dennis, 760-2400

Charles Moore Arena, O'Connor Way, Orleans, 255-5902

Art Galleries

The jewels in Cape Cod's crown are its art galleries. The quality of work exhibited within them—oils, acrylics, watercolors, mixed media, sculptures, and photography—is comparable in excellence to what one would find in large cities such as New York, Boston, Chicago, and San Francisco. Works range from realistic scenes of Cape Cod to still lifes and portraits. Both well-established and new talents are represented. You'll find the highest concentration of galleries in Provincetown, long regarded as a dynamic center of American art. Nearby Wellfleet is also growing in importance as more galleries open up for business there. The following is a partial listing of the many art galleries you will find on Cape Cod. Most are open every day during regular business hours; some are also open in the early evening. Receptions to celebrate the opening of special shows are frequent occurrences at galleries and are highlights of the Cape's social life. During the summer many towns have festive, outdoor art exhibitions, featuring paintings from both professional and amateur artists, where some excellent buys can be had.

HYANNIS

Angles & Art Galleries, 362 Main Street, 778–6800
Cape Cod Guild of Fine Arts Gallery, 248 Stevens Street, 775–0900
Richard's Galleries (featuring Edna Hibel), 337 Main Street, 771–8350
William R. Davis Fine Art, 778–0009

BARNSTABLE

Cape Cod Art Association, 3480 Route 6A, Barnstable Village, 362–2909
Cummaquid Fine Arts, 4275 Route 6A, 362–2593
The Evans Gallery, 3236 Main Street, 375–6300
The Whippletree, Route 6A, West Barnstable, 362–3320

BREWSTER

Aries East Gallery, Route 6A, 896–7681
Maddocks Gallery, 1287 Main Street, 896–6223
Sola Gallery II, Lemon Tree Village, 896–1882
Underground Art Gallery, 673 Satucket Road, 896–3757
Winstanley-Roark Fine Arts, 2759 Main Street, 896–1948

CHATHAM

Chatham Art Gallery, 464 Main Street, 945–4699
Creation Creations, Route 28, 945–3302
Falconer's, 880 Main Street, 945–2867
The Gallery at Chatham, 595 Main Street, 945–5449
The Hearle Gallery, 488 Main Street, 945–2406
The Kingsley-Brown Gallery, 499 Main Street, 945–6035
The Munson Gallery, 880 Main Street, 945–2888

DENNIS

Around A Square Gallery, 766 Route 6A, 385–9321
The Artist's Gallery, 593 Route 6A, 385–4600
Grose Gallery, 524 Route 6A, 385–3434
Starfish Craft Gallery, 766 Route 6A, 385–4444
Waldo-Moakley Art Studio, 766 Route 6A, 385–8084

FALMOUTH

The Barron Gallery, 311 Main Street, 640–8884
Falmouth Artists Guild, 774 Main Street, 540–3304

Gallery 333, 333 Old Main Road, North Falmouth, 564-4467

Market Barn Gallery, 15 Depot Avenue, 540-0480

Woods Hole Gallery, 14 School Street, Woods Hole, 548-4329

MASHPEE

Thomas Kinkade at the Mashpee Commons Gallery, Routes 28 and 151, 539-0009

Woodruff's Art Center, Mashpee Commons, 477-5767

HARWICH

The Bradford Trust, 66 Miles Street, 430-1482

Cape Art & Frame, 115 Route 137, 432-0880

Cove Art, 115 Route 137, 432-0880

VI-KING Studio, 118 Church Street, 432-2788

ORLEANS

Nauset Painters, watch for announcements of juried outdoor art shows

Addison Holmes Gallery, 43 South Orleans Road, 255-6200

Hogan Art Gallery, 39 Main Street, 240-3655

Neal Cotton Studio, 255-2369

Star Galleries, 76 Route 6A, 240-7827

Tree's Place, Routes 28 and 6A, 255-1330

TRURO

Secrest Studios, Old Kings Highway, 349-6688

Textures, 300 Route 6, 487-8922

PROVINCETOWN

Albert Merola Gallery, 424 Commercial Street, 487-4424

Annie Dew Original Art, 385 Commercial Street, 487-1655

Antonelli Giardelli Gallery, 416 Commercial Street, 487-9693

Bangs St. Gallery, 432 Commercial Street, 487-0743

Berta Walker Gallery, 208 Commercial Street, 487-6411

Clibbon Gallery, 120 Commercial Street, 487-3563

Cortland Jessup Gallery, 432 Commercial Street, 487-4479

DNA Gallery, 288 Bradford Street, 487-7700

Dorian Studios, 322 Commercial Street, 487-9602

Doug Marr Gallery, 134 Commercial Street, 487-6605

Dream-A-Little, 144 Commercial Street, 487-9725

The Driskel Gallery at the Schoolhouse Center, 494 Commercial Street, 487-4800

Fowler Gallery, 423 Commercial Street, 487-3388

Galleria Artemisia, 167 Commercial Street, 487-8300

Harvey Dodd Gallery, 437 Commercial Street, 487-3329

Hilda Neily Gallery, 432 Commercial Street, 487-6300

Julie Heller Gallery, 2 Gosnold Street, 487-2169

Kennedy Studios, 353 Commercial Street, 487-3898

Kiley Court Gallery, 445 Commercial Street, 487-4496

Memories of Provincetown, 169 Commercial Street, 487-9911

Musselman Gallery, 379-A Commercial Street, 487-9954

Passions Gallery, 336 Commercial Street, 487-5740

Pearson Stained Glass Studio, 241 Commercial Street, 487-2851

Provincetown Art Association & Museum, 460 Commercial Street, 487-1750

Provincetown Group Gallery, 465 Commercial Street, 487-8841

Rice Polak Gallery, 430 Commercial Street, 487-1052

Romanos Rizk Studio, 8 Kiley Court, 487-1229

Silas-Kenyon Gallery at the Schoolhouse Center, 494-4800

Simie Maryles Gallery, 435 Commercial Street, 487-7878

Song of Myself Portrait Studio & Gallery, 349 Commercial Street, 487-5736

Taqwa Glass Studio & Gallery, 349 Commercial Street, 487-9180

TJ Walton Gallery, 173 Commercial Street, 487-0170

Trista Gallery, 148 Commercial Street, 487-3939

William-Scott Gallery, 439 Commercial Street, 487-4040

Wohlfarth Galleries, 234 Commercial Street, 487-6569

SANDWICH

Collections Unlimited, 365 Route 6A, East Sandwich, 833-0039

Giving Tree Gallery, Route 6A, East Sandwich, 888-5446

Sandwich Arts and Crafts, School and Water Streets, 888-0232

Sandwich Art Gallery, 153 Main Street, 833-2098

WELLFLEET

Blue Heron Gallery, 20 Bank Street, 349-6724

Brehmer Graphics, 130 Commercial Street, 349-9565

Cape Impressions Gallery, 313 Main Street, 349-6479

Cove Gallery, 15 Commercial Street, 349-2530

Customs House Gallery, 5 Commercial Street, 349-2299

The Davis Gallery, Route 6, 349-0549

Eccentricity, Main Street and Holbrook Avenue, 349-7554

Golden Cod Gallery, East Commercial Street, 349-2247

Herring River Gallery, 3566 Route 6, 349-6812

Jacob Fanning Gallery, 25 Bank Street, 349-9546

Kendall Art Gallery, 40 Main Street, 349-2482

Left Bank Gallery, 25 Commercial Street, 349-9451

Narrow Land Pottery, 11 West Main Street, 349-6308

The Nicholas Harrison Gallery, 275 Main Street, 349-7799

Salty Duck Pottery, 115 Main Street, 349-3342

The Wellfleet Artisans Cooperative, Commercial Street, 349-0100

The Wellfleet Collection Gallery, 355 Main Street, 349-0900

The Works Gallery, Briar Lane, 349-0024

Crafts

Cape Cod's ethos of self-reliance has produced a tradition of excellence in the crafts that is several centuries old, as old, in other words, as America itself. Past Cape Codders made things of utility, everything from home furnishings to sailing ships; then they added style and beauty to them. Today's Cape craftspersons continue this tradition by emphasizing individual style, the beauty of the object being made, the quality of materials and workmanship, and an unfailing utility. In the past, form followed function. Today both qualities are intertwined. Excellent craftspersons and their work in all media can be found in every town on Cape Cod.

Specialty Shops

These specialty shops are fascinating just to visit. Many feature locally made crafts. Most are open all year but may have limited hours or days. Call first.

ARTISTRY ON THE CAPE

It's been almost one hundred years since Sandwich Glass production ended. But the exquisite, pressed, and free-blown glass objects the company produced are still treasured by collectors. No visit to Sandwich would be complete without a stop at the museum that celebrates these American treasures.

Artistry in glass is still a highly honored craft on the Cape. Just down the road in the shadow of the Sagamore Bridge is Pairpoint Crystal, which claims to be America's oldest glassworks. There you can find hand-painted crystal worthy of any collection. Collectors especially treasure its Christmas bells and plates.

Another stop for art glass collectors is the Sydenstricker Galleries on Route 6A in Brewster. The original owner, William Sydenstricker, discovered an ancient Egyptian method of glassmaking while doing research at MIT in Cambridge. Although Sydenstricker died in 1994, his studio still produces some of the most colorful and fascinating glass designs you'll ever come across. Visitors are welcome to watch the craftspeople produce these pieces. It's an unusual process, as two sheets of glass with a colorful design between them is heated to exactly 1,500 degrees Fahrenheit (glassblowing calls for a much higher temperature), allowing the glass to melt into a thermoplastic state, locking the design within.

BOURNE

Pairpoint Crystal, 851 Route 6A (just behind the Christmas Tree Shop), Sagamore, 888–2344 or (800) 899–0953. America's oldest glassworks. Richly colored, handblown items, crystal, Christmas collectibles.

Bournedale Country Store, 26 Herring Pond Road off Route 6, Bourne, 833–0700. This classic country store has been around for 200 years.

SANDWICH

Glass Studio, 470 Route 6A, 888–6681. You can watch Michael Magyar creating glass items using modern and old techniques. Among his creations, Venetian goblets, handblown Christmas ornaments, and "sea bubbles."

Titcomb's Book Store, 432 Route 6A, East Sandwich, 888-2331. A barn filled with books by Thornton W. Burgess ("Peter Rabbit"), Cape and maritime books.

Green Briar Jam Kitchen, 6 Discovery Hill, 888-6870. For almost one hundred years this kitchen has been filled with wonderful aromas of jams and jellies cooking. Pick up some beach plum jelly or other delicious flavors to bring home.

The Museum Shop at the Sandwich Glass Museum, 129 Main Street, 888-0251. More than 400 different reproductions of Sandwich glass.

The Jewel Box, 5 Merchants Square, 888-3251. Solid brass ornaments of Cape Cod town landmarks from the Chatham lighthouse to the Eastham Windmill.

The Weather Store, 146 Main Street, 888-1200. As everyone should know, if you don't like the New England weather just wait a minute. Here you can get the instruments you need to watch for changes, even "weather sticks" that indicate when a storm is heading your way.

FALMOUTH

Woods Hole Handworks, 68 Water Street, Woods Hole, 540-5291. An artists' cooperative with a fine selection of handmade jewelry, weavings, tiles, and other items.

Signature Gallery, Mashpee Commons, Routes 151 and 28, 539-0029. A fine selection of works by Cape Cod artisans.

Kensington's, 156 Main Street, Falmouth, 548-7940. Nantucket lightship handbags.

BARNSTABLE

West Barnstable Tables, Route 149, 362-2676. Tables are made using wood scavenged from nineteenth-century buildings.

Isaiah Thomas Books & Prints, 4632 Falmouth Road, 428-2752. More than 60,000 books, ranging from first editions to used.

The Blacks Handweaving Shop, 597 Route 6A, 362-3955. Beautiful woolen pieces have been created in this shop since the 1950s.

Salt & Chestnut Weathervanes, 651 Route 6A, 362-6085. New England-style weathervanes, custom-made ones also available.

Oak & Ivory, 1112 Main Street, Osterville, 428-9425. The place to find a Nantucket lightship basket if you don't have the time for the ferry crossing.

Tern Studio, Route 149, 362-6077. Bowls and vases made from driftwood.

Maps of Antiquity, 1022 Route 6A, 362-7169. Antique maps as well as reproductions, especially of Cape Cod towns and area.

The Whippletree, 600 Route 6A, 362-3320. Specializes in Cat's Meow Village collectibles.

The Bird Cage, 1064 Main Street, 362-5559. Sports collectibles including shooting memorabilia, bamboo fly rods, duck stamps, and more.

HYANNIS

Play It Again Sports, 25 Route 28, 771-6979. In case you've forgotten something, here's a good place to look. Both used and new items.

Stephanie's, 382 Main Street, Hyannis, 775-5166. "Largest collection of swimwear in New England."

YARMOUTH

Pewter Crafters of Cape Cod, 933 Route 6A, Yarmouthport, 362-3407. Pewter made on the premises in both traditional and contemporary designs.

Parnassus Book Service, 220 Route 6A, 362-6420. So many books are here that the supply overflows to the outside of the building—under cover, of course, but available on the honor system twenty-four hours a day.

Hallet's, 139 Route 6A, Yarmouthport, 362-3362. From the outside it looks like just another village store, but step inside and it's like stepping into the past. It's a genuine 1889 drugstore with all the original fixtures, including a marble soda fountain that still dishes out frappes and floats. Upstairs there's a display area with old apothecary items and photos.

DENNIS

Scargo Pottery, 30 Dr. Lord Road South, 385-3894. Pottery in every size and shape from birdhouses and fountains to cups.

Dennisport Dollhouse, 497 Upper County Road, 398-9356. Dollhouses, furnishings, and kits to make your own.

Raspberry Thistle, 79 Main Street, West Dennis, 398-8200. Fine fabrics and notions for those who love to sew.

BREWSTER

Brewster Pottery, 437 Harwich Road, 896-3587. Work done on the premises includes pottery, porcelain, and stoneware.

Underground Gallery, 673 Satucket Road, 896-6850. Watercolors on display in an underground working studio.

Eve's Place, 564 Route 6A, 896-4914. If you want pearls, this is the place to buy and learn all about them.

Spectrum, 369 Route 6A, 385-3322. Two floors of wonderful crafts from around the country.

Sydenstricker Galleries, 490 Route 6A, 385-3272. The glass from here is found in embassies and museums. Glass-fusing demonstrations at various times.

Great Cape Cod Herb, Spice & Tea Company, 2628 Route 6A, 896-5900. Large variety of herbs from around the world.

HARWICH

Thompson's Farm Market, 710 Route 28, 432-5415. A fancy market and deli. Good place to find picnic fixings. Also a cafe with baked goods and coffee.

Allen Harbor, 335 Lower County Road, Harwich Port, 432-0353. Precision wind and weather indicators.

Cape Cod Cooperage, 1150 Old Queen Anne Road, 432-0788. A barn full of furnishings and containers. The coopers use one hundred-year-old methods in their work. Also Adirondack chairs.

Orvis, Harwich Commons, East Harwich, 432-1200. A Cape Cod branch of the famous Vermont company, this is a fisherman's heaven. Also sponsors a fly-fishing school.

Monahan, 540 Route 28, 432-3302. Jewelry from estate auctions and on consignment. Said to be the oldest family-owned jewelry shop in the country.

Pleasant Lake General Store, Route 124, 432-5305. An old-fashioned store that is also a nice stop on the Rail Trail bike route.

Doctor Gravity's Kite Shop, 564 Route 28, 430-0437. Great collection of kites to take to the beach.

CHATHAM

Cape Cod Specialties in North Chatham, 945-9705 or (800) 998-9708. Offers gift packages of Cape-made specialties, from jams and clam chowder to potato chips. Also stoneware, cups, and other gift items.

Tale of the Cod, 450 Main Street, 945-0347. Two floors of gifts and furniture.

Chatham Jewelry, 532 Main Street, 945-0690. Nice collection of jewelry, also custom designing and fabricating on premises.

Mayflower, 475 Main Street, 945-0065. Nice selection of gifts, newspapers, magazines, and office supplies.

Yankee Ingenuity, 525 Main Street, 945-1288. An eclectic collection of items. Great for browsing.

Chatham Pottery, 2058 Route 28, South Chatham, 430-2191. Pots, tiles, pitchers, plates, bowls, and more, all made on the premises.

Chatham Glass Company, 756 Main Street, 945-5547. Wonderful glass items from candlesticks and goblets to marbles. Also glassblowing demonstrations.

Simpler Pleasure, 393 Main Street, Chatham, 945-4040. Unique, quilted travel bags.

The Dead Zone, 647 Main Street, 945-5853. A museum of the Grateful Dead and their era. Music, novelty gifts, and tie-dyed clothing. Needless to say, owner Patty Rice is a true "Dead head," having attended more than 120 of their concerts. As a bumper sticker in the shop says, "Old hippies never die they just flashback."

Chatham Sign Shop, 40 Kent Place, 945-1909. The place to buy a hand-carved sign.

Journey on a Small Planet, 746 Main Street, 945-1771. Offers a collection of unique gifts, books, antique prints, model boats, and specialty foods.

Forest Beach Design, 402 Main Street, 945-7334 or (888) 792-7353. The goldsmiths here create wonderful designs that are sure to keep the Cape Cod memory alive for years. You'll find the Cape lighthouses, some with a diamond for the light, the Chatham bandstand, hermit crabs, Nantucket lightship baskets, and a Cape Cod mother's pin all in sparkling gold.

ORLEANS

Orleans Carpenters, Commerce Drive, 225-2646. Reproduction Shaker and other museum-quality furnishings. Has a "seconds" section.

Nauset Lantern Shop, 169 Route 6A, 899-2660. Handcrafted brass and copper Colonial-style lanterns. Most for outdoor use.

Kemp Pottery, Route 6A, 255-5853. Bird feeders, sinks, garden items, and more, all using Nauset Beach sand.

Goose Hummock Shop, Route 6A, Orleans, 255-0455. Marine and sporting supplies store.

Bird Watcher's General Store, Route 6A, 255-6974. This place is really for the birds, everything from seeds to information on where to spot them.

The Clock Shop, 430 South Orleans Road Route 28, 240-0175. Beautiful grandfather clocks, music boxes, Black Forest cuckoos, and nautical and tide clocks.

EASTHAM

Collector's World, Route 6, 255-3616. Grand and unusual collection of antiques and collectibles.

Chocolate Sparrow, 4205 Route 6, 240-0606. Hand-dipped chocolates and homemade fudge.

WELLFLEET

Wellfleet Pottery, Commercial Street, 349-6679. Original designs using various methods, all handpainted.

Chocolate Sparrow, Main Street, 349-1333. Not only hand-dipped chocolates but also penny candy.

Abiyoyo, 313 Main Street, 349-3422. Creative toys and stuffed animals.

TRURO

Whitman House Quilt Shop, Route 6, North Truro, 487-3204. Lots of wonderful quilts.

Truro Crafters, South Highland Road, 487-3239. Pottery, scrimshaw, and wood carvings.

Atlantic Spice Co., Route 6 at Route 6A, 487-6100. Great buys on herbs, spices, teas, and potpourri.

PROVINCETOWN

Tiffany Lamp Studio, 432 Commercial Street, 487-1101, Tiffany lamps made and sold.

Impulse, 188 Commercial Street, 487-1154. Kaleidoscopes, wind chimes, glass creations.

Marine Specialties, 235 Commercial Street, 487-1730. Unusual items, some salvage, not everything marine related.

Outer Cape Kites, Ryder Street Extension, 487-6133. Just what you need for the beach.

Puzzle Me This, 336 Commercial Street, 487-1059. Lots of mind-teasing goods.

Wineries

Cape Cod Winery, 681 Sandwich Road, Falmouth, 457-5592,
   www.capecodwinery.com. Six varieties, including Merlot, cranberry
   blush, and whites. Wine-tasting room open seasonally.
Truro Vineyards of Cape Cod, Route 6A, North Truro, 487-6200.
   Chardonnay and other varieties. Wine shop open seasonally.

Shopping

Many people come to Cape Cod not to stake a claim to a swath of
beach but to shop at the local outlet and bargain stores, boutiques, and
antiques emporiums. Eventually, everyone vacationing on Cape Cod
gets bitten by the shopping bug, especially during rainy days or when
they feel the need to bring souvenirs to loved ones back home. Cape
Cod has a plethora of stores selling goods that accommodate all spend-
ing limits.

Hyannis is Cape Cod's major center for shopping. On Route 132—
Iyanough Road—there's the Cape Cod Mall, the largest on the peninsula. This enclosed mall has three major department stores, a variety of
specialty stores, several eating places, and various services. Across Route
132 from this mall are additional stores. Main Street in Hyannis has
many stores, too—army and navy surplus, many souvenir places, clothing stores, and candy shops.

West Yarmouth, Dennis, Falmouth, and Orleans also have large
shopping malls. The main shopping streets of Provincetown, Chatham,
Osterville, New Seabury, and Falmouth village are also very popular
with visitors for their charm and diversity of offerings.

Stop and Shop is a large supermarket chain serving Cape Cod.
Shaw's and A&P are other supermarkets. Food prices are higher on
Cape Cod than on the mainland, but there are also many daily bargains
and specials. Many of the large supermarkets and some convenience
stores are open twenty-four hours a day. A large number of stores are
open all day Sunday. Liquor stores are open daily except Sundays, and
close at 10:00 P.M.

Shopping centers include:

Cape Cod Mall, Route 132 and 28, Hyannis, 771-0200. More than eighty
   stores, the largest indoor shopping center on Cape Cod. Includes
   five major department stores and lots of dining options.
Falmouth Mall, Route 28, Falmouth, 540-8329. More than thirty-five
   shops.

Mashpee Commons, Routes 28 and 151, Mashpee, 477-5400. More than eighty shops, along with restaurants and movie theaters. Free outdoor concerts and special events throughout the year.

Patriot Square, Route 134, South Dennis, 394-4129. Twenty-plus stores.

For information on shopping in Osterville, call 428-6327.

The following is a listing of some places for good buys or just for the fun of browsing:

Factory Outlets

Cape Cod Factory Outlet, 888-8417, includes stores such as Corning/Revere, Van Heusen, Bugle Boy, American Tourister, Bass, London Fog, Carters, and Izod; in Sagamore

Christmas Tree Shops, Cape Cod's most popular discount stores offering a variety of merchandise; in Falmouth, Sagamore, Hyannis, West Yarmouth, West Dennis, Yarmouthport, and Orleans

The Basket Shoppe, baskets and wicker; in Dennisport

Cuffy's Factory Store, casual clothing for the whole family; in South Yarmouth

Ocean State Job Lot, a variety of merchandise; in Falmouth, Hyannis, Bourne, and South Yarmouth

Corning Factory Store, Corning Ware and Pyrex; in Sagamore

Dansk Factory Outlet, Dansk products such as cookware, kitchen items, giftware, and dishes; in Hyannis

Europa, importer of interesting clothing and furnishings; in Hyannis and West Falmouth

Van Heusen Factory Store, shirts and sportswear for men and women; in Sagamore

Auctions

There are many auction houses located throughout the Cape; the larger ones are listed below. Check the local papers to get the most up-to-date auction information, especially during the summer.

Eastham Auction House, Holmes Road, North Eastham, 255-9003

Atlantic Auction Gallery, Factory Outlet Road, Sagamore, 888-7220

Mainsail Auction Co., 70 Industrial Road, Marston Mills, 420-6046

Robert C. Eldred Company, Inc., Route 6A, East Dennis, 385-3116

Sandwich Auction House, 15 Tupper Road, Sandwich, 888-1926

Flea Markets

Dick and Ellie's Flea Market, Route 28, Mashpee, 477-3550. More than
200 dealers set up on fourteen acres, five days a week.

Wellfleet Drive-in Flea Market, Route 6, South Wellfleet, 349-2520

Antiques

Cape Cod is an antiques maven's heaven. The shops are all over the
peninsula. Your best bet is to tour around, poke in and out, and keep a
sharp eye out for good buys.

A popular stop, especially with international visitors, is the Hyannis
Antique Center, 500 Main Street, Hyannis, which covers a wide variety
of items, from furnishings to collectibles. In June Heritage Plantation in
Sandwich holds a large show with dealers from throughout the Cape
and elsewhere. The Cape Cod Antique Dealers Association has a listing
of member dealers and their offerings. For a copy, send a business-sized
envelope with 55 cents postage to Betsy Hewlett, P.O. Box 191,
Yarmouthport, 02675. Copies can also be found at information centers.

Here is a sampling of dealers:

BARNSTABLE

Barnstable Stove Shop, Route 149, West Barnstable, 362-9913

Barnstable Village Antiques, 3267 Main Street, 362-6633

Cotuit Antiques, 4404 Route 28, Cotuit, 420-1234

Esprit Decor, 3941 Main Street, 362-2480

Hyannis Antique Coop, 500 Main Street, Hyannis, 778-0512

S. Barber Antiques & Fine Arts, 248 Stevens Street, 775-0900

Sow's Ear Antiques, Route 28 at Route 132, Cotuit, 428-4931

BOURNE

The Marketplace, 61 Main Street, Buzzards Bay, 759-2114

BREWSTER

Barbara Grant, 1793 Main Street, 896-7198

Breton House Antiques, 1222 Stoney Brook Road, 896-3974

Donald B. Howes Antiques, 1424 Main Street, 896-3502

Eve's Place, 564 Main Street, 896-4914

King's Way Books & Antiques, 774 Route 6A, 896-3639

Kingsland Manor Antiques, Route 6A, West Brewster, 385-9741

Monomoy Antiques, 3425 Route 6A, 896–6570

The Punkhorn Bookshop, 672 Main Street, 896–2114

Shirley Smith and Friends, 2926 Main Street, 896–4632

Swensen Pianos & Antiques, 219 Magnet Way, 896–5560

Tymeless Antiques and Collectibles, 3811 Main Street, 255–9404

Wisteria Antiques Etc., 1199 Main Street, 896–8650

Yankee Trader, 2071 Route 6A, 896–7822

CHATHAM

Amazing Lace, 726 Main Street, 945–4023

Aquitaine Antiques, 35 Cross Street, 945–9746

Bob's Antiques, Shop Ahoy Plaza, 945–4606

Chatham Antiques, 1409 Main Street, 945–1660

House on the Hill Antiques, 17 Seaview Street, 945–2290

Ivy Cottage Shop, 416 Main Street, 945–1809

Monomoy Salvage, 1134 Main Street, 945–6055

The Spyglass, 618 Main Street, 945–9686

Teacher's Antiques and Oriental Rugs, 1323 Main Street, 945–0681

DENNIS

Antiques Center of Cape Cod, 243 Main Street, 385–4600

Audrey's Antiques, 766 Route 6A, 385–4996

Central Market II, 292 Main Street, 760–1028

Gloria Swanson Antiques, 632 Route 6A, 385–4166

Leslie Curtis Antiques & Designs, 838 Main Street, 385–2921

Main Street Antique Center, 691 Route 28, 760–5700

Red Lion Antiques, 601 Main Street, 385–4783

South Side Antiques Center, 691-A Route 28, 394–8601

EASTHAM

Antiques Warehouse of Cape Cod, 3700 Route 6, 255–1437

The Birches Antiques, 60 Depot Road, 240–1936

Country Road Antiques, 2425 Route 6, 255–7084

FALMOUTH

Antiques in West Falmouth, 634 West Falmouth Highway, 540–2540

Aurora Borealis Antiques, 104 Palmer Avenue, 540–3385

Peg Wills Antiques, 144 Jericho Path, 548–3555

MASHPEE

Mashpee Antiques & Collectibles, Routes 28 and 151, 539–0000

HARWICH

The Barn at Windsong, 243 Bank Street, 432–8281

The Bedford Trust, 66 Miles Street, 430–1482

Diamond Antiques and Fine Art, 103 Main Street, 432–0634

Harwich Antiques Center, 10 Route 28, 432–4220

A London Bridge Antiques, 9 Pleasant Lake Avenue, 432–6142

Mews Antiques at Harwich Port, 517 Main Street, 432–6397

The Mews at Harwich Port, Route 28 at Ayer Lane, 432–6397

New to You Shop, 543 Main Street, 432–1158

ORLEANS

Antiques Center of Orleans, 32 Main Street, 240–5551

Continuum, 7 Route 28, 255–8513

Countryside Antiques, 6 Lewis Road, East Orleans, 240–0525

East Orleans Antiques, 204 Main Street, 255–2592

Lilli's Antique Emporium, 255 Route 6A, 255–8300

Peacock Alley Antiques, Route 28, 240–7799

Pleasant Bay Antiques, Inc., 540 Chatham Road, South Orleans, 255–0930

PROVINCETOWN

444 Shop, 444 Commercial Street, 487–0444

Clifford-William Antiques & Gifts, 255 Commercial Street, 487–4174

Dinsmore Scott Antiques & Fine Jewelry, 179 Commercial Street, 487–2236

Provincetown Antiques Market, 131 Commercial Street, 487–1115

Remembrances of Things Past, 376 Commercial Street, 487–9443

West End Antiques, 146 Commercial Street, 487–6723

SANDWICH

H. Richard Strand Jr. Antiques, 2 Grove Street, 888–3230

Henry T. Callan Fine Antiques, 162 Quaker Meeting House Road, 888–5372

Horsefeathers Antiques, 454 Route 6A, 888–5298

H. Richard Strand Antiques, Town Hall Square, 888–3230

Maypop Lane, 161 Route 6A, 888-1230

Sandwich Antique Center, 131 Route 6A, 833-3600

WELLFLEET

The Farmhouse, Route 6A, 349-1708

OSTERVILLE

The Farmhouse Antiques, 1340 Main Street, 420-3170

A. Stanley Wheelock Antiques, 870 Main Street, 420-3170

YARMOUTH

Constantine Goff Antiques, 161 Main Street, Yarmouthport, 362-9540

Minden Lane Antiques, 175 Main Street, 362-0220

Ryan M. Cooper Maritime Antiques, 161 Main Street, 362-1604

Town Crier Antiques, 153 Main Street, 362-3138

Thrift Shops

At these shops you never know what bargains or treasures—antiques, handcrafts, clothing, and more—you might find.

Not only are you finding great buys, but you're also helping good causes. All have limited hours, most are open year-round. All also accept donations. For general information, call the Cape Cod Council of Churches Thrift Shop in Dennis at 394-6361.

BARNSTABLE

Cape Cancer Thrift Shop, Route 6A, 362-2848

Hospice of Cape Cod Thrift Shop at the Schoolhouse, Route 6A, 362-8532

Kit 'n' Kaboodle, Unitarian Church, Route 6A, 362-6381

BREWSTER

Garret Treasures Consignment Shop, First Parish Church, 1969 Main Street, Route 6A, 896-5577. Open summer only.

Our Lady of the Cape Thrift Shop, Luke's Plaza, Route 6A, 896-5377

The Sea Captains Thrift Shop, Brewster Town Hall Annex, 896-8180

BUZZARDS BAY

St. Peter's Consignment Shop, 167 Main Street, 759-5623

CENTERVILLE

The Thrifty Niche, South Congregational Church, Main Street, 775-8332

CHATHAM

The Benefit Shop, South Chatham Community Church, Route 28, 432–3719

St. Christopher's Gift & Consignment Shop, 625 Main Street, 945–2211

COTUIT

St. Vincent de Paul Clothing Center, Christ the King Parish, 4463 Route 28, 420–0949

DENNIS

Cape Cod Council of Churches Thrift & Gift Shop, 355 Main Street/Route 28, 394–6361

New Beginnings Boutique and Thrift Shop, 466 Main Street/Route 28, 394–2600

Northside Thrift Shop, 635 Main Street / Route 6A, 385–4300

R.L.D.S. Thrift Shop, 185 Sea Street, 394–5990

EASTHAM

Friends of the Eastham Council on Aging, 580 Massasoit Road, 255–0264

FALMOUTH

Falmouth Hospital Auxiliary Thrift Shop, Route 28 and Ter Heun Drive, 457–3992

North Falmouth Congregational Church Thrift Shop, 149 Old Main Road, 563–2177

Second Hand Rose Thrift Shop, 6B Alphonse Street, 540–0570

Susan's Thrift Shop, 286 Teaticket Highway, 548–7086

HARWICH

The Corner Thrift Shop, First Congregational Church, 697 Main Street, 432–1053

Holy Trinity Thrift Shop, 240 Route 28, 432–7625

Noah's Ark Thrift Shop, Christ Church, Route 28, 432–1787

United Methodist Thrift Shop, 1 Church Street, 432–3734

HYANNIS

Annie's Closet Consignment, 393 West Main Street, 228–8844

Cape Cod Hospital Auxiliary Thrift Shop, 690 Main Street, 775–0078

The Friendly Thrift Shop, Hyannis Federated Church, 320 Main Street, 771–5395

ORLEANS

Cape & Island EMS Thrift Shop, Orleans Market Place, Old Colony Way, 255-1166

Elite Repeat Consignments, 213 Main Street, 255-1824

The Goody Bag Consignment Shop, 121 Route 6A, 240-5444

St. Joan of Arc Thrift Shop, 63 Canal Road, 255-4476

OSTERVILLE

Clothes Encounters Consignment, 805 Main Street, 428-9265

Rainbow's End, United Methodist Church, 1056 Main Street, 428-5304

SAGAMORE

Red Roose Thrift Shop, Swift Memorial Church, 82 Old Plymouth Road, 888-9808

SANDWICH

St. John's Episcopal Thrift Shop, 159 Main Street, 888-2828

WELLFLEET

A.I.M. Thrift Shop, Main Street, 349-6622

YARMOUTH

Cape Cod Cancer Consignment Exchange, 133 Main Street, Route 6A, 362-3416

Ditty Box, First Congregational Church of Yarmouth, 329 Main Street/Route 6A, 362-6977

Fishermen's House Thrift Shop, 322 Old Main Street, 398-2972

St. David's Thrift Boutique, 205 Main Street, 394-4222

West Yarmouth Congregational Church, Route 28, Corner of Lewis Road, 775-0891

Bookshops

Barnes & Noble, Route 132, Hyannis, 771-1400

Booksmith, Musicsmith, Skaket Corners, Orleans, 255-4590. Good selection of books, CDs.

Borders Book & Music, 990 Iyannough Road, Hyannis, 862-6363

Brewster Book Store, 2648 Main Street, Brewster, 896-6543

Cabbages and Kings (children's books), 628 Main Street, Chatham, 945-1603

Cape & Dagger, 357 Commercial Street, Provincetown, 487-0848. Mystery books, new and used.

Compass Rose Book Shop, Main Street, Orleans, 255-1545

Eight Cousins Children's Books, 189 Main Street, Falmouth, 548-5548

Isaiah Thomas Books & Prints, 4632 Falmouth Road, Cotuit, 428-2752. Everything from antiques and first editions to used books; also appraisals, repair service.

Paperback Cottage, 927 Route 28 at Route 134, 760-2101. Books are also available for rent.

Parnassus Book Service, 220 Route 6A, Yarmouthport, 362-6420. A book lover's heaven. Great place for browsing, even books outside the building available on honor system twenty-four hours a day.

Yellow Umbrella Books, 501 Main Street, Chatham, 945-0144. New and used, antique editions, everything.

Calendar of Special Events

Every town on Cape Cod schedules some special event for the enjoyment of residents and visitors alike—bazaars, bingo, festivals, sporting events, parades, fireworks displays, arts-and-crafts fairs, band concerts, painting exhibitions, cookouts, clambakes, open houses, and tours. The following calendar lists just some of these events. Call local chambers of commerce for more information.

FEBRUARY

Cape Cod Bay Seabird and Seal Cruises, through April, Wellfleet Bay Wildlife Sanctuary, Wellfleet

MARCH

Annual Hat Parade and Tea Party, Falmouth

APRIL

Woods Hole Model Boat Show and Workshop, Woods Hole

Daff O'Ville Day, Osterville

Brewster in Bloom, Brewster

Patriots Day Weekend, while not celebrated with any special events on the Cape, it is a three-day holiday weekend for many in Massachusetts

Whale-watching begins, Provincetown, Barnstable

MAY

Cape Maritime Week, Open house at Cape Cod lighthouses, Coast Guard stations, walking tours, Cape-wide

Green Briar Herb Festival, Sandwich

Cape Cod Canal Striped Bass Fishing Tournament, Buzzards Bay

Memorial Day Celebrations, all towns

Figawi Race (ocean sailboat race) from Hyannis to Nantucket and back

Johnny Kelley ½ Marathon and 5-mile Road Race (Kelley is a famed Boston Marathon runner having not only run and won the race for years but did so in his eighties.)

Lighthouse Tour, Chatham

JUNE

Heritage Week, one of the best times to be on Cape Cod to learn of its history, take part in cultural events, join in walking tours of historic sites, learn of the Cape's environment, house, and lighthouse tours, and more than 100 other events, Cape-wide.

Antiques Show, Heritage Plantation, Sandwich

Elegant Harborside Tea, Fridays through August, Community of Jesus, Rock Harbor, Orleans

Run for the Earth, 5-kilometer run on tidal flats, Cape Cod Museum of Natural History, Brewster

Cape Cod Canal 10 Kilometer Road Race, Buzzards Bay

Provincetown Portuguese Festival, Provincetown

Gardens and Homes of Brewster Tour, Brewster

Secret Garden Tour, Dennis

Harbor Festival, along the Hyannis waterfront, includes a blessing of the fleet, Hyannis

JULY

Independence Day celebrations in all Cape Cod towns

Star-Spangled Spectacular, Community of Jesus, Rock Harbor, Orleans

Annual Orleans Rotary Antiques Show, Orleans

Osterville Village Day, annual community celebration and parade, Osterville

Barnstable Country Fair, Barnstable County Fairgrounds, Route 151, East Falmouth

Mashpee Powwow, Native Americans in full regalia from across North America join in the celebration, Mashpee

Annual Antique Car Show and Competition, Heritage Plantation, Sandwich

Bayberry Quilters of Cape Cod Annual Quilt Show, Harwich

AUGUST

Cape Cod Air Show, Otis Air Force Base, Bourne

Chatham Festival of the Arts, Chatham

Pops by the Sea, concert by the Boston Pops with guest conductors, Hyannis

Dennis Festival Days, a five-day celebration, Dennis

Katharine Lee Bates Day Celebration (she wrote the words to "America"), Falmouth

Mentadent Tennis Tournament of Champions, Mashpee

Falmouth Road Race, a world-class 7.1-mile race that draws thousands, Falmouth

Provincetown Carnival Week, a Mardi Gras–type celebration, Provincetown

Annual Dennis Antiques Show and Sale, Yarmouth

Pops in the Park, Cape Cod Symphony Orchestra, Orleans

SEPTEMBER

Annual Bourne Scallop Festival, Bourne

Harwich Cranberry Festival, Harwich

Windmill Festival, Eastham

Fall Arts Festival, Provincetown

Truro's Treasures, crafts, parade, beach bash, and dump dance, Truro

O'Neill-by-the-Sea Festival, playwright Eugene O'Neill's works performed, Provincetown

Annual Bird Carvers Festival, Brewster

Fall for Orleans Festival, Orleans

OCTOBER

Seafest, Chatham

Osterville Fall Festival, Osterville

Yarmouth Seaside Festival, Yarmouth

NOVEMBER

Lighting of Pilgrim Monument on Thanksgiving Eve, Provincetown

DECEMBER

Christmas Shoppers Stroll, Hyannis

Christmas by the Sea, Falmouth

Holly Days, fresh greens for sale at Ashumet Holly and Wildlife Sanctuary, Falmouth

Lighting the Pilgrim Monument, into early January, Provincetown

Victorian Christmas Open House, Thornton W. Burgess Museum, Sandwich

Christmas in Sandwich, a three-week celebration in one of the Cape's prettiest towns, Sandwich

Yarmouthport Christmas Stroll, Yarmouth

Holiday Seal Cruises, Ashumet Holly and Wildlife Sanctuary, Falmouth

First Night, Chatham

Popular Attractions

Cape Cod is well endowed with all kinds of attractions besides beaches. Some are educational; others are just for fun; each provides interesting experiences for all ages. There's so much to do on Cape Cod that even bad-weather days can be fascinating and enjoyable.

The Major Sites

Cape Cod National Seashore, Lower Cape from Chatham to Provincetown, 255-3421. Attractions include beaches, bike and hiking trails, historical and ecological interpretive programs, fishing, surfing, historic homes and sites, and visitors centers. See "Cape Cod National Seashore" in the Outdoors section for more detailed information. Be sure to visit the Province Lands Visitors Center on Race Point Road in Provincetown (487-1256), which offers environmental, canoe, and surf-casting programs.

Marine Biological Laboratory, 100 Water Street, Woods Hole, 289-7623 (call at least one day in advance to be included on a tour). Although summer is its busiest season, with scientists and students converging here from all over the world to do research and study, MBL nev-

ertheless extends itself to the public by offering daily tours. It is the only scientific institution in Woods Hole to do so. You'll visit a laboratory, talk to a researcher, and see both the holding tanks where live marine specimens are kept and a slide show on what MBL is and how it contributes to science. Tours during the summer only. Admission is free.

Woods Hole Oceanographic Institution Exhibit Center and Gift Shop, 15 School Street, 289-2663. Also offers one-hour walking tours in season.

National Marine Fisheries Service Aquarium, Albatross Street, Woods Hole, 495-2001. the first aquarium in the country is showing its age, but it still is interesting. Touch tanks and seals.

Woods Hole Historical Museum and Collections, Woods Hole Road, 548-7270. Contains a library on marine topics, oral histories by townspeople, a diorama of Woods Hole in the 1800s, and historic small boats.

John F. Kennedy Hyannis Museum, 397 Main Street, Hyannis, 790-3077. Primarily a collection of photographs, along with a video on the Kennedys covering the period 1934 to 1963. The museum recorded a record 40,000 visitors in the summer of 1999 after John F. Kennedy Jr. died in a plane crash off Martha's Vineyard.

Falmouth Historical Society, Palmer Avenue near the Village Green, 548–4857. The historical society supervises two important buildings in Falmouth: the Julia Wood House, with its beautiful furnishings and garden; and the Conant House, a museum filled with rare glass and china, sailor's valentines, and items belonging to Katherine Lee Bates, author of the poem "America the Beautiful." Miss Bates first published her poem on 4 July 1895 in *The Congregationalist*. It was later set to the music of "Materna," composed by Samuel A. Ward in 1882. Miss Bates's house can be seen on Main Street, but it is not, at present, open to the public. Guided tours of the Conant and Wood houses are available. Open mid-June to mid-September in the afternoon. Admission charged.

New England Fire & History Museum, Route 6A in Brewster, 896–5711. This fascinating museum features hand- and horse-drawn fire equipment; old firemarks, helmets, and trumpets; a diorama of the "Burning of Chicago—1871"; an old-time firehouse; an eighteenth-century New England Common; an old-fashioned apothecary shop; and a 1929 Mercedes-Benz Nurburg 460. It also has the Arthur Fiedler (late conductor of the Boston Pops) fire-memorabilia collection. Open Memorial Day weekend to Columbus Day weekend. Admission charged.

The Cape Cod Museum of Natural History, Route 6A in Brewster, 896–3867 or (800) 479–3867. This excellent museum has exhibits on whales, geological survey maps, Native American artifacts, seashells, minerals, birds, and fossils. It also has a working weather station, a live-turtle tank, and saltwater tanks containing several species of marine invertebrates and fish. The museum's Clarence Hay Library is one of the finest natural-history circulating libraries in New England. The museum is also at the starting point of three interesting walking trails (see "Best Cape Walks" in the Outdoors section). Open all year. Admission charged.

Sandwich Glass Museum, 129 Main Street, Sandwich, 888–0251. This unique museum exhibits beautiful decorative and table glassware produced by companies operating in Sandwich from 1825 into the twentieth century. Featured are pressed glass with a stippled background; patterned glass of various designs in colors of amethyst, canary, green, and blue; and enameled, etched, and cut glass. There are also historical items from the lives of Daniel Webster, the actor Joseph Jefferson, Thornton W. Burgess, and the historian Frederick Freeman. Open daily, 9:30 A.M. to 4:00 P.M., from early April to late

October; open Wednesday through Friday, 9:30 A.M. to 4:00 P.M., all other months. The museum is closed for holidays and during the month of January. Admission charged.

Hoxie House, 888–1173, Route 130 in the center of Sandwich. Here is Cape Cod's oldest house and one of the oldest dwelling places in all of North America. It was built in 1637, or only seventeen years after the first landing of the English Pilgrims at Plymouth. The Hoxie House features an authentic saltbox roof, which has become a rare sight on Cape Cod. Open from mid-June to the first of October, Monday through Saturday. Admission charged.

Thornton W. Burgess Museum, Water Street, next to Dexter's Grist Mill in Sandwich, 888–4668. The author and naturalist Thornton Burgess wrote children's stories about the adventures of Peter Rabbit, Digger the Badger, Reddy Fox, Jimmy Skunk, and Chatterer the Red Squirrel. This museum honors Mr. Burgess's life and work and his immortal characters. Burgess wrote more than 170 books and 15,000 daily columns. On exhibit is the largest known collection of Burgess's writings and original Harrison Cady illustrations. The museum holds a story hour, using live animals, daily at 1:30 P.M. in July and August. Open April until Christmas. Donations accepted.

Green Briar Nature Center, Discovery Hill Road off Route 6A in East Sandwich, 888–6870. Green Briar Nature Center not only has a live Peter Rabbit but also a Briar Patch trail along which you can walk. One of the best parts of this center is the kitchen where on any given day fresh jams, jellies, and relishes are cooked and poured into glass jars. Give in to temptation and buy a few of your favorite jams. The center, open year-round, also sponsors lectures, field trips, and workshops. Donations accepted.

Heritage Plantation of Sandwich, Grove and Pine Streets, off Route 130, Sandwich, 888–1222. Heritage Plantation is Cape Cod's finest and most beautiful privately operated attraction. It features a round Shaker barn, which contains a priceless collection of thirty-four mint-condition antique cars built from 1899 to 1937—Mercer, Stutz, Cord, Packard, Pierce-Arrow, Peerless, an American-made Rolls-Royce, and Gary Cooper's snappy yellow 1930 Duesenberg Model J Tourester. There is also an old Cape Cod windmill, a military museum, a collection of antique firearms, military miniatures, Native American artifacts, a collection of American flag replicas, an art museum, an old-fashioned carousel restored and running, exhibits of early tools, American folk arts, and one of the country's largest displays of original Currier and Ives lithographs.

Heritage Plantation is situated on seventy-six acres of land-scaped grounds, flower beds, and nature trails. There are more than a thousand varieties of trees, shrubs, and flowers. During May, June, and July, thousands of Dexter rhododendrons bloom, and in summer 550 varieties of daylilies turn the grounds into blankets of bright, warm colors. The plantation presents three major exhibits a year. It also has a varied program of live entertainment. Don't leave Cape Cod without visiting Heritage Plantation. It's that special. Open daily from mid-May to Columbus Day. Admission charged.

State Fish Hatchery, off Route 6A in Sandwich. Trout by the thousands and in all sizes are raised here to inhabit the streams of Massachusetts and provide fine sport for anglers. You are welcome to walk among the holding tanks and get close looks at the trout in their various stages of development. Fish-food pellets are available in vending machines for feeding the trout, an enjoyable experience for all ages. Open daily throughout the year. Admission is free.

The Cape Cod Canal. The Cape Cod Canal extends 17.4 miles from Cape Cod Bay to Cleveland Ledge at Buzzards Bay. It has a controlling depth of 32 feet at mean low water and a minimum bottom width of 480 feet. It is the world's widest sea-level canal. In 1985 the Cape Cod Canal was designated a National Historic Engineering Landmark.

The first settler to see good sense in building a canal linking Cape Cod Bay with Buzzards Bay was Myles Standish, of Pilgrim fame, back in the early 1600s. He figured that the canal would help to increase trade between Plymouth Colony and the other European colonies, such as New Amsterdam (New York City), that were developing along the Atlantic seaboard. Several generations later George Washington also saw the economic and military advantages of a canal at Cape Cod. A canal would make sea transport between Boston and southerly ports not only faster and cheaper, but also safer. Until a canal was actually built, thousands of vessels were lost on dangerous shoals and in fierce storms trying to make it around the Cape.

It was not until the early 1900s, however, that the first Cape Cod Canal was completed, thanks to the vision and bankrolling of the millionaire August Belmont, who incidentally had familial roots on the Cape. The Cape was linked to the Massachusetts mainland by two drawbridges over this early canal. Belmont, however, lost money on this venture because the canal did not generate the volume of traffic anticipated. It had major limitations, being too narrow and allowing only one-way traffic, and the drawbridges caused a number of accidents to ships attempting to get through. In 1928 the canal was bought by the federal government, and the U.S. Army Corps of Engineers was given the task of making it better. The corps realigned and deepened the canal so that it could accommodate two-way traffic. Army engineers developed and continue to improve upon a state-of-the-art traffic control system as well as a system to monitor tide and wind conditions, which ensures safe navigation.

Under the direction of the engineers, the present Bourne and Sagamore bridges were constructed and opened to motor vehicle traffic in the mid-1930s. These bridges are high enough to allow the largest ship to pass with more than enough clearance. Today the Cape Cod Canal is used by both commercial shipping and pleasure craft. You, too, can sail through the Cape Cod Canal on a tour boat operating from Onset (see "Sightseeing and Cruises" in the Outdoors section for details). There are canal overlooks and rest and picnic areas flanking both sides of the canal. Visitors center open Monday through Friday. Admission is free.

The Aptucxet Trading Post, Aptucxet Road, Bourne, 759-9487. In 1627 the leaders of Plymouth Colony had a trading post built here for the purpose of exchanging their goods for furs brought in by natives and trappers. Within a short time, this commercial enterprise was sending considerable amounts of fur worth many thousands of pounds in British currency to merchants in the "olde country." The trading post was rebuilt by the Bourne Historical Society in 1930 on the original foundation. It now contains many artifacts from early settlers and Native Americans, a saltworks, and a gristmill. There is also the railroad station that was built for President Grover Cleveland, who spent his summer vacations in Bourne; inside is a model of the Cape Cod Canal. Open mid-April to mid-October. Closed Tuesdays. Admission charged.

Pairpoint Glass Works, 851 Sandwich Road, Route 6A, Sandwich, 888-2344 or (800) 899-0953. Pairpoint Glass Works uses age-old glass blowing and shaping techniques to create beautiful and useful objects. You can watch master craftspeople at work and purchase their creations at the store on the premises. Pairpoint continues a long-honored Sandwich tradition. The blowing room is open Monday through Friday. Admission is free. Store open daily.

Pilgrim Monument and Museum, Town Hill off Bradford Street, Provincetown, 487-1310. The Pilgrim Monument commemorates the landing of the Pilgrims in America in 1620, an event that took place before they set foot on Plymouth Rock. If the land had been more receptive to agriculture here at land's end on Cape Cod, Provincetown could have been the Pilgrim's first settlement. The monument rises 352 feet above sea level, and it is considered the highest granite structure in the United States. There is an observation area on top, reached by stairs, from where you can see Cape Cod Bay, the open Atlantic Ocean, the sand dunes of Provincetown and North Truro, the curving land of Cape Cod at its most northerly point, and the distant shoreline of mainland Massachusetts. Conversely, the monument, on a clear day, can often be seen from the mainland, across Cape Cod Bay, off Duxbury Beach.

At the base of the monument is a museum containing exhibits depicting Pilgrim life, their ship the *Mayflower,* and the signing of the Mayflower Compact, which took place in Provincetown harbor. The museum also has memorabilia of both Admiral Donald B. MacMillan, the famous Arctic explorer and longtime resident of Provincetown, and Eugene O'Neill, the immortal American playwright who spent many summers in Provincetown and was a central figure in its cultural life. Seasonal. Admission charged.

Ashumet Holly Reservation and Wildlife Sanctuary, Ashumet Road off Route 151, East Falmouth, 563-6390. This forty-five-acre sanctuary was given to the Massachusetts Audubon Society by Wilfred Wheeler, who brought together and made flourish many species of American, European, and Oriental hollies. This beautiful and tranquil sanctuary is also lush in season with magnolia, dogwood, rhododendron, and wildflowers. Easy hiking trails take you through the stands of hollies and other plantings and around a lovely pond. During the summer, Ashumet Holly sponsors sightseeing cruises to the Elizabeth Islands. In addition, various courses are taught during the year—for example, Oriental brush painting and dried-flower arranging. In late September Ashumet celebrates its Franklinia Festival, one of the few trees to flower in autumn and named in honor of Benjamin Franklin. Activities include hay rides, guided walks, slide programs, and refreshments. Open all year. Admission charged.

Wellfleet Bay Wildlife Sanctuary, Route 6, South Wellfleet, 349–2615. An extensive wildlife sanctuary on Cape Cod Bay operated by the Massachusetts Audubon Society, Wellfleet Bay features a number of self-guided nature trails to marsh, beach, woodland, and island areas. There are interesting courses and lectures on natural history and conservation. This facility sponsors the best tours of the tern and other seabird habitats of remote Monomoy Island. It also operates a summer day camp for children. A gift shop is on the premises. Open all year. Admission charged.

Cranberry World Visitors Center, on the harbor in Plymouth, 747–1000. Although off the Cape, Cranberry World offers fascinating exhibits showing how cranberries were cultivated historically, how they are harvested now, and how they are processed into different kinds of delicious foods. Free samples of cranberry drinks are offered. Cranberries are Cape Cod's major agricultural crop, and Cranberry World in Plymouth tells the story best.

The best time to see the harvesting of cranberries on Cape Cod and in other southeastern Massachusetts areas is from mid-September to the end of October. The old way of harvesting was done by stoop labor using a wooden hand rake with an attached box; the berries were scooped up and collected into the box. Today the cranberry bogs are flooded, and the cranberries float to the top, forming brilliant scarlet lakes; the berries are then harvested by machines. It's a very interesting and colorful sight, so bring your camera. Cranberry bogs can be seen throughout the Upper Cape and the Mid-Cape. They are easily identified as low, flat, open areas with vegetation growing close to the sandy soil, and appearing like a thick green carpet. The bogs are extensive spaces, rectangular in shape and bordered by 2-to-3-foot-high dikes.

Most cranberry growers do not mind if you hike along their bogs. Stay on top of the dikes and don't walk on the bogs themselves, however, as your footsteps will crush the plants and their fruit. Cranberry World is open daily from the first of April to the end of November. Admission is free.

Historic Homes and Other Noteworthy Places

Visitors should call local chambers of commerce for more information.

BOURNE AREA

Cataumet Methodist Church, County Road, Cataumet. Built at a nearby location in 1765 and originally a missionary church among the local Native Americans, the church conducts services that are open to the public.

Briggs-McDermott House and Alonzo Booth Blacksmith Shop, 22 Sandwich Road, Bourne, 759-6120. A Greek Revival home, furnished circa 1830–1910, has period gardens, working forge. Admission charged.

Buzzards Bay Railroad Bridge, at the western end of the canal. This vertical bridge is 270 feet high, 540 feet long, and the third longest vertical railway bridge in the world. While not used very often, it is quite a sight to see. With free parking, it is a good place to begin a canal bike ride.

Bournedale Herring Pond, Route 6, an artificial course built to provide fish a way to reach the pond at spawning time. Herring season is mid-April to mid-June.

National Marine Life Center Visitors Center, 120 Main Street, Buzzards Bay, 759-8722. Exhibits on dolphins, whales, and seals. Future home for a rehabilitation hospital for marine animals that become stranded and need care before being returned to the ocean.

Massachusetts Military Reservation, Otis Air Force, Bourne, 968-4003. Tours of this sprawling military center can be arranged if done so well in advance.

Wampanoag Indian Burial Hill, Bournedale Road, Bourne. Christian Native Americans were buried here until the early nineteenth century. A man named King Saul was the last one. Many of the natives in this area were converted by Thomas Tupper and Richard Bourne.

Massachusetts Maritime Academy (830-5000), at the end of Academy Drive, Buzzards Bay. The state's major training facility for seafaring officers, the academy carries on a centuries-old maritime tradition in Massachusetts. Visitors are welcome; good views of ships entering and leaving the Cape Cod Canal are plentiful.

FALMOUTH

Bourne Farm, Route 28A, West Falmouth. This working, forty-acre farm features a restored 1775 farmhouse, barn, and other buildings; fields cultivated with various vegetables; a pumpkin patch open to all in autumn; walking trails; and peach, pear, and apple orchards. The farm is a delightful oasis of tranquillity. Admission is free.

Friends Meeting House, Route 28A, West Falmouth. Quaker worship was held in this area as far back as 1720. The present building was built in 1775. An old Quaker graveyard flanks the meetinghouse, and across the highway are old horse carriage stalls used by the Friends. You are welcome to attend worship.

The Village Green, a classic New England green with Colonial, Federal, and Greek Revival homes surrounding it; many of the homes now serve as bed-and-breakfasts. On the National Historic Register.

First Congregational Church, 68 Main Street on the Village Green, has a bell, still rings, commissioned by Paul Revere. Engraved on the bell is the inscription, "The living to the church I call, and to the grave I summon all."

Mill Road Cemetery, off Mill Road, Falmouth. Historic burial ground contains the remains of early settlers and Revolutionary War soldiers. The cemetery is located near where Mill Road meets the main road to Woods Hole. There is a wooded lane that leads to this historic place, set a short distance from the road.

Saint Barnabas Church, on the Village Green in Falmouth. This beautiful Episcopal church reminds the visitor of similar structures gracing the small villages of England. You are welcome to attend services.

WOODS HOLE

Nobska Light, Church Street, the light commands a high point and is visible for 17 miles. Built in 1876, it is now automated. A great place for ocean views (especially the "hole" of Woods Hole) and sunsets.

Spohr's Garden, Fells Road, a three-acre private garden that is open all year thanks to the generosity of Charles and Margaret Spohr. Daffodils, lilies, azaleas, magnolias, and more.

St. Joseph's Bell Tower, Millfield Street on Eel Pond. A Romanesque tower built in 1929 by a student at the marine labs to remind all of a higher power. The bells ring twice daily.

Church of the Messiah, Church Street. This lovely Episcopal church is beloved by the scientists and residents of the Woods Hole area. You are welcome to attend services.

SANDWICH

Nye Homestead, Old County Road, East Sandwich. This unique house dates from 1685 and features exposed construction details to give you an idea of how well people in that period built their homes. The antique furnishings are of interest to most visitors. Open from July to mid-October; closed Saturdays and Sundays. Admission charged.

Yesteryears Doll Museum, Main and River Streets, 888-1711. Housed within a Gothic Revival meetinghouse are dolls ranging from a seventeenth-century Queen Anne to Barbies. Admission charged.

Wing Fort House, 69 Spring Hill Road, 833-1540. A circa 1641 house considered the country's oldest continuously lived in by the same family. Admission charged.

Dexter's Grist Mill, Town Hall Square, 888-1173. This seventeenth-century mill has been restored to working order. It grinds cornmeal fine enough to make excellent muffins or Indian pudding, and you can buy it right at the mill. Open mid-June to mid-October.

Quaker Meeting House and the Steven Wing House, Spring Hill Road, East Sandwich. Worship has been held here continually since 1657, making this site the oldest meeting place for Quakers in this hemisphere. The present meetinghouse was built in 1815. Visitors are welcome. Also in this area is the historic Steven Wing House, a portion of which was built in 1641. It is furnished with colonial and Victorian period antiques. Open from mid-June to mid-October. Admission charged.

MASHPEE

The Old Indian Meeting House, at Meeting House Pond, near cemetery off Route 28, Mashpee. Considered to be the oldest standing place of Christian worship on Cape Cod, this meetinghouse was built in 1684, moved to this location in 1717, and served the spiritual and social needs of the Native Americans of the Upper Cape for many generations. Open mid-June to the beginning of September on Wednesday, Friday, and Saturday. Admission is free. For more information, call Tribal Office at 477-0208.

Wampanoag Indian Museum (477-1536), Route 130, Mashpee. This interesting museum is housed in a 1793 building. It features early Native American artifacts and exhibits portraying Wampanoag life. Open from May to the beginning of October on Friday, Saturday, and Monday; open all year by appointment. Admission is free.

BARNSTABLE AREA

Colonial Court House (362-8927), Route 6A, Barnstable Village. This was the English king's courthouse in the eighteenth century. English justice was administered from here, as was opposition to the king's rule. The courthouse contains many historic items and memorabilia from the bicentennial celebration.

Cahoon Museum of American Art, 4676 Falmouth Road, Hyannis, 428-7581. A 1775 Georgian colonial house filled with the works of two popular primativists, Ralph and Martha Calhoun. Admission is free.

Trayser Museum on Cobb's Hill, Route 6A, Barnstable Village, 362-2092. A historical and maritime museum located in a nineteenth-century customs house. Donation requested.

Centerville Historical Society Museum, 513 Main Street, 775-0331. Located in an 1840 house with Victorian period rooms, a Colonial kitchen, and exhibits on Centerville's history, art, and industry. Admission charged.

Osterville Historical Society Museum, 155 West Bay Road, 428-5861. Includes a Boat Shop museum, Captain Parker House, and 1790 Cammett House, along with items related to Osterville's history. Admission charged.

Captain Jonathan Parker House, on Parker Road, Osterville. Built in 1795 and now housing the Osterville Historical Society, this lovely Cape Cod home features displays of Victorian furnishings, Sandwich glass, nineteenth-century photos of Osterville life, a children's room with dolls, and many other period artifacts. Open from late June through September on Thursday and Sunday, 3:00 to 5:00 P.M. Admission charged.

Crosby Yacht Yard, via West Bay Road from Osterville center. The famous Crosby Cat Boat, a favorite of fishermen and leisure sailors, originated here in the mid-1880s. There's a plaque in honor of Horace Crosby here. The yacht yard now provides services to some of the most expensive sailing vessels found anywhere in the United States.

Dottridge Homestead, Ocean View Avenue, Cotuit. Built in the early 1880s, this home contains period furnishings and memorabilia. The house was moved to Cotuit from Harwich over log rollers pulled by oxen. Open from late June to Labor Day on Thursday and Sunday (afternoon). Donations accepted.

Saint Francis Xavier Church, South Street, Hyannis. This Roman Catholic church has long been associated with the Kennedy family, especially with Rose Kennedy, their beloved matriarch. John F. Kennedy worshipped here, and there's a plaque in honor of his memory on a pew in the chapel. You are welcome to attend services.

The Kennedy Compound, Hyannisport. This is a private enclave of homes belonging to the Kennedy family. The compound is closed to the public, although harbor tours (see "Sightseeing and Cruises") will take you by it.

John F. Kennedy Memorial, Ocean Street, Hyannis. The memorial in a park overlooking Lewis Bay, it consists of the presidential seal, a decorative fountain, and a pool. This memorial is emblematic of the late president's love for the sea and for sailing.

Mary Lincoln House, Main Street, Centerville. Built in 1840, this house contains rare Sandwich glass, Revolutionary War uniforms and many other period costumes, bird carvings by Elmer Crowell, ship models, and beautiful quilts. Open from the first of June to early October; closed Monday and Tuesday. Admission charged.

Sachem Iyanough's Grave, Route 6A in Cummaquid. This is the burial site of the famous Native American chief who assisted the Pilgrims when they scouted settlement and trade possibilities in Barnstable. Iyanough was forced to seek refuge from Myles Standish and his force, who were exacting retribution against those native people who dared to challenge white dominance in this "new-found-land."

Reverend John Lothrop House/Sturgis Library (362-6636), Route 6A, Barnstable. Built originally in 1644 by Reverend John Lothrop, the famous minister and patriarch of Barnstable, this house was expanded in 1782 by Captain William Sturgis, a mariner of considerable note. The library contains important genealogical material and the original 1605 Lothrop Bible. Open during the week all year.

West Parish Meetinghouse, Route 6A and Meeting House Way. Considered to be the oldest Congregational church in America (established in Scituate, Massachusetts, in 1634 and in Barnstable in 1639). The West Parish Meeting House was originally built in 1717; it was restored in the 1950s. The cock at the top of the steeple was made in England and has overlooked this bit of Cape Cod since 1723, and the meetinghouse's bell was made by Paul Revere in the first decade of the 1800s. West Parish Meetinghouse is an architectural classic.

YARMOUTH

Bass Hole in Yarmouth. Some historians speculate that the Viking warrior Thorvald, Leif Ericsson's younger brother, was killed by natives here. No evidence pertaining to the Vikings, however, has ever been found. In the mid-1800s this area was the site of a major shipbuilding enterprise operated by the Bray family. Today nature has taken over and converted the area back to its original beauty, but you can imagine that the sails of Viking longboats are out on the horizon.

Winslow Crocker House, 362–4385, Route 6A, Yarmouthport. A Georgian-design home built in 1780, the house contains many exceptional antiques and is a prime showplace for the Society for the Preservation of New England Antiquities. Open from the first of June to mid-October; closed Monday, Friday, and Saturday. Admission charged.

Friends Meeting House, Station Avenue, South Yarmouth. Built in 1809 after local persecution of the Quakers ceased, the meetinghouse offers services open to the public.

Captain Bangs Hallet House (362–3021), off Route 6A, Yarmouthport. This early Greek Revival home of a sea captain engaged in the China trade houses a fine collection of early maritime artifacts and memorabilia: logs, charts, and chronicles; antique furnishings; and a 1740 kitchen. Open from early July to Labor Day. Admission charged.

Church of the New Jerusalem, Route 6A, Yarmouthport. This lovely Swedenborgian church, which possesses an exceptional organ, is noted for the emphasis on music during services. You are invited to attend worship.

Hallet's, 139 Route 6A, Yarmouthport, 362-3362. A genuine old apothecary built in 1889 and filled with reminders of yesterday.

Judah Baker Windmill, Yarmouth. Built in 1791 and kept in operation until 1891, this windmill was also used in a signaling system to announce the arrival and departure of Boston–Cape Cod packet ships.

Pawkanawkut Village Graves, Indian Memorial Drive, South Yarmouth. On this site was a native village that existed until the late 1700s. The inhabitants were killed off by smallpox, and their remains are buried in unmarked graves according to ancient custom.

Yarmouth Port Village Pump, Summer Street, Yarmouthport. Built in 1886, the pump served as the main source of fresh water for the village. Pumps such as this one were common in Cape Cod towns in the nineteenth century.

DENNIS

Jericho House Museum, Trotting Park Road, Dennis. Built in 1801 for a Cape Cod sea captain, the structure now houses a fine collection of nineteenth-century antiques. An adjacent barn features tools and household implements used during the nineteenth century, exhibits of early saltworks and a general store, equipment used in cranberry cultivation and harvest, and a display of driftwood sculpture. Open from the first of July to Labor Day on Wednesday, Friday, and Saturday from 2:00 to 5:00 P.M. Donations accepted.

Hokum Rocks, Hokum Rock Road, Dennis. This rock pile was once the home of a native hermit who greeted visitors with the salutation, "Ho kum?"—meaning "Who comes here?"

Josiah Dennis Manse (385-2232), Whig Street, Dennis. Built in 1736 and furnished with period antiques, including Reverend Josiah Dennis's portable pulpit/writing desk, the manse also has a fine collection of books and manuscripts relating to Cape Cod history. The oldest schoolhouse in Dennis is on the grounds of the manse. Open from July through August on Tuesday and Thursday from 2:00 to 4:00 P.M. Donations accepted.

Cape Museum of Fine Arts, Route 6A, 385-4477. More than 800 works by Cape Cod artists. Located on the grounds of the Cape Playhouse. Open all year.

Scargo Lake and Tower, off Scargo Road, Dennis. This 28-foot-high tower, built in 1902, offers good views of the surrounding landscape; the grounds have picnic facilities and nature trails. This area is rich in Native American legends concerning Princess Scargo and that of Maushop, a friendly giant. Here also is the burial ground of the Nobscusset tribe and their chief Mashantampaine.

Shiverick Shipyards (historical plaque), Sesuit Neck Road in East Dennis. This was one of the largest shipyards on Cape Cod during the nineteenth century. Shiverick schooners and clippers sailed throughout the world.

South Parish Congregational Church, Main Street, South Dennis. Built in 1835, the church had many sea captains in its congregation. Its organ was made in 1762 in London by a craftsman who also built one for the composer George Frideric Handel. The church's chandelier is made of 1835 Sandwich glass. You are welcome to attend worship.

BREWSTER

Stony Brook Grist Mill and Museum and Herring Run, 830 Stony Brook Road. A picturesque spot where in spring the herring run is the main attraction. The country's first water-powered mill was located here. The present gristmill is on its foundation.

The Brewster Store, 1935 Route 6A, 896-3744. Selling goods since 1866, this classic country store has been serving generations of Cape Codders. It was originally built as a church, and customers can still sit on pews to enjoy coffee or the newspaper.

HARWICH

Harwich Historical Society Museum at Brooks Academy, 80 Parallel Street, 432-8089. Exhibits on the cranberry farming industry, seafaring, coopering, and a general store. Donations accepted.

CHATHAM

Atwood House, 347 Stage Harbor, 945-2493. Built in 1752, the home contains period antiques, an extensive seashell collection, Sandwich glass, and Cape Cod books. In an adjoining shed are murals of Chatham painted by Alice Stalknecht-Wight. Open from mid-June to the end of September on Monday, Wednesday, and Friday from 2:00 to 5:00 P.M. Admission charged.

Chatham Light, Main Street between Bridge Street and Shore Road. A popular place to view the ocean. While the lighthouse is open only during Cape Heritage Week, the view from the parking area is of

Chatham Break, where, in 1987, waves crashed through the protective barrier beach that protected Chatham Harbor. Many homes were destroyed.

Chatham Fish Pier, off Main Street. Watch the fishing boats unload their catches of fresh seafood from a special observation deck. Best time to experience this typical Cape Cod event during weekdays is after 2:00 P.M.

Mayo House, 540 Main Street, 945-4084. A three-quarter Cape that has been on the site since 1818. Exhibits of the period. Admission is free.

Godfrey Windmill, at Chase Park. Dating back to 1797. Open July through August; closed on Tuesday. Donations accepted.

Monomoy Island Wildlife Refuge, 945-0594, off Chatham Harbor and accessible only by boat.

Railroad Museum, 945-0342, Depot Road. Built in 1887 and now in the National Register of Historic Places, the structure was restored as a country depot and contains railroad memorabilia, models, equipment, and photographs. Open from the end of June to the Friday after Labor Day, 1:30 to 4:30 P.M.; closed Saturday and Sunday. Donations accepted.

ORLEANS

First Universalist Meeting House, 255-1386 Main Street, Orleans. Built in 1834, it now houses the Orleans Historical Society and contains exhibits of Native American, local history, and lifesaving artifacts. Open July through August, Thursday and Friday, 2:00 to 4:00 P.M. Donations accepted.

French Cable Museum, 240-1735, Route 28 and Cove Road, Orleans. Built in 1890, the structure housed cable and transmission gear for transatlantic communications between North America and France. Open from July to mid-September, Tuesday through Sunday, 2:00 to 4:00 P.M. Admission charged.

Jonathan Young Windmill, Route 6A, 240-1329. The works are fully operating, and the windmill has been restored authentically. Admission is free.

Orleans Historical Society, 3 River Road, 240-1329. Native American artifacts, early photographs, marine items, and lifesaving equipment. Admission charged.

EASTHAM

Doane Homestead, off Doane Road, Eastham. A marker here notes where the first English settlers in Eastham established their habitation.

Rock Harbor, Cape Cod Bay, the town's first maritime center was the scene during the War of 1812 of town militiamen turning back the British HMS *Newcastle*.

First Encounter Beach (historical plaque), Samoset Road, Eastham. This is where a party of Pilgrims under the leadership of Myles Standish was attacked by natives. The attack took place shortly after the Pilgrims made their first landing in the New World in 1620 and before they finally set ashore at Plymouth. The reason for the attack was that, a few years before, an Englishman had come into this area, captured some of the natives, and sold them as slaves to buyers in Spain. The natives were obviously concerned that these new settlers had similar intentions. Although this "first encounter" was a conflict involving flying arrows and discharging muskets, it is said that no one was killed or injured. In a very real sense this "first encounter" was the advent of the decline of Native American cultures in New England.

1741 Swift-Daley House, 255-3380, Route 6, Eastham. Once the home of Nathaniel Swift, one of the founders of the Swift Meat Packing Company, this historic house is furnished with antiques dating from the late eighteenth century and other artifacts of interest. Open July through August, Wednesday and Friday, 1:30 to 4:30 P.M. Admission is free.

Old Cove Cemetery, Cove Road, Eastham. The first cemetery in Eastham, the site contains the graves of early settlers and memorials to three who came over on the *Mayflower*. This area was also the site of the first meetinghouse in town, which was built shortly after settlement in 1644.

Captain Penniman House, Fort Hill Road, Eastham. A palatial Victorian home built in 1876 by a prominent whaling captain, the house is now an attraction within Cape Cod National Seashore.

Schoolhouse Museum, Nauset Road, Eastham. Built in 1869 and used as an Eastham school until 1905, it now serves as a museum of local history. Open July through August, Wednesday and Friday, 2:00 to 5:00 P.M. Admission charged.

Eastham Windmill, Route 6, Eastham. Built in 1680 and still in good working order, the mill is open from the end of June to Labor Day.

WELLFLEET

First Congregational Church, Main Street, Wellfleet. The building contains a clock that strikes ship's time and a Tiffany stained-glass window illustrating a ship reminiscent of the Pilgrim's *Mayflower*. You are invited to attend worship here.

Nauset Light and Three Sisters Lighthouses, Cable Road and Ocean View Drive. The lighthouses date from the 1800s. Nauset Light was recently moved to protect it from ocean erosion.

Wellfleet Historical Society Museum, Main Street, Wellfleet. This excellent maritime and local history museum is open from late June to early September, Tuesday through Sunday, 2:00 to 5:00 P.M. Admission charged.

Samuel Rider House, Gull Pond Road, Wellfleet. Built in the early 1700s, the home is characteristic of a Lower Cape farm of that period. Open from late June to early September, Monday through Friday, 2:00 to 5:00 P.M. Admission charged.

Marconi Wireless Station, off Route 6 in Cape Cod National Seashore. From transmission towers built on these cliffs overlooking the open Atlantic, Guglielmo Marconi sent the first transatlantic wireless message in January 1903. There is little left of Marconi's towers. There is, however, a memorial to Marconi, as well as an observation pavilion from which to view the panorama of the cliffs and ocean. Open all year. Admission is free.

TRURO

Bell Church, Meetinghouse Road, Truro. Built in 1827, the church has a Paul Revere–made bell and Sandwich glass windows. You are welcome to attend services.

Truro Historical Museum at Highland Light, Highland Road, North Truro. An interesting collection of maritime, farming, and whaling artifacts is housed in what was once an early Lower Cape inn. Also here are artifacts from shipwrecks, antique firearms, Sandwich glass, and bird carvings. Open from June to September. Admission charged.

Cape Cod Light, South Highland Road. The original lighthouse was built in 1798. Rebuilt in 1853, Henry David Thoreau stayed here during one of his Cape walks. In 1996 the light was moved back 450 feet from the sea to protect it from erosion. Where Thoreau stayed is now about 150 feet offshore.

Jenny Lind Tower, off Lighthouse Road, North Truro. The "Swedish Nightingale" used this tower in 1850 to sing to people in Fitchburg, Massachusetts, who couldn't get into a concert that was oversold by unscrupulous wheelers and dealers. The 55-foot tower was brought to Truro by Harry Aldrich and set on high ground as a memorial to his father.

PROVINCETOWN

MacMillan Wharf, off Commercial Street, downtown Provincetown. Named in honor of the late Admiral Donald B. MacMillan, famous Arctic explorer and longtime resident, the wharf is where the fishing fleet brings in its catch and where whale-watching and Cape Cod Bay cruises originate. Every day it's a busy place and one of the most enjoyable attractions in Provincetown. The annual "Blessing of the Fleet" takes place at MacMillan Wharf toward the end of June.

Old Harbor Life-saving Museum, Race Point Beach, 487-1256. Tells the story of the nineteenth-century stations committed to saving the lives of those shipwrecked. More than 100,000 lives were saved by thirteen stations.

Oldest Cemetery in Provincetown, Shank Painter Road, Provincetown. A good place for cemetery buffs to wander, the grounds contain many markers from the eighteenth century and a memorial plaque honoring four who passed away when the *Mayflower* was anchored in the nearby harbor in 1620.

Expedition Whydah, 16 MacMillan Wharf, 487-7955. A museum that chronicles the *Whydah*, the only pirate ship ever salvaged. It sank off Wellfleet in 1717 and was recovered in 1984.

Mayflower Compact Memorial (historic bas-relief plaque), adjacent to Town Hall, Provincetown center. This plaque commemorates one of the earliest documents in American history, whereby a group of people sought to govern themselves by majority rule for their mutual prosperity and well-being. The Mayflower Compact—or "The Agreement," as the Pilgrims called it—which was signed on board the *Mayflower* in Provincetown harbor on November 21, 1620, is considered by many to be as revered a document of liberty as the Magna Carta, the Declaration of Independence, and the United States Constitution. It was a strong step forward in the development of democracy in the political entity that would become the United States of America.

Heritage Museum, 356 Commercial Street, Provincetown. Housed in what was an 1860 Methodist church, this local museum contains historical artifacts, old lifesaving equipment, fire apparatus, fishing gear, antique furniture, and books. It also features exhibitions of contemporary painting, photography, and sculpture created by area artists. Open from the beginning of April to mid-October. Admission charged.

Seth Nickerson House, 72 Commercial Street, Provincetown. Built in 1746, this house is considered to be the oldest one in Province-town; its rooms are furnished with antiques. Open from May through October. Admission charged.

Famous Photogenic Lighthouses

Nobska Light, via Church Street and Nobska Road, Woods Hole. This is my favorite lighthouse on the entire Atlantic coast because of its site high on top of Nobska Point. From here you have magnificent views of Nantucket and Vineyard sounds, Woods Hole, Martha's Vineyard Island, and the Elizabeth Islands. Nobska Light, originally built in 1828 and rebuilt in 1876, is an important lighthouse because of all the traffic sailing in these waters—island ferries, fishing boats, pleasure vessels, and oceanographic research ships. It's not unusual to see cruise liners, such as the QE II, and tall-masted, full-rigged ships representing a bygone era. There are times during July and August when the sea-lanes around here seem as thick with traffic as the cross streets of Times Square in New York City. The sunsets from here are breathtaking. Snap a good photo of Nobska, get it blown up, and you'll have one of the finest souvenirs of your trip to Cape Cod.

Chatham Light, Main Street, Chatham. Two wooden lighthouses, known as the Twin Sisters of Chatham, were built here in 1808 but were destroyed in the storm of 1879. Angeline Nickerson was the keeper after her husband died. The present lighthouse is electronically operated. A very popular site for viewing. Limited parking time.

Nauset Light, Ocean View Drive, off Route 6 via Cable Road, Eastham. Three stone light towers were built here in 1838, and they became known to mariners rounding the Cape as the Three Sisters. They eventually collapsed due to the eroding soil and were replaced by wooden towers in the 1890s. The current steel tower is automated.

Highland Light, via Highland and Lighthouse Roads, Truro. Highland
Light is better known to mariners around the world as Cape Cod
Light. It is one of the first lights seen on the American mainland by
mariners sailing in from Europe. The first lighthouse was built in
1797 to keep vessels away from the shoals known as the "graveyard
of ships." Literally thousands of ships went aground or disappeared
around these cliffs. The current, automated lighthouse is a popular
attraction within Cape Cod National Seashore. Visitors centers in
Eastham, South Wellfleet, and Provincetown will be happy to provide you with more information on visiting lighthouses within
Cape Cod National Seashore.

Scenic Drives

Route 6A—"The Old King's Highway." This scenic drive takes you
through the towns of Sandwich, Barnstable, Yarmouth, Dennis,
Brewster, and Orleans on a journey past lovely, old villages of historic homes, fine inns and B&Bs, gourmet restaurants, marshlands,
beaches, forests, estuaries, antiques and crafts shops, museums, and
major attractions. Always close by are the beaches and harbors of
Cape Cod Bay. Route 6A, along the north coast of Cape Cod, is our

longest and most satisfying scenic drive. Along this route you will experience the Cape without a lot of commercialization. The traffic is usually more relaxed and not as thick nor as frenetic as in other parts of the Cape. You can't help falling in love with Cape Cod when you tour Route 6A. This truly is quintessential Cape Cod, where nostalgia and reality blend together in harmony.

Route 28A. Pocasset to West Falmouth—access off the Otis rotary. This portion of Route 28A, heading toward Falmouth and Woods Hole, takes you through the charming villages of North and West Falmouth, near Old Silver and Chapoquoit beaches on Buzzards Bay, and past fine restaurants and B&Bs, historic sites and homes, old Cape Cod farms, and harbors. In many respects Route 28A here is similar in environment and pace to Route 6A. You can meander along, enjoying the scenery, without the pressures persisting on the major highway. Route 28A will bring you to Palmer Avenue in the Sippewissett area. Sippewissett Road off Palmer is another lovely, scenic drive that takes you past Wood Neck Beach on Buzzards Bay, to Quissett Road and Quissett Harbor, and into Woods Hole Village.

Woods Hole to Menauhant. Take Woods Hole Road to the village of Woods Hole. Find a parking place, which may be difficult in this small, extremely busy community, and see the sights (islands ferry terminal, Woods Hole Oceanographic Institution, Marine Biological Laboratory, etc.), visit the shops, and eat a good meal of fresh seafood. Go back on Woods Hole Road and turn right on Church Street, which takes you past the Church of the Messiah, down to the beach, and up to Nobska Point with its well-known lighthouse offering superb views of Martha's Vineyard Island, the Elizabeth Islands, Vineyard Sound, and Nantucket Sound. Walk along the cliff and take pictures of the lighthouse. Continue east on Nobska Road, which merges with Fay Road, then Oyster Pond Road, then Surf Drive Road. There are beaches along Surf Drive Road on Nantucket Sound. At the end of Surf Drive, turn onto Shore Road and right onto Clinton Avenue, then Scranton Avenue, which goes along Falmouth Inner Harbor, where there are restaurants, charter-fishing operations, and band concerts at Marine Park. Turn right onto Robbins, at the end of the harbor, then right onto Manchester Avenue, which takes you past the Martha's Vineyard Island ferry terminal. This road merges with Grand Avenue and Menauhant Avenue, taking you past some of the most popular beaches in the town of Falmouth.

Mashpee to Cotuit. Not far from Mashpee Circle, heading east on Route 28 toward Hyannis, take a right on Quinaquisset Road and continue until you reach the center of Cotuit. The beauty of Cotuit center is that it is one of the least commercial villages on the Cape, a place where it seems that time has stood still. Tour the center, using Main Street and Ocean View Avenue, and go out to the beach on Nantucket Sound at the end of Main Street; there are many fine vistas along the way. Then go back on Main Street, which will take you past some fine old homes to Route 28.

Osterville to Hyannis. Heading east on Route 28, take a right on County Road, which merges into Main Street. Main will take you into Osterville center, one of the most affluent communities on the Cape, where you can take a meal at Wimpys, a Cape tradition. You can see some of the palatial homes and seaside estates on Wianno Avenue and along Seaview Avenue. West Bay Road will take you to the yacht marinas and to the well-guarded entrance to the exclusive Oyster Harbor section. From Osterville continue east on Main Street, which will bring you to the public beaches on Main Street. Just before turning off Main Street, continue on and stop for ice cream at Four Seas, the oldest ice cream shop on Cape Cod.

Marston Mills to West Barnstable. Route 149 north/south takes you across the Cape Cod peninsula from Route 28 to Route 6A. This is a rural road with pleasant scenery. Highlights along the way are a herring run with tame waterfowl to feed, the Whelden Library, an old-fashioned general store, and West Parish Congregational Church, a classic white New England Protestant church with an aesthetically perfect interior (its first service was held on Thanksgiving Day, 1719; services now feature superb choir and organ music). There is also a small, private airport off Route 149 where, occasionally, sailplane rides are offered in the summer.

Chatham Harbor. The center of beautiful Chatham, reached via Route 28, can be toured by motor vehicle or on foot. There are many charming shops, inns, B&Bs, and restaurants in town. Chatham is what "outlanders," or visitors, imagine a perfect Cape Cod town to be like: small, friendly, quaint, weather-beaten shingled, bright, cheery, and at the edge of the sea. Main Street brings you to Chatham Light, the fish pier overlooking Chatham Harbor, and the lower extension of Nauset (barrier) Beach and Nantucket Sound; to the south is Monomoy Island Wildlife Refuge. Following first Shore

Road and then Main will take you past Tern Island, a Massachusetts Audubon Society sanctuary; along Chatham Harbor to Norris Road; and then to Morris Island. At the northern end of town, take Fox Hill Road to Nickersons Neck and the Chatham Port area. Barn Hill Road, off Main Street, leads to Hardings Beach.

Ocean View Drive and Wellfleet Harbor Drive. To view the drama of the open Atlantic from the top of high cliffs and broad, fine sand beaches, take Le Count Hollow Road, which runs east off Route 6 in South Wellfleet. This road leads to Le Count Hollow Beach. Doubling back from the beach, take your first right onto Ocean View Drive, which parallels the ocean; it brings you to White Crest and Newcomb Hollow beaches. All three beaches are town managed and within Cape Cod National Seashore. Another scenic drive in Wellfleet is on the west side of Route 6; it leads to attractive, downtown Wellfleet, Wellfleet Harbor on Cape Cod Bay, scenic Chequesset Neck Road, the Great Island Trail, and Duck Harbor Beach.

Province Lands. In Provincetown explore the vast sand areas of the Province Lands area of Cape Cod National Seashore by taking Province Land and Race Point roads. These roads also lead to Herring Cove and Race Point beaches, bike and nature trails, horseback-riding stables, and the Province Lands Visitor Center. There are many splendid vistas of sea, rolling sand dunes, and beach grass. Also explore the side roads on either side of Route 6 in North Truro and Provincetown for access to spectacular sand dunes and super beaches.

Family Amusements

Cape Cod Discovery Museum, 444 Main Street, Dennisport, 398–1600 or (800) 298–1600 in Massachusetts. A hands-on museum for children from toddlers to elementary school kids. Exhibits range from a photo-sensitive wall that lets kids leave their shadow behind, to an "invention Convention" where children can take apart common appliances to see what makes them tick. The museum was developed by two former teachers. Open all year. Admission charged.

Zooquarium of Cape Cod, Route 28, West Yarmouth, 775–8883. This marine aquarium and zoological park presents dolphin and sea lion shows. It has a petting zoo of gentle animals for young children and live exhibits of lions, cougars, bears, piranhas, alligators, sea turtles, and snakes. There are pony rides, antiques and farm exhibits, an extensive seashell collection, a gift shop, and a picnic area. Open from February to November. Admission charged.

Bassett Wild Animal Farm, Tubman Road, off Route 6A, Brewster, 896-3224. A favorite with young children, Bassett Wild Animal Farm has a number of wild and farm animals. It also offers a petting zoo, hay and pony rides, a gift shop, and an area for picnics. Open from mid-May to mid-September. Admission charged.

Yesteryears Doll Museum, corner of Main and River Streets, downtown Sandwich, 888-1711. The museum houses a fascinating collection of antique dolls, dollhouses, miniature furnishings, and toys. Open from early May to the end of October. Admission charged.

Cape Cod Potato Chip Factory, Breed's Hill Road, off Route 132, Hyannis, 775-7253. See them made, then have some free samples.

Cape Cod Children's Museum, Falmouth Mall, Route 28, Falmouth, 457-4667. Hands-on learning center with a toddler castle, submarine, pirate ship, and planetarium. Admission charged.

Pirate Adventures on the *Sea Gypsy*, sailings from Hyannis and Orleans, 430-0202. With painted faces and pirate dress, youngsters set sail on a fun adventure.

Cuffy's Wearhouse Outlet, Dupont Avenue off White's Path, South Yarmouth, 394-1371. Cuffy's is the place for sweatshirts and T-shirts, but the factory store makes shopping fun, with its animated exhibits. See how more than a million T-shirts and sweatshirts are screenprinted every year. Also some good deals not found elsewhere.

Ryan Family Amusements, 200 Main Street, Buzzards Bay, 759-9892, with bowling and game room; 1067 Route 28, South Yarmouth, 394-5644, with bowling and game room; Cape Cod Mall, Hyannis, 775-5566, with game room; 291 Commercial Street, Provincetown, 487-3015, with game room

Artmosphere has a kids camp and a Friday night supper club where the kids create their own ceramic masterpieces. Locations in Hyannis, 575 Main Street, 790-9110, and Mashpee, at Mashpee Commons, 539-4242.

Other Amusements

Cartwheels, 11 South Gages Way, South Dennis, 394–6755. The latest in go-carts.

Storyland, 70 Center Street, Hyannis, 778–4339. Bumper boats and miniature golf.

Bass River Sports World, Route 28, South Yarmouth, 398–6070. Softball and baseball batting cages, golf driving range, game room, and mini golf.

Bud's Go-Karts, 9 Sisson Road at Route 28, Harwich Port, 432–4964.

Trampoline Center, Route 28, Harwich Port, 432–8717.

Grand Slam, Route 28, Harwich Port, 430–1155. Baseball and bumper boats.

Game Zone, 54 Main Street, Orleans, 240–3800. Video games pinball machines, more.

T-Time Family Sports Center, Route 6, Eastham, 255–5697. Game room, batting cages, driving range, and mini golf.

For more ideas, check the *Cape Cod Times* Friday edition for its weekly listing of entertaining ideas for all ages.

The Best of Cape Cod

Spelling out the best of Cape Cod is not an easy task, but if you still can't decide where to go, we'd like to suggest a few of our favorites.

Cape Cod National Seashore. You haven't seen Cape Cod unless you visit here. Cape Cod National Seashore reveals and preserves the natural beauty of the Cape. The Visitors Center is in Eastham.

Villages. Sandwich offers a classic Cape Cod experience. Provincetown, where the Pilgrims first landed, still retains its fishing heritage.

Lodgings. Cape Cod is very accommodating to every taste from campgrounds and lovely inns and bed-and-breakfasts to grand resorts. The Chatham Bars Inn is a classic resort fully restored to its original elegance. Another resort, smaller and also on the waterfront, is the Lighthouse Inn in West Dennis. The Sheraton in Hyannis is more modern with just about everything one could want within steps.

The Kennedys. Hyannisport is home to the Kennedy family. President John F. Kennedy also used his home there as a summer White House. It is best seen from a Hy-Line boat tour from Hyannis.

Fishing. World-class fishing for everything from bluefin tuna to bass and flounder. In addition to saltwater fishing, the Cape is home to 365 freshwater lakes, for even more fishing.

Beaches. The Cape's beaches are among the best in the nation. Coast Guard in Eastham is best for the surf. Sandy Neck in West Barnstable is 6 miles long. Craigville in Centerville is for families.

Golf. Little Highland Golf Course in Truro has only nine holes, but its design, like a Scottish course, offers grand Atlantic Ocean views.

Dining. Chillingsworth in Brewster, with its classic French cuisine, is known worldwide, but for a Cape Cod dining experience consider the Regatta by the Sea, for clam chowder check out Captain Parker's in West Yarmouth, and for clams head to Baxter's on the water in Hyannis Harbor. For ice cream, Four Seas in Centerville is the Cape's oldest and tastiest.

Nightclubs. Christine's in West Dennis.

Walk. Fort Hill in Eastham follows the sea and has Native American sites along the path.

Car trip. Route 6A from Sandwich to Orleans, the King's Highway, has been rated one of the best in the country.

Lighthouses. Cape Cod Light in Truro.

Sunsets. Try Sunset Hill in Hyannisport or Barnstable Harbor from the end of Millway Street.

Museums. Heritage Plantation in Sandwich can't be beat. It has great classic cars, an old-fashioned carousel, beautiful grounds, and lots of Americana.

Bike Trail. Dennis to Eastham or along the Cape Cod Canal service roads.

Bird-watching. Monomoy National Wildlife Refuge in Chatham.

Bookstores. Don't miss Parnassus on 6A in Yarmouthport. The books overflow the store.

Theater. The Dennis Playhouse is the oldest in the country. Many famous celebrities got their start here.

Whale-watching. Get to see these giants of the sea up close. Provincetown is the closest jumping off place to their feeding grounds.

CHAPTER FOUR

Guide to Towns, Accommodations, and Dining

Cape Cod consists of fifteen towns and a number of villages. The organization of Cape Cod towns and villages is confusing to both visitors and residents alike. For example, there's this anomaly: Barnstable is the county that encompasses all of Cape Cod; it is also a town and a village within this town; the town of Barnstable has seven villages, one of which is Hyannis, the most populous community on the Cape and large enough in importance to be a city. There are, however, no cities on Cape Cod, nor will there ever be any as long as Cape Codders remain fixed in the nostalgia of living in small communities, where the fantasy, if not the reality, of society on a human scale is retained.

Every Cape Cod town has a long and distinguished history. Many have been published in thick volumes filled with fascinating information, not only about local persons and events, but also about the very development of the United States from colonial times to the present. Persons interested in their family roots and/or American history can wade through a rich treasure trove contained in the public libraries and historical societies of Cape Cod as well as at Cape Cod Community College in Barnstable, which has one of the largest collections of books and manuscripts.

The following descriptions of individual Cape Cod towns also contain aspects of local history, but they appear only as highlights to emphasize each community's uniqueness. My purpose is not to tell you everything about an individual town, just enough so that, when you explore it on your own, each community will already have a distinct image in your mind.

As a guide to costs, the following price range is offered in the listings. On accommodations: inexpensive, $60 to $120; expensive, more than $120 a night. For dining: inexpensive, under $12; moderate $12 to $25; expensive, more than $25 for a meal. These are prices for in-season; off-season prices can be much lower. Many places on Cape Cod have specials on accommodations and dining that can lower the cost of a vacation. Always ask if there are any special deals.

Bourne

Town offices—24 Perry Avenue, Bourne, 759-0613; Cape Cod Canal Area Chamber of Commerce Information Center, 70 Main Street, Buzzards Bay, 759-0600.

The following villages, with their postal zip codes, are within the town of Bourne: Bourne—02532; Pocasset—02559; Cataumet—02532; Sagamore—02561; Sagamore Beach—02562; Buzzards Bay—02532; and Monument Beach—02553.

Regardless of what road you take, Bourne is the "Gateway Town" to Cape Cod. Bourne is located both on the mainland side of the Cape Cod Canal and on the peninsula itself. The two highway access bridges to the Cape are the Bourne and the Sagamore and are located in the town of Bourne. Within Bourne are the Massachusetts Maritime Academy in Buzzards Bay and the Massachusetts Military Reservation, which consists of Otis Air Base; Camp Edwards, a training area for National Guard units; and a base for contingents of the Coast Guard, Marines, and Navy. The Massachusetts National Cemetery (563-7113) is also located in Bourne.

The village of Buzzards Bay, on the mainland side, has several motels and restaurants for the convenience of travelers. Interstate 495 to Route 25 connects directly with the Bourne Bridge, bypassing congested Route 6 through Wareham. If you need restaurants, service stations, and souvenir shops, the diversion to Route 6 is easy to make from Route 25. The village of Sagamore provides access to the Sagamore Bridge, the Mid-Cape Highway—Route 6—and scenic Route 6A, "The Old King's Highway," which goes through the charming villages along the north coast of Cape Cod. There are motels, restaurants, and shops in Sagamore. The Christmas Tree Shop, with its huge thatched roof and windmill, at the Sagamore Bridge and a complex of outlet stores across from it have become popular stops for bargain-hungry travelers. The villages of Pocasset, Cataumet, and Monument Beach are reached from the Bourne Bridge via Route 28. The villages continue to retain the traditional rural charm and simplicity of Cape Cod and offer many pleasant scenic drives and vistas.

Historically, Bourne is important to the development of Cape Cod because it contains the isthmus between Buzzards Bay and Cape Cod Bay.

Bourne was part of the Town of Sandwich until 1884, at which time it separated and became a town in its own right. In the early 1600s a trading post was established by the Pilgrims in Bourne at Aptucxet. Natives and trappers brought in furs and were paid in the manufactured goods they needed. Aptucxet Trading Post flourished until the middle of that century, then declined in importance as similar trading operations sprouted along the Atlantic and within the wilderness of North America. During early settlement, Protestant ministers, such as Richard Bourne and Elisha Tupper, converted many natives to Christianity.

Through much of its history, Bourne was an agricultural and fishing town. When the railroad connected the large cities of America with Cape Cod, though, Bourne also became a summer oasis for the wealthy of Boston, Hartford, New York City, Philadelphia, Baltimore, and Washington, D.C. Affluent people from these cities sought to escape oppressive heat and find comfort by a pleasant seaside. Although today the presidency of John F. Kennedy is closely associated with Cape Cod, it was President Grover Cleveland who first established, at his Gray Gables estate in Bourne, a Summer White House on the Cape. Warm waters and cooling breezes off the Bourne coast also attracted many other notables, such as the actor Joseph Jefferson, one of Cleveland's fishing buddies.

With the evolution of better means of transportation, the dominance of Bourne as a preferred vacation place diminished somewhat in favor of other Cape Cod towns. Bourne, however, retains a committed and growing contingent of loyalists who know that everything they want from Cape Cod is right here and not necessarily farther down the peninsula.

Bourne Accommodations

Bourne Scenic Park, Buzzards Bay, Route 6, 759-7873. *Campground.* Near the Cape Cod Canal. Open from early April to late October. 437 sites. Outdoor pool, inexpensive.

Best Western Bridge Bourne Motel, 100 Trowbridge Road, 759-0800 or (800) 675-0008. *Motor inn.* Overlooks the canal. Indoor pool, some kitchenette-equipped units. Open all year. Restaurant, indoor pool. Moderate to expensive.

Bay View Campgrounds, Route 28, 759-7610. *Campground.* Hot showers, swimming pool, tennis, and playground. Open May 1 to October 15; 415 sites.

Eastern Inn, 6 Bourne Bridge Approach, 759-2711. *Motor inn.* Convenient location on the canal's mainland side. Restaurant, indoor pool, sauna, and whirlpool. Open all year. Moderate.

Bay Motor inn, 233 Main Street, Buzzards Bay, 759-3989. *Motor inn.* In town center; restaurants nearby, pool. Inexpensive.

Ship's Way Motel, 51 Canal Street, Buzzards Bay, 888-0208. *Motor inn.* Kitchen available; walk to beach; pool; restaurants nearby. Inexpensive.

Bourne Dining

Quintal's Restaurant, 343 Scenic Highway Route 6, Buzzards Bay, 759-7222. Open all year. Family dining, take-out available, breakfast through dinner. Inexpensive to moderate.

Lindsey's Family Restaurant, 3138 Cranberry Highway, Buzzards Bay, 759-5544. Open all year. Family-style restaurant with seafood and other dishes. Inexpensive to moderate.

Shaw's, North Bourne Rotary, Buzzard's Bay, 759-1111. Family-operated restaurant featuring fish, lobster, ice cream, and pies. Moderate.

The Courtyard Restaurant and Pub, Route 28A, Cataumet, 563-1818. A very nice restaurant offering an eclectic menu: broiled scallops with sherry-buttered crumbs, marinated boneless breast of chicken grilled with crushed peppercorns, grilled swordfish with dill butter, and cioppino—clams, mussels, white fish, shrimp, and scallops simmered in tomatoes, fresh vegetables, and white wine. Also an equally creative luncheon menu. Open all year. Moderate.

The Chart Room, Shore Road in Cataumet, 563-5350. A comfortable dining room overlooking the water and serving fine seafood and meat dishes. Live entertainment. Open end of May to mid-October. Moderate.

Falmouth

Town offices—173 Main Street, Falmouth, 548-7611; Falmouth Chamber of Commerce, Academy Lane, Falmouth, 548-8500 or (800) 526-8532.

The following villages, with their postal zip codes, are within the town of Falmouth: Falmouth—02540; East Falmouth—02536; North Falmouth—02556; North Falmouth (Old Silver Beach)—02565; West Falmouth—02574; Woods Hole—02543; Teaticket—02536; Waquoit—02536; Falmouth Heights—02536; and Hatchville—02536.

Falmouth was settled by English colonists in 1660. Its roots were planted by those dissatisfied with the prevailing religious order in the colony of the late seventeenth century. They included a group of dissident Congregationalists, under the leadership of Isaac Robinson, and another strain represented by Jonathan Hatch, whose disgust with the persecution of the Quakers in Barnstable motivated him and many members of the Society of Friends to settle in the western areas of Falmouth.

The gem of Falmouth is its triangular village green. It was cleared and set aside as common land in 1749. Here, as a war for independence from Great Britain became inevitable, Falmouth's militia drilled under Colonel Joseph Dimmick and Captain John Grannis. During the war, British ships attempted to send landing parties ashore to subdue the inhabitants of Falmouth and requisition without pay their stores of food and other supplies; but the British were driven off by heavy fire from townsmen defending home and hearth. The British again tried to take Falmouth during the War of 1812, but artillery batteries under the command of Captain Weston Jenkins battered them back and away. During the same war, the captain of the British warship *Nimrod* demanded that Jenkins give up his cannon. Jenkins told him to "come and get 'em!" After a torrid exchange of fire and some minor damage to shore facilities, the *Nimrod* sailed away—without the cannon.

When peace took hold, Falmouth settled down to developing and prospering from its manufacturing industries, agriculture, and fisheries. Within this solid Yankee environment, Falmouth's most noteworthy citizen was born and raised. Katherine Lee Bates later traveled through this immense country and was so inspired by what she saw that she composed "America," a favorite patriotic hymn. In the late nineteenth century, Falmouth emerged from its tranquil insularity into a popular summer vacation town. In addition to the affluent people who could afford extended warm weather stays here came eminent scientists such as Louis Agassiz, who was among those founding a research colony in 1888 that became the internationally famous Marine Biological Laboratory. In the 1930s, Woods Hole Oceanographic Institution was established and is now considered one of the world's premier research facilities in the ocean sciences.

Falmouth, the second largest town on Cape Cod, is a community of contrasts. It is a place of solid, long-established wealth; a center of basic research and stunning discoveries on the leading edge of science; a sports town of runners, swimmers, boaters, and bikers; a place of culture where visual art, dance, music, and theatricals are performed at all levels of expertise; a town of bountiful farms and gorgeous gardens, a collection of picture-book New England villages with lovely churches, historic homes, and peaceful greens; a place of gaudy shopping centers and bargain outlets; a collection of excellent inns, B&Bs, and gourmet restaurants; the main embarkation point for the islands of Martha's Vineyard and Nantucket; and a necklace of beaches both packed sardinelike with humanity in the summer, and vacant, with hardly a soul to be seen in the winter.

Falmouth is a place of infuriating traffic tie-ups and gridlocks, especially on Woods Hole Road, Route 28 in the east end, and downtown, but also of less frequented back roads where the scenery is often far better.

North and West Falmouth and the Sippewissett area are special because they have not been spoiled by the intensive commercialization affecting many parts of Cape Cod. They continue to have the coziness of what most people imagine small communities in New England to be like. They are located along the warm waters of Buzzards Bay, where Old Silver, Chapoquoit, and Wood Neck beaches are open to the public. Even during the height of summer, it is a pleasure to drive along scenic Route 28A and tour the side roads. You really feel that you're on Old Cape Cod in these parts. There are nice B&Bs, restaurants, and shops along the way. In West Falmouth there's a historic Quaker meetinghouse and cemetery and the 1775 Bourne Farm, restored, continuing in operation, and welcoming you to walk about. On Palmer Avenue, in the Sippewissett area, is Peach Tree Circle with its magnificent gardens, a veritable horticulturist's paradise.

The west end of Falmouth has perhaps the finest example of a coherent Cape Cod village scene. At the center is the triangular village green. Surrounding the green are many historic homes, including the birthplace of Katherine Lee Bates; the buildings of the Falmouth Historical Society; the white, tall-steepled Congregational church with its Paul Revere bell; beautiful Saint Barnabas Episcopal Church and its lovely grounds; and the main post office.

Main Street in downtown Falmouth, from the post office to Shore Street, is flanked by many small shops, restaurants, and offices. This area is the most aesthetically pleasing part of commercial downtown and is enjoyed by visitors for its slow pace, personal service, and human scale. Here are also the public library, statue of Katherine Lee Bates, and town offices. South of downtown are public beaches. East of downtown, Falmouth has its collection of shopping malls, convenience stores, bargain and factory outlets, motels, and fast-food places. Within this area are Falmouth Inner Harbor with its ferry to Martha's Vineyard; band concerts at Marine Park; and beaches, motels, and restaurants at Falmouth Heights. Adjacent areas are Maravista, Menauhant, Green Harbor, Davisville, and East Falmouth. Heading north and inland from downtown is rural Falmouth with farms, cranberry bogs, horse stables, golf courses, and freshwater ponds. This inland area of Falmouth includes the Hatchville section and borders on the Massachusetts Military Reservation.

Woods Hole, famous throughout the world for its Woods Hole Oceanographic Institution, Marine Biological Laboratory, and summer headquarters of the National Academy of Sciences (at Quissett Harbor), is also a village in the town of Falmouth. Woods Hole is the primary terminal for year-round ferries to Martha's Vineyard and also to Nantucket during the peak vacation season. It is a tiny, quaint village with several excellent seafood restaurants and handicrafts shops. Many interesting events are open to the public during the year, including scientific lectures and programs, concerts, art exhibitions, and poetry readings. Most events take place at the community hall, next to the drawbridge, or in facilities at the scientific institutions.

Young people are attracted to Woods Hole because they perceive it to be an avant-garde place, an extension of Greenwich Village and Harvard Square in miniature with easy access to the beach and islands. A walk along Water Street will bring you to a book shop, boutiques, crafts shops, restaurants, a rustic drawbridge, yacht basin, and the buildings of Woods Hole Oceanographic Institution, Marine Biological Laboratory, and the National Marine Fisheries laboratories. The building with the sailing ship model coming out of its granite facade is Candle House, in which candles were made and whale oil stored. It is now the administrative center for the Marine Biological Laboratory. Nearby is a small public park overlooking the harbor. From here you can see the research vessel *Knorr* (when she is home from an expedition), on which Robert Ballard and his team found the remains of the *Titanic* off Newfoundland.

Straight ahead, beyond the WHOI docks, are Uncatena, Nonamesset, and Naushon islands of the Elizabeth archipelago. Naushon is the largest of the Elizabeth Islands and is privately owned. Boaters, however, can anchor in Naushon's Tarpaulin Cove, where swimming and picnicking, but no fires, are allowed. The buildings and docks farther down Water Street belong to the National Marine Fisheries. One of these is an aquarium open to the public. In its outdoor pool are harbor seals whose antics in the sun delight visitors. On Millfield Street, overlooking Eel Pond filled with expensive yachts, is Saint Joseph's Tower, with bells named for the scientists Louis Pasteur and Gregor Mendel. Here also is a flower garden, which invites the walker to rest and contemplate. A short drive or bike ride from Woods Hole center, via Quissett Avenue, will bring you to pretty Quissett Harbor and the seaside walk to The Knobb on Buzzards Bay. Or take Church Street to Nobska Point and its lighthouse overlooking Nantucket Sound and Martha's Vineyard Island.

Two points of caution are worth noting when visiting Falmouth. First, finding a parking space in the center of Woods Hole is extremely difficult. Illegally parked cars are ticketed and towed. Best bet is to find parking on streets away from the center, then walk to attractions and dining spots. During evenings a parking lot on Water Street, near the drawbridge, is open to the public. Second, be sure you have advance reservations for accommodations during the week in mid-August when the Falmouth Road Race takes place. Thousands of runners converge on Falmouth during this exciting period, and all tourist facilities in town are stretched beyond their limits.

North Falmouth Accommodations

Sea Crest Resort, off Quaker Road in Old Silver Beach area, 540-9400 or (800) 225-3110. *Resort*. Fine accommodations with ocean-front location on private portion of Old Silver Beach. Resort offers outdoor and indoor pools, saunas, steam and exercise rooms, tennis, ocean-view dining, dancing and entertainment, and cocktail lounge. A popular Cape Cod resort. Open all year. Expensive.

Silver Shores on-the-Beach, Old Silver Beach, 548-0846. *Motor inn*. Ocean-front rooms at one of the Upper Cape's most popular beaches. Seasonal. Inexpensive to moderate.

Captains Inn, Old Main Road, 564-6424. *B&B*. Historic Cape Cod estate, large rooms, gardens, croquet, horses; near beaches. Gourmet breakfasts and afternoon tea served. Highly recommended. Open all year. Moderate to expensive.

North Falmouth Dining

Bill Weaner's Silver Lounge Restaurant, Route 28A in North Falmouth, 563-2410. Known for friendly, casual dining; steaks, seafood, and daily specials are featured. Open all year. Inexpensive to moderate.

West Falmouth Accommodations

Inn at West Falmouth, 66 Frazar Road, 540-6503 or (800) 397-7696. *B&B*. A 1900s bed-and-breakfast furnished with antiques from many lands. Most rooms have a private deck, bath, and fireplace. Also pool and tennis courts; beach is a ten-minute walk. Open year-round. Expensive.

The Elms, Route 28A, 540-7232. *B&B*. A comfortable home that emphasizes great food. Breakfasts include Irish bread, eggs Benedict, and homemade codfish cakes; also serves dinner. Near Chapaquoit Beach and Woods Hole. Open all year. Moderate.

Sjoholm, 17 Chase Road off Route 28A, 540-5706. *B&B*. Fine accommodations in a quiet, lovely area. Near beaches, Falmouth center, and Woods Hole. A bountiful, all-you-can-eat buffet breakfast featuring Swedish dishes. Open all year. Moderate.

The Ideal Spot Motel, Route 28A at Old Dock Road, 548-2257 or (800) 269-6910. *Motor inn*. Motel and efficiency units near Chapaquoit and Old Silver beaches. In nice village area of boutiques and restaurants. Open all year. Moderate.

Woods Hole Accommodations

The Nautilus Motor Inn, Woods Hole Road, 548-1525. *Motor inn*. Fine accommodations near Martha's Vineyard ferry terminal. Dining and lounge at the adjacent Dome Restaurant; tennis, swimming pool, and lovely grounds. Seasonal. Moderate to expensive.

The Marlborough, 320 Woods Hole Road, 548-6218. *B&B*. A lovely home tastefully decorated with many romantic touches, just up the road from Martha's Vineyard ferry and near beaches and bike trails. French spoken here. Breakfast buffet served with many gourmet items, such as ham poached in beer and hot fruit soup. Open all year. Moderate to expensive.

Woods Hole Passage, 186 Woods Hole Road, 548-9575. *B&B*. Convenient to Woods Hole and Falmouth. Has a Southwestern touch in decorations, breakfast. Attached barn has four rooms. Open year-round. Moderate to expensive.

Sands of Time Motor Inn, Woods Hole Road, 548-6300. *Motor inn*. Fine accommodations overlooking Woods Hole Harbor. Swimming pool and many other guest amenities. Near Dome Restaurant, Martha's Vineyard ferry terminal, and beautiful ocean drive to Nobska Point. Seasonal. Moderate to expensive.

Sleepy Hollow Motor Inn, Woods Hole Road, 548-1986. *Motor inn*. Comfortable accommodations, swimming pool; near beaches, Dome Restaurant, and ferry terminal to the islands. Seasonal. Moderate to expensive.

Woods Hole Dining

Shuckers World Famous Raw Bar, 91A Water Street, down Cobble Way, 540-3850. A Woods Hole favorite on Eel Pond for raw and steamed seafood, king crab legs, and lobster. Fresh fruit drinks. Seasonal. Inexpensive.

Fishmongers Cafe, 56 Water Street, 548-9148. Very popular Woods Hole seafood restaurant overlooking harbor. Seasonal. Inexpensive to moderate.

Landfall Restaurant, Luscombe Avenue, near Ferry Terminal, 548-1758. A busy but efficient seafood restaurant overlooking the water. Great food—Cape Cod fish-k-bob, seafood Newburg, Nantucket swordfish; maritime decor, good service. Open June through October. Moderate.

Captain Kidd, 77 Water Street, 548-8563. A popular eating and drinking place for the Woods Hole crowd; focus on seafood—pasta and scallops Provençal, grilled native tuna. Closed from January to April. Inexpensive to moderate.

Falmouth Village Accommodations

Spring Garden Motel, 578 Route 6A, 888-0710 or (800) 303-1751. *Motor inn.* Modest looking but charming motel with marsh and river views. Seasonal. Moderate.

Coonamessett Inn, Gifford Street and Jones Road, 548-2300. *Inn.* The Coonamessett is one of the Upper Cape's finest places for accommodations and dining, and it has been that way for years. It is on the banks of a pretty pond and near a golf course. This is what a New England inn should look like and how it should be operated. Beautiful grounds surround it. Downtown Falmouth and the beaches are within a few minutes' drive. Open all year. Moderate to expensive.

Shoreway Acres Resort, Shore Street, 540-3000 or (800) 352-7100. *Motor inn.* A popular place located on one of the most beautiful streets in Falmouth. Within easy walking distance of Surf Drive Beach and shops, restaurants, and attractions in the village. Gourmet dining, indoor pool, sauna, and lovely grounds. Open all year. Moderate to expensive.

Sippewissett Campground and Cabins, 836 Palmer Avenue in the Sippewissett area, 548-2542. *Campground.* Also cabins and cottages. Free shuttle service to Woods Hole. Near beaches and downtown attractions and eateries. Open May 1 to end of October; 120 sites.

The Admiralty Inn, Route 28, 548-4240. *Motor inn.* Nice accommodations at a convenient location. The Admiralty has been recently enlarged and improved. Swimming pool, restaurant, lounge, and live entertainment. Package plans available. An excellent value. Open all year. Moderate to expensive.

Best Western Marina Trade Winds, Robbins Road at the Harbor, 548-4300. *Motor inn.* Overlooks Falmouth Harbor, within a short walk of Martha's Vineyard ferry, shops, and restaurants. Heated swimming pool and efficiency apartments. Seasonal. Moderate to expensive.

Mostly Hall, 27 Main Street at the Village Green, 548-3786 or (800) 682-0565. *Inn and B&B.* A very palatial home, near all conveniences in town. Moderate to expensive.

Ramada Inn on the Square, 40 North Main Street, on the way to Woods Hole, 457-0606. *Motor inn.* Near downtown and Woods Hole.

Lounge and restaurant; indoor pool and exercise room. Open all year. Moderate to expensive.

Capt. Tom Lawrence House, 75 Locust Street, on the way to Woods Hole, 540-1445. *B&B.* An 1861 sea captain's house located on the road to Woods Hole, near village green and downtown shops and restaurants. Once hosted Jacques Cousteau. Serves full breakfasts featuring many gourmet items. Open all year. Expensive.

The Inn at One Main Street, One Main Street, on the way to Woods Hole, 540-7469. *B&B.* Lovely home built in 1892 located at the beginning of the road to Woods Hole and within steps of the village green and downtown shops and restaurants. Continental breakfast served; take-out breakfasts supplied to those catching early ferries to the islands. Open all year. Moderate.

Palmer House Inn, 81 Palmer Avenue at the village green, 548-1230. *B&B.* A comfortable, lovely old home adjacent to the village green and downtown conveniences. Interesting breakfast menu includes Finnish pancakes and cheese blintzes. Open all year. Moderate.

The Village Green Inn, 40 West Main Street at the village green, 548-5621. *B&B.* Originally built in the eighteenth century, this home was later made more elegant in the nineteenth-century Victorian style. Located across the street from the village green and within walking distances of shops and restaurants. Continental breakfast. Free beach-parking stickers. Open all year. Moderate.

Cape Colony on-the-Ocean, Surf Drive, 548-3975. *Motor inn.* Accommodations with beach on Nantucket Sound. Landscaped grounds, swimming pool; morning coffee. Seasonal. Moderate.

Falmouth Inn, Main Street, 540-2500 or (800) 255-4157. *Motor inn.* A large motel offering good accommodations, indoor pool, restaurants, and lounge. Near downtown, shopping centers, ferry to Martha's Vineyard, and beaches. Owns Falmouth Country Club, championship eighteen-hole course. Golfing packages are available. Open all year. Moderate to expensive.

Falmouth Village Dining

Coonamessett Inn, Jones Road and Gifford Street in Falmouth, 548-2300. A visit to Cape Cod should include a lunch or dinner at the Coonamessett. Great food, impeccable service, and lovely interior. The Coonamessett also offers nightly entertainment and dancing. Open all year. Moderate to expensive.

Regatta of Falmouth, 217 Scranton Avenue, 548-5400. Popular restaurant with creative dishes, great views of harbor and Vineyard Sound. Seasonal. Moderate to expensive.

Golden Swan, 323 Main Street, 540-6580. A favorite Falmouth restaurant with attentive service. Its facade and interior remind one of a charming place found in a small town in England. The cuisine is continental with an emphasis on excellent veal dishes—from Wiener schnitzel to shrimp and veal Française. Early bird specials. Open all year. Moderate.

The Nimrod, Dillingham Avenue, 540-4132. An extensive menu of seafood and meat dishes. Excellent Sunday brunch that can include broiled sea scallops, baked haddock, and broiled scrod. Fresh baked pies, cakes, and breads. Inexpensive to moderate.

The Box Lunch, 781 Main Street, 457-7657. Ideal place for packing a picnic for anytime. More than fifty selections for all tastes—kids, vegetarian, seafood lovers. Seasonal.

Betsy's Diner, 457 Main Street, Falmouth, 540-0060. Extensive menu. Inexpensive, breakfast anytime.

The Flying Bridge, 220 Scranton Avenue at Falmouth Harbor, 548-2700. The Flying Bridge, located on Falmouth's inner harbor, has two restaurants: Portofino, serving continental cuisine such as medallions of beef Siena and fettucine Portofino—expensive; and The Cafe, featuring steaks, chicken, seafood, and gourmet pizzas—moderate. Nightly entertainment. Great location for yacht watching. Open all year.

McMenamy's Seafood Restaurant, Route 28, 540-2115. A popular place, located near shopping malls, offering seafood plates, lobster rolls, scallop casserole, and daily specials. Open all year. Inexpensive.

Christopher's Restaurant and Pub, Route 28, 540-7176. Popular family dining place offering good value, though the service tends to be slow. Clam chowder and kale soup, Greek lamb and vegetable gyros, hash and eggs, and roast turkey with stuffing. Open all year. Inexpensive.

Falmouth Heights Accommodations

The Red Horse Inn, 28 Falmouth Heights Road, 548-0053 or (800) 628-3811. *Motor inn.* Award-winning flower gardens, swimming pool; location convenient to shops, restaurants, and beaches. Open all year. Moderate.

Gaslight Inn, 9 Fairmont Avenue, 457-1647. *Inn.* An 1880 Victorian with antique furnishings and ocean views. Walk to ferry and restaurants. Open May to November. Moderate to expensive.

Park Beach Motel, 241 Grand Avenue, 548-1010 or (800) 341-5700. *Motor inn.* Located near popular sandy beach. Heated pool and many guest amenities. Seasonal. Moderate.

Falmouth Heights Motor Lodge, 146 Falmouth Heights Road, 548-3623 or (800) 468-3623. *Motor inn.* Conveniently located near Martha's Vineyard ferry and Falmouth Heights beaches. A good value. Seasonal. Moderate.

Falmouth Heights Dining

Wharf Restaurant, 228 Grand Avenue, Falmouth Heights, 548-0777. Open year-round, serves seafood. Moderate to expensive.

Cherrystones, Route 151, 477-4481. Popular full-service restaurant. Open all year. Moderate.

Ninety Nine, 8 Ryan's Way, 477-9000. Popular Boston-area eatery. Features dishes ranging from sirloin tips to scrod. Inexpensive to moderate.

East Falmouth Accommodations

Surfside Resort, 134 Menauhant Road, 548-0313 or (800) 582-6100. *Motor inn.* Popular motel where all units have balconies or patios. Private beach on Nantucket Sound, two swimming pools, putting green, shuffleboard, fishing jetty, children's play area. Efficiency units available. Continental breakfast served. Seasonal. Moderate.

Green Harbor Waterfront Motor Lodge, Acapesket Road, 548-4747 or (800) 548-5556. *Motor inn.* Excellent family accommodations with many features. Tranquil country setting but close to Route 28 and ocean beaches. Swimming pool, boating, fishing, sun deck, and lovely lawns. Open all year. Moderate to expensive.

Carleton Circle Motel, 579 Sandwich Road, 548-0025 or (800) 434-8150. *Motor inn.* Rooms and efficiencies, pool, near beaches. Open all year. Moderate.

East Falmouth Dining

Oysters Too, Route 28, 548-9191. A popular seafood restaurant on the road between Falmouth and Hyannis—baked stuffed shrimp, fish and chips. Open all year. Inexpensive to moderate.

Iguana's Restaurant, Route 28, 540-6000. Mexican, Southwestern dishes, plus steaks to burgers. Large microbrew selection. Open all year. Inexpensive.

Pat's Pushcart, 339 Main Street, 548-5090. Wonderful and hearty Italian dishes (also a Boston North End eatery). Dinners only. Seasonal. Inexpensive to moderate.

Sandwich

Town offices—145 Main Street, Sandwich, 888-0340; Cape Cod Canal Area Chamber of Commerce, 70 Main Street, Buzzards Bay, 759-6000.

The following villages, with their postal zip codes, are within the town of Sandwich: Sandwich—02563; East Sandwich—02537; and Forestdale—02644.

Settled in 1637, Sandwich is Cape Cod's oldest town. The land was cleared and homes built by Edmund Freeman and his compatriots. They were colonists who came to Cape Cod from Saugus, a community north of Boston. After the landing of the Pilgrims at Plymouth and the successful establishment of their colony, more English emigrants sailed to Massachusetts. As the population expanded along the mainland coast and good land was taken, enterprising individuals such as Freeman saw better possibilities for themselves south on Cape Cod. The governor of Plymouth Colony gave Freeman and nine other men permission to create a settlement of sixty families on Cape Cod. As was the case elsewhere, once the settlement was established other families came in from places such as Duxbury and Plymouth, and the town grew into some significance. In 1669 this burgeoning habitation was incorporated and named Sandwich after the town in Kent, England, from which a number of the settlers originated.

The established religion of Sandwich was, as it was throughout the colony, that of the Congregational Church. Quaker missionaries arrived peacefully enough to live and, if possible, gain converts, but they were readily condemned and persecuted as heretics. The people of early Sandwich were Puritans ("Roundheads") from the same theological mold as Oliver Cromwell. Their intolerance was no different from that of the Anglicans in Virginia and that of the Roman Catholics in Mexico and French Canada. After the restoration of the monarchy in England, King Charles II ordered that members of the Society of Friends should not be persecuted, but it took some years for toleration of the Quakers to take hold in Sandwich. As with other evolutionary changes in American society, the acceptance of diverse beliefs did come in the eighteenth century, and today Sandwich is as proud of its Quaker heritage as it is of its Puritan.

The early economy of Sandwich was based on agriculture and whaling on Cape Cod Bay. In the early nineteenth century, a number of companies began making glass in Sandwich and fashioned beautiful and useful objects. These were among the first industrial plants in a largely agricultural-commodity-producing America. Among the reasons why the glassmaking industry flourished in Sandwich was that the town was the source of the two basic ingredients—silica (the fine sand at Sandwich) and sodium chloride (deriving salt from the sea was itself a mainstay industry for many a Cape Cod town). Although glassmaking faded away, the remaining examples of Sandwich glass today are highly valued by collectors of early Americana. In addition to glass, Sandwich factories produced stagecoaches, prairie schooners, and railroad cars. One can say that the town was a "hub of American transport manufacturing" long before Detroit assumed that title.

All the early factories of Sandwich are gone, and what remains is a peaceful, charming town much beloved by its residents and those who visit. Over many years, I have found Sandwich to be one of Cape Cod's friendliest towns. Within the Main and Water Streets area of the town center are a number of Sandwich attractions that you can reach on foot: Shawme Lake, with its resident population of geese and ducks eager for handouts from generous visitors; the 1637 Hoxie House, oldest home on Cape Cod; town hall; Dexter's Mill, built in the 1650s; the Sandwich Glass Museum; the Thornton W. Burgess Museum; Yesteryears Doll Museum; and The Dan'l Webster Inn, highly recommended for dining and overnight stays. Heritage Plantation, one of Cape Cod's "must see" attractions, can be reached via Grove Street from the town hall. While in the center of town, stroll along Main Street and visit the lovely Congregational, Episcopal, and Roman Catholic churches. This area of Sandwich seems to have remained within the nineteenth century, with only horse-drawn carriages, ladies in long skirts and bonnets, and prudent gentlemen in stovepipe hats missing from the scene. On Route 6A, heading east, are other attractions: the state fish hatchery and game farm, the 1685 Nye Homestead, the Quaker Meeting House, and the Stephen Wing House.

Sandwich Accommodations

The Dan'l Webster Inn, Sandwich Village Center, 888-3622. *Inn.* A superb Upper Cape inn in every respect—accommodations, dining, service, atmosphere, and interior and exterior environments. In the center of Sandwich, within walking distance of attractions and a short drive from Heritage Plantation and beaches. Open all year except Christmas Day. Moderate to expensive.

Scusset Beach Reservation, Scusset Beach Road off Route 3 (mainland side of Cape Cod Canal), 888-0859 or (877) 422-6762 (reservations). *Campground.* Near Cape Cod Canal and Sandwich attractions. Campers are allowed to use Scusset State Beach as part of the daily rate. Open from mid-April to mid-October; 98 sites.

Shawme-Crowell State Forest, Route 130, 888-0351 or (877) 422-6742 (reservations). *Campground.* Near Cape Cod Canal and Heritage Plantation in Sandwich. Open from mid-April to mid-October; 260 sites.

The Belfry Inne & Bistro, 8 Jarves Street, 888-8550 or (800) 844-4542. *Inn.* Situated in a former church and the next-door rectory. Many rooms have whirlpool baths. In town location, great for strolling. Moderate to expensive.

Shady Nook Inn, 14 Route 6A, 888-0409. *Motor inn.* Good value; some efficiencies and cottages. Swimming pool; coffee shop. Open all year. Moderate.

Captain Ezra Nye House, 152 Main Street, 888-6142 or (800) 388-2278. *B&B.* 1829 sea captain's house in a lovely area of historic Sandwich. Decorated with fresh-flower bouquets. Homemade muffins a specialty for breakfast. Open all year. Moderate.

Spring Garden Motel, 578 Route 6A, 888-0710 or (800) 303-1751. *Motor inn.* Modest looking but charming motel with marsh and river views. Seasonal. Moderate.

The Earl of Sandwich Motor Manor, 378 Route 6A, 888-1415 or (800) 442-3275. *Motor inn.* Fine accommodations with a Tudor feel. Open all year. Moderate.

Old Colony Motel, 436 Route 6A, 888-9716 or (800) 786-9716. *Motor inn.* Good value. Swimming pool. Open all year. Moderate.

Sandwich Lodge & Resort, 54 Route 6A, 888-2275 or (800) 285-5353. *Resort.* Excellent lodging, including indoor and outdoor pools, Jacuzzis, dining. Open all year. Moderate to expensive.

Sandy Neck Motel, 669 Route 6A, 362-3992 or (800) 564-3992. *Motor inn.* Good value; located at the entrance of Sandy Neck Beach area on Cape Cod Bay. Near several restaurants. Open early April to end of November. Moderate.

Peters Pond Park, Cotuit Road, 477-1775. *Campground.* Freshwater-lake swimming, fishing, and boating. Open mid-April to mid-October; 500 sites.

Sandwich Dining

The Dan'l Webster Inn, Sandwich Village Center, 888-3622. Fine dining, service, and environment in the heart of the oldest town on Cape Cod. Creative cookery at its finest. Excellent wine list. Live entertainment. Highly recommended. Open all year. Moderate to expensive.

Capt. Scott's Seafoods, 71 Tupper Road, 888-1675. Popular seafood restaurant with take-out. Open all year. Inexpensive.

Marshland Restaurant, 109 Route 6A, 888-9824. This little eatery is not much to look at on the outside, but inside they create gourmet breakfasts, luncheons, and dinners. A favorite of mine and many others. Open all year. Inexpensive.

Horizons on Cape Cod Bay, on Town Neck Beach, Sandwich, 888-6166. Fresh seafood, great chowders, big sandwiches, and bountiful salads. Open all year. Inexpensive.

The Dunbar House & Tea Shop, 1 Water Street, 833-2485. Open 10:00 A.M. to 5:00 P.M. Featuring seafood quiche and other lunches. Authentic English teas, and high tea on Sundays. Outdoor dining in summer. Open all year. Inexpensive to moderate.

Bee Hive Tavern, 406 Route 6A, 833-1184. This restaurant has the feel of a comfortable, old tavern. Delicious seafood and meat dishes. Open all year. Inexpensive to moderate.

A HEAVENLY MEAL

The Belfry Inne has been a landmark in Sandwich for years, but not always as an inn. It had once been the village's Catholic church, and the inn is composed of the former church and its next-door rectory.

Christopher Wilson had a vision for the site—creating a wonderful inn and delightful restaurant. Wilson has creatively added inn rooms to the upper level of the church while retaining its former looks and wood paneling. Even the confessionals are used; stop by and see how. My favorite room is Monday, with a beautiful original stained-glass window framed in wood to resemble a ship's wheel.

To further lift the spirit, chef Peter Martin has created some delightful dishes (the dining room is open to the public). Here is a dish using two popular Cape treats—lobster and scallops.

LOBSTER AND SCALLOP ALLA PANTELLERIA

Serves two.

You'll need two 1¼ pound lobsters, cooked and shelled, 8 ounces of sea scallops, 2 tablespoons of capers, one clove, chopped garlic to taste, ½ teaspoon of mixed crushed red pepper and cracked black pepper, two medium tomatoes seeded and chopped, 2 tablespoons olive oil, and ⅓ pound cooked fettuccine (al dente).

In a 12-inch saute pan add the 2 tablespoons of olive oil and heat on medium high. Add scallops and saute. Turn scallops and add garlic. Cook one minute. Add tomatoes and capers and cook two minutes. Add lobster; toss together and heat two minutes. Add pasta, peppers, and toss. Heat all on medium for four minutes; add extra virgin olive oil and a pinch of salt. Heat two minutes.

The Belfry Inne & Bistro, 8 Jarves Street, 888-8550. Set in the sanctuary of a former church, this American bistro offers fine dining in a romantic setting. Moderate to expensive.

Aqua Grille, 14 Gallo Road, 888-8889. Overlooking a marina (and not so lovely power plant), fish dishes are the specialty but also plenty of other choices. Open for lunch and dinner. Moderate to expensive.

Mashpee

Town offices—Great Neck Road in Mashpee, 539-1400 or (800) 423-6274 (outside Massachusetts). Mashpee Information Center, Mashpee rotary—Route 28, 477-0792.

The following villages, with their postal zip codes, are within the town of Mashpee: Mashpee—02649; New Seabury—02649; and Popponesset Beach—02649.

Before the arrival of settlers from England, Cape Cod and the islands were inhabited by bands of native people belonging to the Wampanoag Federation. They subsisted on agriculture, fishing, and hunting. They had a culture that gave their lives great meaning and satisfaction. When the English arrived to stay for good in the early seventeenth century, the natives helped these newcomers to survive and encouraged them to share in the bounty of land and sea, sources perceived by them as having more than enough to provide for everyone. Land sharing was the way of Native Americans, but exclusive land ownership was the way of Europeans; these two diametrically opposed concepts soon collided in bloodshed. The natives rebelled against the incessant encroachment of the English, and what is known in the history books as King Philip's War broke out. Although the natives won a few raids and skirmishes, the war was won by the settlers, who possessed superior weapons. As a result of war and new diseases against which they had no immunity, the once abundant and vigorous native population of Cape Cod was decimated and subjugated.

The last remaining, significant concentration of Wampanoags continues on in the town of Mashpee. During the 1970s the Mashpee Wampanoags attempted to regain ownership of large tracts of land in the town, basing their claim on aboriginal rights and treaties made with the early settlers. Adding insult to the many injuries the Mashpee Wampanoags had suffered for so long, the courts ruled that they were not a tribe in the legal and anthropological sense and therefore could not claim ownership of the land they sought.

Mashpee today is a community of several distinct groups. There are the Wampanoag families who live in or near the center of town, along Route 130, and on the adjacent roads. Within this general area there are also a number of new home developments catering to the affluent retired, summer camps for young people, and enclaves of vacation homes on freshwater lakes.

The eastern portion of the Massachusetts Military Reservation (Otis Air Base and Camp Edwards) extends into Mashpee. At Mashpee rotary, where Routes 28 and 151 merge, a major shopping center has been created that is based on a nostalgic version of a New England village main street. The land south of Route 28 and on Nantucket Sound has been developed into several exclusive vacation communities. The most notable of these, in architecture, landscaping, and amenities, is New Seabury. Within New Seabury are stunning, expensive vacation/retirement homes, inns, luxury boutiques, a championship golf course, beautiful beaches, and other facilities. Here also is the Popponesset Beach area, where the affluent vacationed long before New Seabury was built. Mashpee attractions include Old Indian Meeting House, built in 1684, off Route 28; Mashpee Indian Museum, on Route 130; and the Lowell Holly Reservation, off South Sandwich Road. Swimming in the warm waters of Nantucket Sound can be enjoyed at South Cape Beach, reached via Great Oak Road (off Mashpee rotary and past New Seabury).

Mashpee Accommodations

New Seabury, Great Neck Road, New Seabury, 477-9111 or (800) 999-9033. *Resort.* A 2,300-acre resort fronting on Nantucket Sound. Its thirteen villages offer a wide variety of accommodations from one- to two-bedroom townhouse units to cottages. Two golf courses, health club, two outdoor pools, tennis courts, private beach, shopping, children's programs. Open all year. Expensive.

South Cape Resort & Club, Route 28, 477-4700. *Resort.* Accommodations in luxury condos. Indoor and outdoor swimming pools, tennis courts, steam room, and sauna. Open all year. Expensive.

Otis Trailer Village—John's Pond Campground, Sandwich Road, 477-0444. *Campground.* Private lake beach; swimming, boating, fishing. Open mid-April to mid-October; ninety sites.

Mashpee Dining

The Flume, Lake Avenue, off Route 130 near Center Mashpee, 477-1456. Popular seafood restaurant within a wooded setting overlooking a pond. Open all year. Inexpensive.

Popponesset Inn, 1 Mall Way in New Seabury, 477-1100. Overlooking the ocean; seafood and beef dishes; live entertainment and dancing. Open all year. Expensive.

Cherrystones, Route 151, 477-4481. Popular full-service restaurant. Open all year. Moderate.

Ninety-Nine, 8 Ryan's Way, 477-9000. Popular, well-known Boston-area eatery. Features dishes ranging from sirloin tips to scrod. Inexpensive to moderate.

Gone Tomatoes, Mashpee Commons, 477-8100. Features pastas, pizza, and Italian dishes. Located within earshot of the summer band concerts. Moderate.

Bobby Byrne's Pub, in shopping center at Routes 151 and 28 in Mashpee, 477-0600. British-pub atmosphere for food and drink. Live entertainment. Popular drinking and munching place. Open all year. Inexpensive.

Barnstable

Town offices—397 Main Street, Hyannis, 790-6240; Hyannis Chamber of Commerce, 1471 Route 132, 362-5230 or (800) 449-6647; Cape Cod Chamber of Commerce Information Center at junction of Routes 132 and 6A, 362-3225.

The following villages, with their postal zip codes, are within the town of Barnstable: Barnstable—02630; West Barnstable—02668; Marstons Mills—02648; Cotuit—02635; Osterville—02655; Centerville—02632; Hyannis—02601; Hyannisport—02647; West Hyannisport—02672; Craigville—02636; Cummaquid—02637; Santuit—02635; and Wianno—02655.

Barnstable is Cape Cod's largest town. It also has within its boundaries the Cape's most diverse collection of villages. Hyannis is Cape Cod's tourism, commercial, transportation, and shopping center. More visitors come to Hyannis throughout the year than to any other Cape Cod village. Hyannis is not as aesthetically pleasing as the smaller, quainter villages, but it offers more of everything—accommodations, dining, entertainment, and shopping. Because of its central location on the Cape, Hyannis is within easy reach of other popular areas: Woods Hole to the southwest and Cape Cod National Seashore and Provincetown to the northeast. Because it is the Cape's transportation hub, all buses converge on Hyannis; plane travel is available from here to the islands, Boston, and New York; rail service is offered during the summer; and ferries run to the islands of Martha's Vineyard and Nantucket.

The Cape Cod Mall on Route 132, the largest shopping center, encompasses under one roof many well-known large stores and smaller shops in which to spend time and money on dismal days when even the gulls and terns abandon the beach. The mall is now joined by a number of shopping centers along Route 132. Main Street is always busy with people strolling, browsing, and enjoying the many stores, souvenir shops, and places of entertainment and dining. At the west end of Hyannis is the Cape Cod Melody Tent, the Cape showplace. In and near Hyannis are a number of public beaches on the warm waters of Nantucket Sound.

Hyannis is also strongly associated in the minds of many with the Kennedy family, although some of its members reside in a private compound in exclusive Hyannisport that was the Summer White House during the late president's administration. Admirers of the Kennedy family can attend services at Saint Francis Xavier Church, where members of the clan worship on occasion, and see their homes in the compound from a boat tour of the harbor and Lewis Bay. Perhaps the most inspiring place on Cape Cod dedicated to JFK is his memorial overlooking Lewis Bay and containing the presidential seal and these words of his: "I believe that this country will sail, and not lie still in the harbor."

Just west of Hyannis are the villages of Craigville, Osterville, and Cotuit. Craigville is well known to many Hyannis visitors for its superb beach on Nantucket Sound and the Craigville Conference Center. At Centerville is the 1840 Mary Lincoln House. Both Osterville and Cotuit are year-round and vacation towns for the rich, although many ordinary people also live in them. Osterville, at Crosby boatyard, is where the popular, quick-responding Cat Boat was designed and built. There are several fine shops and boutiques in Osterville center to drop in on when touring. While in Osterville visit the 1795 Captain Johnathan Parker House, in which the local historical society now has a museum.

Cotuit is famous for its oysters, and these delicious treats from the sea are still harvested here and shipped to markets to the delight of gourmets. Cotuit is also where, in 1916, a sailing organization for youngsters, called the Cotuit Mosquito Club, was founded. The town itself lacks many tourist amenities, but the absence of commercialization at its center makes Cotuit a most attractive village in which to live. The Cotuit Historical Society operates the 1800 Dottridge Homestead with its period furnishings and historical artifacts. Inland from Cotuit and Osterville is the village of West Barnstable with its architecturally superb West Parish Meeting House, which is located on Route 149. There's also an old-time general store in this area just before you come to scenic Route 6A in West Barnstable.

At West Barnstable is one of Cape Cod's best beaches—Sandy Neck on Cape Cod Bay—and extensive salt marshes. Barnstable Village, the administrative and political center of both the town and county, is a place of historic homes and harbor that offers whale-watching cruises and deep-sea fishing charters. The attractions on the Cape Cod Bay side of Barnstable include the 1717 West Parish Meeting House, the 1644 Lothrop House & Sturgis Library—oldest public library building in the country, Cape Cod Community College, the 1834 Barnstable County Court House, and the 1856 Thrayser Memorial Museum (U.S. Customs House from 1856 to 1913). The Barnstable Village area, including West Barnstable and Cummaquid, has several fine bed-and-breakfasts and gourmet dining places. It is the opposite of frenetic, often gaudy Hyannis. There are beaches for swimming and meandering as well as antiques and crafts shops along Route 6A.

The early history of Barnstable was shaped by religious reformers from England who journeyed to the New World in the early seventeenth century. Their purpose was to create the Puritan utopia that existed in their minds and that, they knew, would be impossible to establish in their home country, where the established Anglican Church viewed dissent such as theirs as heresy and treason. The Reverend John Lothrop became leader of these early Puritan utopians in Barnstable. Through the force of Lothrop's vision and character, the community set down roots, grew, and prospered. Another important figure from Barnstable's history is James Otis, known during the Revolutionary War period as "The Great Advocate" and "The Patrick Henry of the North." John Adams said of Otis that he was "the spark by which the child of Independence was born."

Hyannis Accommodations

Ramada Inn Regency, 1127 Route 132, 775-1153. *Motor inn.* Offers 196 rooms, indoor pool, restaurant; handy to area attractions. Open all year. Moderate to expensive.

Roadway Motor Inn, 1157 Route 132, 775-3324. Also has two-room suites, swimming pool. Open all year. Moderate.

Budget Host Hyannis Motel, 614 Route 132, (800) 322-3354. *Motor inn.* Has forty rooms, some efficiencies, pool. Walking distance to shops, theaters. Inexpensive to moderate.

Anchor-In Motel on the Water, 1 South Street, 775-0357. *Motor inn.* Beautiful rooms overlooking the water. Walk to island ferry, restaurants. Open all year. Moderate to expensive.

Heritage House Motor Hotel, 259 Main Street, 775-7000 or (800) 352-7189. *Motor inn.* Fine in-town accommodations. Indoor and outdoor swimming pools, saunas, Jacuzzi, and whirlpool; restaurant and lounge. Open all year. Moderate to expensive.

Four Points Hotel, Route 132 and Bearse's Way, 771-3000 or (800) 325-3535. *Hotel.* A Sheraton hotel with 261 rooms, heated indoor and outdoor pools, restaurant, fitness center. Moderate to expensive.

Hyannis Harbor Hotel, 213 Ocean Street, 775-4420 or (888) 810-0044. *Motor inn.* Fine accommodations, some with balconies overlooking harbor. Indoor and outdoor swimming pools, saunas, whirlpool, and exercise room; restaurant, coffee shop, and lounge. Open all year. Moderate to expensive.

Comfort Inn Cape Cod, 1470 Iyanough Road, 771-4804 or (800) 228-5150. *Hotel.* Over one hundred rooms, indoor heated pool and spa, fitness center, complimentary continental breakfast. Inexpensive to moderate.

Anchor-In, 1 South Street, 775-0357, *Motor inn.* Overlooks the harbor, convenient to attractions, outdoor pool. Moderate to expensive.

Captain Gosnold Village, 230 Gosnold Street, 775-9111. *Motor inn and cottages.* Comfortable accommodations within walking distance of beaches and island ferries. Seasonal. Moderate to expensive.

Sheraton Hyannis Resort, at West End Circle, 775-7775. *Motor inn and resort.* Excellent accommodations and amenities. One of the most popular places on Cape Cod. Rooms have patios or balconies. Excellent eighteen-hole golf course, tennis, indoor and outdoor swimming pools, playground, rental bikes, and health club. Fine restaurant and popular nightclub. Located across the road from the Cape Cod Melody Tent. Open all year. Expensive.

The Inn on Sea Street, 358 Sea Street, 775-8030. *Inn.* A nice Victorian inn in the heart of town offering comfortable accommodations and gourmet breakfasts. Open all year. Moderate.

Seacoast on the Towne, 33 Ocean Street, 775-3828 or (800) 466-4100. *Motor inn.* In-town location; near ferry, other attractions. Free continental breakfast. Inexpensive to moderate.

Hyannis Inn Motel, 473 Main Street, 775-0255 or (800) 922-8993. *Motor inn.* In-town location; has heated indoor pool, some rooms with whirlpools. Moderate.

Hyannis Dining

Penguins Sea Grille, 331 Main Street, 775-2023. A restaurant serving seafood and Italian dishes in the heart of downtown Hyannis. Open all year. Moderate.

Cape Cod Central Railroad, 252 Main Street, 771-3800. Has dinner train; call for information. Expensive.

Mooring on the Waterfront, 230 Ocean Street at the docks, 771-7177. A casual dining place located at a busy, interesting harbor. Seafood and beef dishes. Open all year. Moderate.

The Paddock, West Main Street traffic rotary, 775-7677. Victorian environment. Fresh flowers and candlelight on tables. Eclectic menu of American and continental dishes. Open mid-April to mid-November. Next to Melody Tent shows. Expensive.

Sam Diego's, Iyanough Road—Route 132, 771-8816. Mexican dishes and drinks. Open all year. Inexpensive.

Bobby Byrne's Pub, Route 28 and Bearse's Way, 775-1425. British-pub atmosphere. Live entertainment. Popular drinking and munching place. Open all year. Inexpensive.

Up The Creek, 36 Old Colony Boulevard, 771-7866. Lobster, seafood, and steaks; cheery tavern setting. Open all year. Moderate.

Mitchell's Steak and Rib House, Iyanough Road—Route 132, 775-6700. Great chowder, steaks, and seafood. Irish music and entertainment. A popular place with visitors. Open all year. Moderate.

Roadhouse Cafe, 488 South Street, 775-2386. Fine dining, lunch, dinner, Sunday brunch. Outdoor dining. Early bird specials. Open all year.

Baxter's Boat House, 177 Pleasant Street, 775-4490. A Cape Cod favorite since the 1950s, Baxter's has been pleasing people with its fried and broiled seafood and location on an old dock near the ferry landing. There's also an indoor dining room and lounge. Beware of losing your meal to a gull. Seasonal. Moderate.

The Egg & I, 521 Main Street, 771-1596. Definitely a place for breakfast; open from 11:00 A.M. to 1:00 P.M. Other dishes available. Hours vary with season. Inexpensive.

Old Country Buffet, Festival Plaza, Route 132, 790-1745. All-you-can-eat buffet with a huge selection from soup and salad to dessert. Open all year. Inexpensive to moderate.

Mildred's Chowder House, Iyanough Road—Route 132, across from airport, 775-1045. Fantastic chowder and good seafood. Popular with families and chowder mavens alike. Open all year. Moderate.

Starbuck's, Iyanough Road—Route 132, 778-6767. Colorful and somewhat zany decor. Interesting yuppie dishes—mesquite-grilled meats, seafood salads, and baked brie. Open all year. Inexpensive to moderate.

Alberto's Ristorante, 360 Main Street, 778-1770. An excellent restaurant for Northern Italian cuisine and homemade pasta. Open all year. Moderate to expensive.

The Black Cat, 165 Ocean Street, 778-1233. Traditional fare for lunch and dinner, across from harbor. Sunday brunch. Moderate.

Hearth 'n' Kettle Restaurant, 412 Main Street, 771-3737. Casual family dining. Inexpensive to moderate.

Tugboats, 21 Arlington Street, 775-6433. Casual dining at Hyannis Marina. Seafood specialties. Moderate.

Hyannisport Accommodations

Simmons Homestead, 288 Scudder Avenue, 778-4999. *B&B*. Elegant sea captain's mansion. Private baths, fireplaces, canopy beds, and quilts. Full breakfast served. Wraparound porch. Near all Hyannis attractions and beaches. Open all year. Expensive.

Harbor Village, Marston Avenue, 775-7581. *Cottages*. Fully furnished accommodations with fireplaces. Private beach, fishing, and canoeing. Open May to October. Moderate.

Centerville Accommodations

Centerville Corners Motor Lodge, South Main Street and Craigville Beach Road, 775-7223. *Motor inn*. Motel and efficiency units; indoor pool and saunas; close to Craigville Beach. Golf, tennis, and restaurants nearby. Open all year. Moderate.

Adam's Terrace Gardens Inn, 539 Main Street, 775-4707. *B&B.* A former sea captain's house. Offers screen decks, afternoon tea. Walk to beach. Open all year. Moderate.

On the Pond Bed & Breakfast, 160 Huckins Neck Road, 775-0417. *B&B.* On the lake. One- and two-bedroom units. Open all year. Moderate.

East Bay Lodge, East Bay Road, 428-5200. *Inn.* A sea captain's house built in 1800. Three floors, free continental breakfast, tennis, refrigerators in rooms. Beach within walking distance. Moderate to expensive.

Craigville Accommodations

Trade Winds Inn, Craigville Beach Road, 775-0365. *Motor inn.* Excellent accommodations overlooking Craigville Beach and Lake Elizabeth. Private beach, coffee room and lounge, putting green, and many other amenities. Seasonal. Expensive.

Ocean View Motel, at Craigville Beach, 775-1962. *Motor inn.* Comfortable accommodations at one of Cape Cod's most popular beaches. Seasonal. Moderate.

Osterville Dining

Wimpy's, Main Street, 428-6300. Popular Osterville restaurant. Fresh swordfish and bluefish daily. Lobster pie and crab imperial. Early bird specials such as baked haddock and pork cutlets Marsala. Live musical entertainment in the lounge. Open all year. Inexpensive to moderate.

Cotuit Accommodations

Salty Dog, 451 Main Street, 428-5228. *Inn.* Near beaches and close to attractions in Hyannis and Falmouth. Bicycles available for guests. Continental breakfast served. Open all year. Moderate.

Cotuit Dining

Regatta of Cotuit at the 1790 Crocker House, Route 28, 428-5715. The Crocker House, a longtime landmark for good dining, is now owned by the owners of the Regatta of Falmouth and features American cuisine. Luncheon, dinner, and Sunday brunch are served. Open all year. Expensive.

Barnstable Village Accommodations

Cobb's Cove, Powder Hill Road in Barnstable Village, 362-9356. *Inn.* Excellent accommodations in a peaceful area on Cape Cod Bay offering many quality amenities. Breakfast and dinner served. Open all year. Expensive.

Ashley Manor, Route 6A, 362-8044. *B&B.* Fine, antique-filled mansion dating from 1699. Secret passage and hiding places used by Loyalists of the British Crown during the American War of Independence. Manicured lawns and diverse plantings highlight a lovely environment. Open all year. All rooms have private baths; there are working fireplaces in most rooms. Amenities include fresh flowers, candy, Crabtree & Evelyn soaps, shampoos and lotions; wine, sherry, or port available in the living room. Full buffet breakfast every morning. Expensive.

Beechwood Inn, 2839 Main Street, 362-6618. *B&B.* Victorian house with antique furnishings. Queen-sized four-poster bed. Paintings by local artists. Home-baked breads and muffins part of breakfast menu. Rocking chairs on veranda. Open early May to November. Moderate to expensive.

Charles Hinckley House, Route 6A and Scudder Lane, 362-9924. *B&B.* A shipwright's house built in 1809. Fine accommodations. Beautiful flowers surrounding the house. I consider the wildflowers growing in front of this historic house to be one of the loveliest floral displays on Cape Cod. Amenities include fresh-flower arrangements, chocolates, and fresh fruit. Open all year. Moderate to expensive.

Henry Crocker House, 3026 Main Street, 362-6348. Lots of history in this circa 1800 former tavern. Three guest rooms, two with an adjoining room to accommodate children or friends. Open all year. Moderate.

Crocker Tavern, 3095 Route 6A, 362-5115 or (800) 773-5359. In the village, with five guest rooms, all with private baths. Once an eighteenth-century stagecoach stop. Open all year. Moderate to expensive.

The Lamb and Lion, Route 6A, 362-6823. *Inn.* Comfortable accommodations. All rooms have private baths. Fine honeymoon suite. Housekeeping units for large families. Swimming pool in atrium. Continental breakfast served. Open all year. Moderate.

Honeysuckle Hill, 591 Main Street, 362-8418. *B&B.* Victorian farmhouse with easy access to Sandy Neck Beach, marshes, village center, and cranberry bogs. Emphasis on making guests feel special. Full breakfast—Scotch eggs and blueberry pancakes. Open all year. Moderate to expensive.

Barnstable Village Dining

The Barnstable Tavern & Restaurant, Route 6A, 362-2355. Creative cookery in a colonial setting in the heart of Barnstable Village. Changing menu; emphasis on fresh ingredients. Open all year. Moderate to expensive.

The Dolphin Restaurant, Route 6A, 362-6610. Offers a creative lunch and dinner menu using the freshest ingredients. All served in a pleasant environment. One of the winners in the Cape Cod Chowder Festival. Open all year, closed on Sundays. Live entertainment Saturday evening. Moderate.

Mattakeese Wharf, Barnstable Village Harbor, 362-4511. Fine seafood restaurant with views of the harbor. Open May to October. Moderate.

Yarmouth

Town offices—Route 28 at Wood Road, Yarmouth, 398-2231; Yarmouth Chamber of Commerce, Route 28, West Yarmouth, 778-1008 or (800) 723-1008.

The following villages, with their postal zip codes, are within the town of Yarmouth: Yarmouth—02675; Yarmouthport—02675; South Yarmouth—02664; West Yarmouth—02673; and Bass River—02664.

Sometimes, along Route 28, it is difficult to figure out where Hyannis ends and the town of Yarmouth begins, because one seems to blend into the other. The Route 28 section of West Yarmouth and South Yarmouth/Bass River is an elongated area of family motels, restaurants, places of entertainment and amusement, and shopping centers and souvenir stores. This strip is one of Cape Cod's most popular tourist centers because of the abundance of these tourist amenities and their proximity to the warm-water beaches on Nantucket Sound. In contrast, Yarmouthport, on the Cape Cod Bay side of the peninsula, exude more history, tranquillity, and the charming nostalgia of a bygone era.

The first settler of note in Yarmouth was Reverend Stephen Bachiler, who arrived from north of Boston in the late 1630s. Bachiler was a womanizer. He was defrocked by his church, married several times, and went to England, dying there when almost a hundred years old. The first permanent settlers of "proper substance" in seventeenth-century Yarmouth were the Thachers, the Crowes (now "Crowell"), and the Howes. Anthony Thacher was the leader of this fledgling community. Quakers also settled in Yarmouth and formed their own enclaves in southern sections.

During the nineteenth century the citizens of Yarmouth, seeking intellectual self-improvement, established lyceums where debates, lectures, and readings from literature and poetry were held. The discussion of religion or politics at these gatherings was not permitted due to their incendiary nature. In 1836 N. S. Simpkins launched his newspaper, the *Yarmouth Register* (still in publication), and wasted no time in taking on the likes of Andrew Jackson and Martin Van Buren. Also during the mid-nineteenth century, Amos Otis placed himself into the local history books as the man who planted a mile of elm saplings on each side of what is now Route 6A. Many decades later, when the high, thickly leafed elm branches arched over the roadway, Otis's trees and the many historic sea captains' homes behind them together form one of the most beautiful, foliage-ensconced, mansion-dotted avenues in America.

Historical attractions in town include the 1780 Winslow Crocker House in Yarmouthport, Friends Meeting House in South Yarmouth, Bass Hole Viking site in Yarmouth, Captain Bangs Hallet House in Yarmouthport, Church of the New Jerusalem in Yarmouthport, Judah Baker Windmill in Yarmouth, the Pawkanawkut Village Indian graves in South Yarmouth, and the Yarmouth Village Pump in Yarmouthport.

West Yarmouth Accommodations

Cape Sojourn, 149 Main Street, 775-3825 or (800) 882-8995. *Motor inn.* Two-story motel with two pools, one indoors. Continental breakfast included. Seasonal. Inexpensive to moderate.

Tidewater Motor Lodge, 135 Route 28, 775-6322 or (800) 338-6322. *Motor inn.* Fine accommodations near downtown Hyannis offering indoor and outdoor swimming pools, sauna, and playground; coffee shop. In-room Jacuzzis. Open year-round. Moderate.

Americana Holiday Hotel, 99 Route 28, 775-5511. *Motor inn.* Good value. Three swimming pools (indoor and outdoor), sauna, whirlpool, putting green, and playground; coffee shop. Open late-March to late-October. Moderate.

American Host Motel, 69 Route 28, 775-2332. *Motor inn.* Good value. Two swimming pools, wading pool, whirlpool, putting green, miniature golf, and playground. Open mid-April to early November. Moderate.

The Mariner Motor Lodge, 573 Route 28, 771-7887 or (800) 445-4050. *Motor inn.* Good value. Two swimming pools (indoor and outdoor), whirlpool, sauna. Open all year. Moderate.

Hunters Green Motel, 553 Route 28, 771-1169 or (800) 775-5400. Large motel with seventy-four rooms, indoor/outdoor pool. Walk to beach, golf, restaurants. Open mid-April to late October. Moderate.

Windrift Vacation Resort, 115 Route 28, 775-4697 or (800) 354-4179. Pool, recreation area. Open all year. Moderate.

Super 8 Motel, Route 28, 775-0962 or (800) 800-8000. Newly renovated. Has heated outdoor pool. Walking distance to attractions. Open all year. Moderate.

Inn at Lewis Bay, 57 Maine Avenue, (800) 962-6679. *B&B.* Overlooking Lewis Bay. Private baths. Walking distance to beach. Open all year. Moderate.

Green Harbor on the Ocean, 182 Baxter Avenue, 771-1126 or (800) 547-4733. *Motor inn.* Excellent accommodations overlooking Nantucket Sound. Swimming pool, boating, fishing, bikes, and miniature golf; landscaped lawns. Open early May to mid-October. Moderate to expensive.

Yarmouth Shores, 29 Lewis Bay Road, 775-1944. *Cottages.* Small cottage colony with its own beach. Seasonal. Moderate.

Flagship Motor Inn, 343 Route 28, 775-5155 or (877) 838-3524. *Motor inn.* Good value. Two swimming pools, saunas, whirlpool, game room, and playground; coffee shop. Open all year. Moderate.

The Cove at Yarmouth Resort, 183 Route 28, 771-3666 or (800) 228-2968. *Motor inn/resort.* Fine accommodations. Tennis, racquetball, squash, health spa, and indoor and outdoor swimming pools; restaurant and lounge. A timeshare. Open all year. Moderate.

West Yarmouth Dining

Yarmouth House Restaurant, 335 Route 28, 771-5154. Steaks, seafood, and prime rib of beef; luncheon and dinner specials. Open all year. Moderate.

Lobster Boat, 681 Route 28, 775-0486. The specialty here is fresh New England lobster. You can get one up to four pounds. Also serves a complete menu of seafood, steaks, and prime rib of beef. Seasonal. Moderate.

Molly's Restaurant and Sports Bar, 585 Main Street, 778-1927. Good selection of dishes, breakfast served seasonally, entertainment Friday and Saturday. Open all year. Moderate.

Salty's Diner, 540 Main Street, 790-3132. Lunch and dinner, classic diner fare, take-out available. Open all year. Inexpensive to moderate.

Giardino's, 242 Route 28, 775-0333. Family-style Italian restaurant. Also take-out. Open all year. Moderate.

Clancys,175 Route 28, West Yarmouth, 775-3322. Casual American-Irish grill. Also take-out. Open all year. Inexpensive to moderate.

Captain Parker's Pub, 668 Main Street, 771-4266. American-style foods. Good menu variety. Also take-out. Open all year. Inexpensive to moderate.

South Yarmouth/Bass River Accommodations

Blue Rock Inn, Highbank Road, 398-6962 or (800) 237-8887. *Motor inn.* Blue Rock golf course; private beach, swimming pool, Jacuzzi, and whirlpool; restaurant and lounge. Open from early April to mid-October. Moderate to expensive.

All Seasons Motor Inn, 1199 Route 28, 394-7600 or (800) 527-0359. *Motor inn.* Good value. Two swimming pools, saunas, whirlpool, and exercise room; coffee shop. Open all year. Moderate.

Ocean Mist, 92 South Shore Drive, 398-2633 or (800) 248-6478. *Resort.* Located on Nantucket Sound with a 300-foot beach; offers thirty-two loft suites, some with full kitchens. Heated indoor pool. Open year-round, except January. Moderate to expensive.

Captain Isaiah's House, 33 Pleasant Street, 394-1739. *B&B.* Restored sea captain's home. Continental breakfast with home-baked breads and cakes. Open June to September. Moderate.

August House, 175 Old Main Street, 760-0412. *B&B.* An eighteenth-century house with three guest rooms. In neighborhood of historic homes. Seasonal. Moderate.

Waterfront Ocean View B&B, 160 South Street, 394-4939. *B&B.* Waterfront rooms have four-poster beds, private baths. Seasonal. Moderate to expensive.

Surfcomber on the Ocean, 107 South Shore Drive, 398-9228. *Motor inn.* Oceanfront location. Some rooms with patios or balconies. Swimming pool and beach. Open late April to late October. Moderate to expensive.

Motel 6, 1314 Route 28, 394-4000 or (800) 341-5700. *Motor inn.* Indoor and outdoor pools, sauna, and whirlpool; restaurant and lounge. Comfortable accommodations. Near beaches, golf, and tennis. Open all year. Moderate.

Best Western Blue Water Resort, 291 South Shore Drive, 398-2288 or (800) 367-9393. *Motor inn.* Located on the ocean. Beach, indoor pool, saunas, putting green, and tennis court; dining room and coffee shop. Live entertainment. Open mid-April to late October. Expensive.

Red Jacket Beach Motor Inn, South Shore Drive, 398-6941 or (800) 672-0500. *Resort.* Excellent accommodations; movies; private beach, swimming pools, tennis, and putting green; dining room and lounge; and many other amenities. One of the best Motor inns on the Cape. Open spring to fall. Expensive.

Riviera Beach Motor Inn, 237 South Shore Drive, 398-2273 or (800) CAPE COD. *Motor inn.* Oceanfront location. Efficiency units; in-room Jacuzzi; sailboats and swimming pools; coffee shop. Open mid-April to late October. Moderate to expensive.

Captain Farris House, 308 Old Main Street, 760-2818 or (800) 350-9477. An 1845 sea captain's home with ten rooms, including four suites. Heated indoor pool. Full services. Expensive.

South Yarmouth/Bass River Dining

The Pancake Man, 952 Route 28, 398-9532. Breakfast all day, dinner available July through August. Inexpensive.

Skipper, 152 South Shore Drive, 394-7406. Views of Nantucket Sound. American and continental cuisine.

Frontier Prime Rib & Lobster House, 769 Route 28, 394-8006. Lobsters, prime rib of beef, steaks, and seafood. Children's menu. Seasonal. Inexpensive to moderate.

Seafood Sam's, Route 28, 394-3504. Good value, features seafood. Moderate.

Longfellows, Old Townhouse Road, South Yarmouth, 394-3663. Pub menu, steak, seafood. Open all year. Inexpensive.

Yarmouthport Accommodations

Land's End Cottage, 268 Route 6A, 362-5298. An eighteenth-century cottage with three guest rooms, each with private bath. Seasonal. Moderate to expensive.

Blueberry Manor, 438 Route 6A, 362-7620. A comfortable, former sea captain's home with four guest rooms. Open year-round. Moderate to expensive.

Liberty Hill Inn, 77 Route 6A, 362-3976 or (800) 821-3977. *B&B*. 1825 Greek Revival home with easy access to beaches, restaurants, and antique shops. Full breakfasts served with many gourmet items. Open all year. Moderate.

The Village Inn, 92 Route 6A, 362-3182. *Inn*. 1790 sea captain's home. Fine rooms, spacious grounds, and screened porch; continental breakfast. Open all year. Moderate.

Colonial House Inn, 277 Route 6A, 362-4348 or (800) 999-3416. *Inn*. Restored sea captain's home decorated with antiques. Heated indoor pool. Price of room includes continental breakfast and dinner. Open all year. Moderate.

Wedgewood Inn, 83 Main Street, 362-5157. *Inn*. 1812 home of maritime lawyer. Near beaches and restaurants. Accommodations include continental breakfast. Open all year. Moderate to expensive.

Yarmouthport Dining

Anthony's Cummaquid, Route 6A, 362-4501. This excellent dining place set within beautiful grounds overlooking marshes and Cape Cod Bay is the Cape Cod branch of Anthony's Pier 4 in Boston, one of America's best-liked restaurants. Superb American and continental cuisine, with emphasis on fresh seafood. Extensive wine list. Open all year. Expensive.

Colonial House Inn, Route 6A, 362-4348. The cuisine of New England. The ambience of a quintessential country inn by the village green. Excellent service. Open all year. Expensive.

Jack's Outback, 161 Route 6A, 362-6690. Popular spot for casual dining. Open breakfast and lunch. Open all year. Inexpensive.

Inaho, Route 6A, 362-5522. Superior Japanese restaurant; elegant environment. One of the Cape's best. Open all year. Moderate to expensive.

Abbicci, 43 Route 6A, 362-3501. Fine dining in a mid-eighteenth-century home. Contemporary Italian cuisine. A culinary treat. Moderate to expensive.

Oliver's, Route 6A, 362-6062. A casual eating and drinking place. Sandwiches and full dinners; live entertainment. Open all year. Inexpensive.

Dennis

Town offices—Main Street, South Dennis, 394-8300; Dennis Chamber of Commerce, Route 28 at Route 134, Dennis Port, 398-3568. For information call (800) 243-9920.

The following villages, with their postal zip codes, are within the town of Dennis: Dennis—02638; Dennis Port—02639; East Dennis—02641; South Dennis—02660; and West Dennis—02670.

As do Barnstable and Yarmouth, the town of Dennis extends to both coasts of Mid-Cape along Cape Cod Bay and Nantucket Sound. Scenic Route 6A, "The Old King's Highway," continues on through the tranquil villages of Dennis and East Dennis, with their beaches on Cape Cod Bay, many historic homes, Sesuit Harbor for deep-sea fishing expeditions, and Scargo Lake for freshwater angling. There are fine B&Bs, restaurants, and shops along this lovely route. Route 134 connects the Dennis villages on Cape Cod Bay with those on Nantucket Sound: West Dennis and Dennis Port. The two are on Route 28, where there is a concentration of motels, restaurants, shops, and amusements. The warm-water beaches of Dennis on Nantucket Sound are very popular with Cape Cod visitors.

In its early days Dennis was part of Yarmouth. Among the original families who settled Dennis were the Nickersons, the Bakers, and the Searses. The first parish was established in 1721, and in 1725 Reverend Josiah Dennis became pastor of this rural, sea-oriented congregation. The reverend did such an outstanding job ministering to the spiritual and civic needs of his congregation that all the town's villages were named in his honor. East Parish, as this area of Yarmouth was known, became incorporated as the Town of Dennis in 1793. Dennis was home port to many a sea captain, and at Sesuit Harbor the Shiverick Shipyards built some of the finest packet boats, schooners, and clippers of the nineteenth century.

Historical places of interest in Dennis include Cape Playhouse, where many famous stars have performed; Hokum Rocks in Dennis; Scargo Lake and Tower in Dennis; the 1801 Jericho House Museum in Dennis; the 1736 Josiah Dennis Manse; Whig Street in Dennis; Shiverick Shipyards in East Dennis South Parish; and the 1835 South Parish Congregational Church, Main Street in South Dennis.

Dennis Accommodations

The Four Chimneys Inn, 946 Route 6A, 385-6317 or (800) 874-5502. *B&B.* Tastefully furnished 1881 Victorian house. Continental breakfast. Across from Scargo Lake. Open mid-March to November. Moderate.

Isaiah B. Hall House, 152 Whig Street, 385-9928 or (800) 736-0160. *B&B.* Warm, homey 1857 Greek Revival house. Near Cape Cod Playhouse, often serving as residence for performers. Art and crafts throughout the house. Breakfast served in dining room festooned with antiques. Open all year. Moderate to expensive.

Dennis Dining

Marshside Restaurant, 28 Bridge Street near junction of Routes 6A and 134, 385-4010. Family dining. Seafood, burgers, beef and chicken dishes, and salads. Open all year. Inexpensive.

Red Pheasant Inn, Route 6A, 385-2133. A long tenure of acceptance on Cape Cod. American and continental cuisine, including game. Comfortable, with good food and service. Open all year. Moderate to expensive.

Dennis Port Accommodations

In addition to the places of accommodation listed here, Dennis Port has a large number of cottage colonies. Most of these are rented by the week, and advance reservations are essential during the months of July and August. For more information about these cottage colonies, contact the Dennis Chamber of Commerce at 398-3568 or (800) 243-9920.

Corsair Resort Motel, 41 Chase Avenue, 398-2279 or (800) 345-5140. *Motor inn.* Oceanfront location with private beach; swimming pool and shuffleboard; in-room movies; free coffee. Seasonal. Moderate to expensive.

Sea Lord, Chase Avenue and Inman Road, 398–6900. *Motor inn.* A one-to three-story unit with twenty-seven rooms. Beach opposite property. Seasonal. Moderate.

The Edgewater, 95 Chase Avenue, 398–6922. *Motor inn.* Fine accommodations; some efficiencies and apartments; indoor and outdoor pools; near beaches. Open end of April to mid-October. Moderate to expensive.

The Soundings, 79 Chase Avenue, 394–6561. *Motor inn.* Private beach, two swimming pools, sauna, putting green, and tennis courts; coffee shop. Most units with balconies overlooking Nantucket Sound. Seasonal. Moderate to expensive.

The Breakers Motel, 61 Chase Avenue, 398–6905 or (800) 540–6905. *Motor inn.* Many rooms with balconies overlooking Nantucket Sound. Private beach and swimming pool. Seasonal. Moderate to expensive.

The Rose Petal, 152 Sea Street, 398–8470. *B&B.* A fine old New England home with spacious rooms. Near beaches, shops, and restaurants. Serves breakfast with home-baked goodies. Open all year. Moderate to expensive.

Dennis Port Dining

The Captain Williams House, 106 Depot Street, 398–3910. A sea captain's house with traditional architectural touches. Features New England dishes from fresh seafood to homemade pasta. Moderate to expensive.

Swan River Seafood, 5 Lower County Road, 394–4466. Casual dining featuring fresh seafood for lunch and dinner. Nice river views. Seasonal. Moderate.

Bob Briggs' Wee Packet, Depot Street, 398–2181. A real Cape treat. The Wee Packet has been around since 1949, dishing up great bay scallops, fried clams, onion rings, sandwiches, and desserts. Family run, the restaurant has a casual atmosphere, exposed kitchen, and small counter area usually filled by regulars. Open for breakfast, lunch, and dinner. Seasonal. Inexpensive.

Clancy's, Upper County Road, 394–6900. With a name like Clancy's, this place could be a pub in Ireland, but it's on Cape Cod overlooking the sea. Good food in a cheery atmosphere. Irish entertainment. Open all year. Inexpensive.

West Dennis Accommodations

Lighthouse Inn, on the Beach, 398-2244. *Inn and cottages.* A complex that includes the Bass River Light, the inn, and cottages. Dining room; outdoor pool, tennis courts, and private beach. Modified American plan (breakfast and dinner). Open May to October. Moderate to expensive.

Pine Cove Inn Cottage, 5 Main Street, 398-8511. Located on the Bass River, these eight modest cottages include use of a private beach and boats. Seasonal. Moderate.

Beachhouse Inn, 61 Uncle Steven's Road, 398-4575. Private beach, guest kitchen. Open year-round. Inexpensive.

Elmwood Inn, 57 Old Main Street, 394-2798. *B&B.* Fine Victorian house located on Bass River. Traditional wicker furniture, spacious grounds, pine groves, and a private beach. Serves full breakfast. Moderate. Open all year.

West Dennis Dining

Lighthouse Inn, 4 Lighthouse Road, 398-2244. Dining room overlooking the sea. Fine seafood and meat dishes. Open May to October. Moderate.

Christine's Restaurant, 581 Main Street, West Dennis, 394-7333. Pasta, seafood, steak. Open all year. Inexpensive to moderate.

East Dennis Accommodations

Sesuit Harbor Motel, Route 6A, 385-3326. *Motor inn.* Good value. Pool. Near restaurants, bike and hiking trails, and beaches. Open all year. Moderate to expensive.

Harwich

Town offices—Main Street, Harwich, 430-7516; Harwich Chamber of Commerce, Main Street, Harwich Port, 432-1600 or (800) 441-3199.

The following villages, with their postal zip codes, are within the town of Harwich: Harwich—02645; Harwich Port—02646; South Harwich—02661; West Harwich—02671; East Harwich—02645; North Harwich—02645; and Pleasant Lake—02645.

Many illustrious individuals have come from, or lived on, Cape Cod. In the early days this area of the Cape was dominated by strong personalities—William Nickerson of Chatham; John Wing, a Quaker from Sandwich; John Dillingham; and John Mecoy. In the later 1660s Gershom Hall built his house in South Harwich and is therefore considered one of the first settlers. In 1694 Harwich was incorporated as a town. The town was divided into South Parish and North Parish. In 1803 North Parish spun off from Harwich and became the Town of Brewster. South Parish continued on as the Town of Harwich.

As was the case in other Cape towns, Harwich became a "burnt over district" of religious denominations and splinter sects contending with each other for a larger share of available souls. The battle between theologies for souls involved Congregationalists, Baptists, New Lighters, Come Outers, and Standpatters. From before the Revolutionary War to well after the Civil War, religious contention raged between people basically cut from the same ethnic cloth on issues as diverse as who would be saved and whether or not slavery should be abolished. It is said that Come Outers, when in a trance, walked on fences and spoke in strange tongues.

The following Harwich attractions are well worth visiting: Brooks Academy Museum and the Harwich cranberry bogs. Auto or bike touring of Wychmere Harbor and the Pleasant Bay area is also recommended.

Harwich Dining

The Cape SeaGrille, 31 Sea Street, 432–4745. Innovative meals, based on daily market. Inexpensive to moderate.

Harwich Port Accommodations

Sea Heather Inn at Troy Court, 28 Seat Street, 432–1275. *Inn.* Has extensive grounds, sea view, one- and two-story units with early American decor. Beach nearby. Open year-round. Moderate to expensive.

Sandpiper Beach Inn, 16 Bank Street, 432–0485. *Motor inn.* On the beach with twenty rooms overlooking Nantucket Sound. Open year-round. Moderate to expensive.

Seadar Inn by the Sea, Braddock Lane at Bank Street, 432–0264. *Motor inn.* Good value. Nantucket Sound beach; breakfast buffet. Open mid-May to October. Moderate.

Harwich Port Dining

L'Alouette, 787 Main Street, 430-0405. Excellent French cuisine; a wide selection of wines. Open all year. Moderate to expensive.

Thompson's Clam Bar, 600 Route 28, 430-1239. Popular restaurant once on the water, now in a new location along Route 28. Still features great clams, seafood, chowders. Also a raw bar. Seasonal. Moderate to expensive.

Bonatt's Restaurant and Bakery, 537 Route 28, 432-7199. Open for breakfast and lunch with nice dishes. Known for its sweet bread. Box lunches also available. Open all year. Inexpensive.

Brax Landing, Route 28 at Saquatucket Harbor, 432-5515. Gourmet seafood. Overlooking the harbor. Open all year. Moderate.

Country Inn, 86 Sisson Street, 432-2769. Casual inn-style setting with fine dining. On the water. Moderate.

South Harwich Accommodations

Handkerchief Shoals Motel, Route 28, 432-2200. *Motor inn.* Good value. Swimming pool; near beaches. Seasonal. Moderate.

House on the Hill, 968 Route 28, 432-4321. Very charming 1832 Federal-style farmhouse with lots of open space around it. Three guest rooms with private bath. Open all year. Moderate.

West Harwich Accommodations

The Commodore Inn, 30 Earle Road, 432-1180. *Motor inn.* Quiet area near Nantucket Sound beach. Swimming pool, putting green, and lawn games; restaurant. Open all year. Moderate to expensive.

Lion's Head Inn, 186 Belmont Road, 432-7766. *B&B.* A sea captain's home close to 200 years old. Antiques and traditional furnishings; interior warm and historical. Fine collection of pewter. Many excellent amenities including private woods, fresh flowers, chocolates, and wine for return guests. Gourmet items on the breakfast menu—omelets with lobster and homemade muffins. Open all year. Moderate.

Tern Inn, 91 Chase Street, 432-3714. *B&B.* Comfortable accommodations in a 200-year-old home within a few minutes' walk of Nantucket Sound beaches. Continental breakfasts served at a "common table." Open early April to the end of November. Moderate to expensive.

Barnaby Inn, 36 Route 28, 432-6789 or (800) 439-4764. *B&B.* A bed-and-breakfast with private baths, some with Jacuzzi, and fireplaces. Moderate.

West Harwich Dining

Bishop's Terrace, 108 Route 28, 432-0253. Fresh seafood, prime rib of beef, and roast duckling among the specialties. Fine food and service in a 1790 sea captain's home. Also dining in the Garden Room and dancing to live music. Open all year. Expensive.

East Harwich Accommodations

Wequassett Inn, Route 28 on Pleasant Bay, near Chatham town line, 432-5400 or (800) 225-7125. *Resort.* Wequassett is superior in all respects and at the top of Cape Cod's finest. Its complex of eighteen separate buildings includes the historic Eben Ryder House and the Warren Jensen Nickerson House. Accommodations include guest rooms, cottages, and suites with fireplaces. All guest rooms have views of Pleasant Bay, Round Cove, or the woods. There are three tennis villas within steps of five courts. Wequassett offers a heated swimming pool, a beach on Pleasant Bay, certified swimming instructors, a sailing school, boating and deep-sea fishing, a jogging path, limousine service, and a country store. The location on a secluded cove and the grounds, architecture, and landscaping are all exceptional. The main dining room is within an elegantly decorated sea captain's home with views of the water; meals are also served on a lovely garden terrace. Its cuisine is American and continental— fresh seafood and prime beef—prepared by an award-winning European chef. The luxury of Wequassett Inn is highly recommended. Open from late spring to fall. Expensive.

Brewster

Town offices—Route 6A in Brewster, 896-3701. For tourist information, call the Brewster Chamber of Commerce at 896-3500.

The following villages, with their postal zip codes, are within the town of Brewster: Brewster—02631; East Brewster—02631; and West Brewster—02631.

Although the Town of Brewster was incorporated as late as 1803, this community was settled much earlier as the North Parish of Harwich. Brewster's claim to fame is that it was home port to many outstanding sea captains such as David Nickerson, who, it is said, brought the dauphin of France out of his revolution-torn country to New England in 1789. Several years later, Captain Elijah Cobb had his vessel taken by the French. Through Robespierre, Cobb obtained release of his ship and stayed long enough to see this disagreeable French revolutionary dispatched by his own Reign of Terror. In 1815 Captain Jeremiah Mayo offered to take Napoleon to America in his ship. Before Napoleon could make it to Mayo's vessel, the *Sally*, however, he was captured; Mayo had to depart without his prize passenger.

Brewster captains defied President Thomas Jefferson's embargo with the British during the War of 1812 by sailing out to sea and continuing on with their business. Brewster even paid a cash ransom to the captain of a British warship, as it saw no need to suffer bombardment and raiding parties in what was to many New Englanders an unpopular war. After hostilities, Brewster-captained ships sailed all over the world, making considerable fortunes for land-based merchants and investors as well as the captains themselves. Throughout the nineteenth century Brewster sea captains were paragons of adventure, commerce, and profit.

Today's Brewster is a quiet, lovely town on scenic Route 6A. The heritage of the sea captains remains in the fine homes they built, many of which have been converted to charming inns and superior restaurants. Brewster is also a town of interesting attractions: Cape Cod Museum of Natural History, New England Fire and History Museum, the 1834 First Parish Church, Brewster Historical Society Museum, Basset Wild Animal Farm, and Nickerson State Park.

Brewster Accommodations

Beechcroft Inn, 1360 Main Street, 896-9534. *Inn.* This fine inn served as a church in the early 1800s. Accommodations include continental breakfast. Bikes available. Open all year. Moderate to expensive.

The Ruddy Turnstone, 463 Route 6A, 385-9871 or (800) 654-1995. *B&B.* A charming bed-and-breakfast with private baths, some rooms have views of the marsh and bay. Moderate to expensive.

The Captain Freeman Inn, 15 Breakwater Road—R.R. 4, 896-7481 or (800) 843-4664. *B&B.* Near the general store and First Parish Church, which convey a small town America feel. An 1860 sea captain's home with many unique architectural details. Swimming pool; bikes. Open all year. Moderate.

The Bramble Inn, Route 6A, 896-7644. *B&B.* Greek Revival home with antique furnishings. Near beaches, bike route, tennis, and shops. Excellent dining room. Closed mid-January to mid-March. Moderate to expensive.

High Brewster Inn, 964 Satucket Road, 896-3636 or (800) 203-2634. Main house has three rooms. Also four cottages. Antiques in buildings, lawn games, superb restaurant. Closed January through March. Expensive.

Isaiah Clark House, 1187 Main Street, 896-2223 or (800) 822-4001. *Inn.* 1780 sea captain's house. Fireplaces, predinner get-togethers, hearty American breakfasts. Near beach and golf. Open all year. Moderate to expensive.

Ocean Edge Resort and Conference Center, One Village Drive, Route 6A, 896-9000 or (800) 626-2688 in state, (800) 343-6074 elsewhere. *Resort.* Ocean Edge is a luxury resort on Cape Cod. Guests stay in fully furnished, two- or three-bedroom villas. It has a fine restaurant, a championship golf course (one of the best on Cape Cod), tennis courts and swimming pools, and overlooks Cape Cod Bay beaches. Its conference center is in the restored Samuel Nickerson mansion (Fieldstone Hall), named for the founder and president of the First National Bank of Chicago. Open all year. Expensive.

Old Sea Pines, 2553 Main Street, 896-6114. *B&B.* On three acres. Started in 1907 as the School of Charm and Personality for Young Women. Some rooms with fireplaces. Open year-round. Moderate to expensive.

Sweetwater Forest, off Route 124, 896-3773. *Campground.* Modern facilities; children's beach; pets welcome. Open all year; 250 sites.

Nickerson State Park, Route 6A, 896-4615. *Campground.* Near beaches, Cape Cod National Seashore, and services within towns of Brewster and Orleans. Open mid-April to mid-October; 420 sites.

Brewster Dining

Chillingsworth, "The Old King's Highway"—Route 6A, 896-3640 or (800) 430-3640. Widely honored as one of the Cape's finest restaurants; many would call it "the Cape's number-one dining place." The emphasis here is on the best available ingredients transformed into elegant French cuisine. Roast tenderloin of beef with truffles in burgundy sauce is among the specialties, and so is lobster in cognac sauce. Service and ambience are superior. The wine list will make oenophiles smack their lips in delight. During the 1987 summer season, Chillingsworth opened for lunch, much to the delight of patrons and newcomers. Luncheon entrées are in the moderate price range and, considering the overall excellence of Chillingsworth, represent some of the finest dining values on the entire Cape. The setting for lunch and dinner is within a lovely estate nearly 300 years old. Dinner at Chillingsworth is expensive. Dinners are served from Memorial Day to mid-December; lunch, throughout the year.

High Brewster, 964 Satucket Road, 896-3636. New American cuisine served within a classic American colonial estate. Operated by the people who run Chillingsworth. Open all year. Moderate.

Brewster Fish House, 2208 Route 6A, 896-7867. Excellent seafood and innovative specials for lunch or dinner. Modest looking from the outside but quite charming inside. Seasonal. Moderate to expensive.

Chatham

Town offices—549 Main Street, Chatham, 945-5100; Chatham Chamber of Commerce, Main Street, 945-5199 or (800) 715-5567

The following villages, with their postal zip codes, are within the town of Chatham: Chatham—02633; North Chatham—02650; South Chatham—02659; and West Chatham—02669.

If Cape Cod is the bent arm of Massachusetts, then Chatham is its elbow. It is difficult not to fall in love with Chatham. Imagine a village of sturdy weather-and-sun-washed homes, rose-covered picket fences, stately churches, centuries-old cemeteries, and the ever-changing sea. All these images converge in Chatham, Cape Cod at its best.

Years before the Puritans settled in Massachusetts, Samuel de Champlain, the French explorer, anchored his vessel in Stage Harbor and came ashore with his men. Champlain considered the land before him as a suitable place to establish a French habitation but was dissuaded by hostile natives and what he considered to be too shallow a harbor with a hazardous entrance on the open Atlantic. Another important person in Chatham's history is Squanto, the English-speaking Native American who was instrumental in helping the first Pilgrims survive by showing them how to fish and farm in this new land. He also helped the Pilgrims negotiate a peace treaty with sachem Massasoit. Squanto died in Chatham on a mission for the colonists and is buried not far from Chatham Light.

Chatham was very much the creation of William Nickerson. He bought the land from the Sachem Mattaquason, then went through several years of wrangling with other colonists, the courts, and even his own son-in-law to gain lawful possession. In seventeenth-century Massachusetts William Nickerson was considered one of the most unscrupulous real estate operators in the colony. You could also say that the man had an ambitious vision and possessed the strength and courage to make it a reality. Part of his vision was to make the lands he owned into a full-fledged, self-governing town. He applied for that status in the late 1670s. Township was not granted because Monomoy, as Chatham was called then, did not have a minister. Nickerson was, however, able to secure the designation of "constable wick," and from this legitimacy he managed his community as an unofficial town. Through much of its early history, Chatham was largely a community of Nickerson families, and many Nickersons continue to reside there.

The people made their living from fishing and farming. It was not until 1711 that the first permanent minister, Reverend Hugh Adams, came to stay for a bit and initiate some progress. He was able to secure town status in 1712, and the name was changed from Monomoy to Chatham. Reverend Adams's life was not to remain tranquil in Chatham. He preached against the evils of strong drink and made enemies of the tavern owners. Adams was subjected to libel suits, nasty gossip, and scurrilous harassment. He relieved himself of this anguish by getting out of town and finding more agreeable parishioners in New

Hampshire. New ministers came to Chatham, however, and were instrumental in helping the community gain a stronger sense of confidence and purpose.

Chatham prospered through an economy based on fishing, agriculture, transportation, and manufacturing. Today fishing continues as an important way of making money, but tourism and real estate are far more valuable to the town's economy. With regard to real estate, the circle has been completed: Chatham came into being through the wheeling and dealing of William Nickerson, and the town continues to grow and prosper through real estate transactions.

Chatham has many superb accommodations and restaurants. The best known is the Chatham Bars Inn, once a seaside lodge for wealthy Bostonians. There are plenty of smart shops for browsing and buying. Don't miss walking along Main Street to see Chatham Light, Chatham Fish Pier, and the splendid views overlooking the harbor, Nauset Beach, and the open Atlantic beyond. Other attractions to enjoy are the 1752 Atwood House, Railroad Museum, Godfrey Windmill, and Wight Murals. Monomoy Island National Wildlife Refuge can be visited by boat. Be sure to take in a Chatham Band concert, held each Friday evening during July and August. These concerts are among the most popular entertainment events on Cape Cod, and they are free. Also take in a theatrical performance by the Ohio University Players at the Monomoy Theater.

In January 1987 a powerful storm unexpectedly created a new attraction for tourists and a pain in the neck for local fishermen and mariners. Chatham harbor is shielded from surges of the open Atlantic by the lower end of Nauset Beach, a barrier beach. Although a barrier beach protects one body of water from another, it is essentially a frail piece of land subject to erosion by fierce winds and powerful tides. A section of Nauset Beach at Chatham harbor has been undergoing this weakening process for a number of years. When the January storm hit, the raging ocean, pushed by an unrelenting wind, tore open the land at this vulnerable point; the Atlantic flowed into the harbor. The phenomenon was somewhat similar to the legendary Dutch boy taking his finger out of the hole in the dike and letting the North Sea flood a part of Holland.

Although Chatham itself was not inundated, a new, widening access from the harbor to the open Atlantic has been created by nature. And it is a hazardous one at that, with unfamiliar, strong currents and breaking waves that cause trouble for vessels. Swimming in this area is dangerous. This breach of the barrier beach has attracted the curious.

Cape Cod Aero Marine provides sightseeing flights over the area, and Art Gould's Boat Livery/The Water Taxi and Outermost Marine will take you to the breach. True to their Yankee antecedents, the entrepreneurs of Chatham have immortalized the breach at Nauset Beach on T-shirts that you can buy.

Chatham Accommodations

Chatham Bars Inn, 297 Shore Road, 945-0096 or (800) 527-4884. *Resort.* The Chatham Bars Inn has undergone extensive renovations. Previously it was open from spring to fall. Now the inn is also open during the winter season for the enjoyment of off-season travelers and for use as a conference center for corporations. Chatham Bars Inn, one of Cape Cod's premier resorts, exudes an exclusive but comfortable feel. It has beautiful grounds overlooking Nantucket Sound and excellent accommodations in lodge and cottages. The inn has a swimming pool, saltwater beach, boats, a nine-hole golf course, and tennis courts as well as two excellent dining rooms and a lounge with live entertainment and dancing. Open all year. Expensive.

Bow Roof House, 59 Queen Anne Road, 945-1346. *Guest house.* Fine accommodations in a 200-year-old bow roof house with original paneling, fireplaces, and other details. Continental breakfast served. Open all year. Moderate.

The Captain's House Inn, 396 Old Harbor Road, 945-0127 or (800) 315-0728. *Inn.* Fine accommodations in an 1839 sea captain's home. Full English breakfast served. Also a carriage house with modern furnishings. Closed December to February. Expensive.

Seafarer Motel, Route 28 and Ridgeville Road, 432-1739. *Motor inn.* The ambience of a country inn combined with modern comforts. Swimming pool and shuffleboard. Near beaches and restaurants. Some units have kitchenettes. Open all year. Moderate.

Hostelling International Mid-Cape, 75 Goody Hallet Drive, 255-2785. Facilities include common kitchen, fifty beds in eight cabins, recreation areas. Seasonal. Inexpensive.

Ye Olde Nantucket House, 2647 Main Street, South Chatham, 432-5641. *B&B.* Fine accommodations in tastefully decorated rooms. Continental breakfast served. Near beaches and restaurants. Open all year. Moderate.

The Bradford Inn, 26 Cross Street, 945-1048. *Inn and motel.* Fine accommodations; heated swimming pool, four-poster canopy beds, fireplaces, and many other amenities. Full breakfast included in room rate and served in the sea captain's house. Open all year. Expensive.

Chatham Town House Inn, 11 Library Lane, 945-2180. *Inn.* An 1881 home in a picture-perfect part of town. Accommodations comfortable and immaculate. Excellent breakfasts and luncheons. Closed from Christmas to Washington's Birthday. Expensive.

Chatham Wayside Inn, 512 Main Street, 945-5550. A 135-plus-year-old landmark that has been completely redone with twenty-four rooms with a light, inviting feeling. Best rooms feature balconies overlooking Kate Gould Park, where the popular band concerts are held. Moderate to expensive.

The Queen Anne Inn, 70 Queen Anne Road, 945-0394 or (800) 545-4667. *Inn.* A lovely old inn with fireplaces in most rooms, antiques, Jacuzzi, heated pool, tennis courts; walking distance to beach, town center. Expensive.

The Dolphin of Chatham Inn and Motel, 352 Main Street, 945-0070 *or (800) 688-5900. Inn.* Located in Chatham historic district near shops, restaurants, and beaches. Spacious accommodations, most with water view. Swimming pool. Breakfast, lunch, and Sunday brunch. Open all year. Moderate.

Hawthorne Motel, 196 Shore Road, 945-0372. *Motor inn.* On the waterfront with sixteen motel rooms, ten housekeeping units, and a two-bedroom cottage. Expensive.

Cranberry Inn, 359 Main Street. 945-9232. Just outside the village, the inn is Chatham's oldest. Easy walk to beach, shops. Most of the eighteen rooms have four-poster beds; many have fireplaces. Expensive.

Pleasant Bay Village, 1191 Orleans Road, 945-1133. *Motor inn.* Motel, efficiency units, suites, or cottages. Beautiful landscaped setting. Swimming pool. Gourmet breakfasts and poolside luncheons. Seasonal. Expensive.

Chatham Dining

Impudent Oyster, 15 Chatham Bars Avenue, 945-3545. Superb seafood and gourmet fare. Live entertainment. Open all year. Expensive.

Champlain's, 26 Cross Street at the Bradford Inn, 945-9151. A culinary experience. Breakfast and dinner. In summer, also an outdoor cafe. Expensive.

Chatham Bars Inn, 297 Shore Road, 945-0096. Excellent American and continental cuisine, elegant environment, fine service, and dancing. Superb water view. A special treat while in Chatham. Open all year. Expensive.

High Tide, 1629 Main Street, West Chatham, 945-2582. Delightful menu with wide selection from seafood to steaks. Music and dancing on weekends. Early bird specials. Moderate to expensive.

The Queen Anne Inn, 70 Queen Anne Road, 945-0394. Elegant surroundings and gourmet selections. Highly recommended. Open April through Thanksgiving. Expensive.

Chatham Wayside Inn, 512 Main Street, 945-5550. Fine food and service in a charming setting. Open all year. Moderate.

Cafe Azure, 1448 Main Street, 945-3930. Casual and intimate dining in a small home. Nice dishes from seafood to vegetarian. Open for breakfast, lunch, and dinner. Friendly British owners. Inexpensive to moderate.

Marley's Restaurant, 1077 Main Street, 945-1700. Casual dining with great seafood. Love their Barbados scallops. Any place named for a cat has to be good. Moderate.

Fleming's Chatham Seafood House, 2175 Main Street, South Chatham, 432-9060. Specialties of clam chowder, seafood, lobster, and chicken. Children's menu. Seasonal. Inexpensive.

Andiamo, 2653 Main Street, South Chatham, 432-1807. A charming Italian bistro offering fine dining in a casual atmosphere. Evenings only. Seasonal. Moderate.

Two Turtles Restaurant, 11 Library Lane, 945-1234. Gourmet dining featuring local seafood, steaks, veal, and poultry specialties. Located in a country inn in Chatham center. Moderate.

Christian's, 443 Main Street, 945-3362. Superb dining for lunch and dinner. Extensive menu plays on movie themes for dishes. Fun upstairs lounge. Open most of year. Moderate to expensive.

Chatham Squire Restaurant, 512 Main Street, 945-0945. Popular downtown spot for breakfast to dinner. Local seafood a specialty. Open all year. Inexpensive.

Pate's, 1260 Main Street, 945-9777. A popular place for steaks and seafood. Open mid-April through Thanksgiving. Moderate.

Orleans

Town offices—School Road, Orleans, 240-3700; Orleans Information
Booth, Eldredge Parkway, 255-1386.

The following villages, with their postal zip codes, are within the town
of Orleans; Orleans—02653; East Orleans—02643; and South
Orleans—02662.

Lovely Orleans is the "gateway town" to the Lower Cape and Cape
Cod National Seashore. It is also the retailing and commercial center
for this part of the Cape. In Orleans you will find many places to stay,
restaurants, and shops. Orleans also offers Nauset Beach, one of Cape
Cod's best and within the boundaries of Cape Cod National Seashore.
Nauset Beach goes on for miles, all the way to Chatham; if you need a
long, solitary beach walk next to a raging surf with wheeling gulls and
terns overhead, this is the place. Orleans also has swimming on Cape
Cod Bay at Skaket Beach, where the water is warmer.

Among the attractions in town are the 1834 First Universalist
Meeting House, home of the Orleans Historical Society, with Native
American, local history, and lifesaving artifacts; the 1890 French Cable
Museum, housing cable and transmission gear for transatlantic communications between North America and France; and the 1873 Academy Playhouse, presenting stage productions throughout the year.
Take the time to do some auto or bike touring of the less-traveled
roads of Orleans. Both the scenery and architecture are pleasing in any
season.

Although strong evidence is lacking, it is believed that Leif Ericsson, that intrepid Viking mariner, and his longboat crew came ashore
at Nauset in A.D. 1003. Bartholomew Gosnold, the English explorer, set
anchor in the waters of Orleans in 1602. Gosnold is also remembered
for giving the peninsula its name—Cape Cod. Samuel de Champlain
also sailed here in 1605. In 1644, when the first colonists settled Eastham, Orleans was part of their land grant. South Parish in Eastham
was established in 1718, and this area became the Town of Orleans in
1797. All other Cape towns have either English or Native American
names. Orleans has a distinctly French appellation, however, and how
it came to be named remains a mystery. Among its momentous historical events was the laying of a transatlantic communications cable
between Orleans and Brest, France. This project was completed in
1898 by Compagnie Française des Cables Telegraphiques. Ironically,

perhaps symbolically, the Orleans end of the cable came in near where the French explorer Champlain had landed several centuries before.

Orleans Accommodations

The Parsonage, 202 Main Street in East Orleans, 255-8217 or (888) 422-8217. *B&B.* Parsonage in the nineteenth century. Within walking distance of downtown shops and restaurants. En route to Nauset Beach. Fresh fruit and flowers; continental breakfast. Open all year. Moderate.

The Farmhouse at Nauset Beach, 163 Beach Road, 255-6654. *B&B.* Nineteenth-century farmhouse within a short walk of Nauset Beach; ocean-view deck. Continental breakfast served. Open all year. Moderate.

Hillbourne House, Route 28, South Orleans, 255-0780. *Motor inn/guest house/cottages.* Main house was built in the late eighteenth century. Private beach and dock, lovely location; continental breakfast. Housekeeping cottages available. Open all year. Moderate.

Ship's Knees Inn, 186 Beach Road, East Orleans, 255-1312. *Inn and cottages.* Fine accommodations in a 150-year-old sea captain's home. Housekeeping apartment and efficiency cottages. Near Nauset Beach. Tennis court and swimming pool. Continental breakfast. Open all year. Moderate.

Seashore Park Manor Inn, Route 6A and Canal Road, 255-2500. *Motor inn.* Fine accommodations in a convenient location. Indoor and outdoor swimming pools, saunas, Jacuzzi, and whirlpool. Seasonal. Moderate.

The Nauset House Inn, 143 Beach Road, East Orleans, 255-2195. *Inn.* Short distance from Nauset Beach. Includes breakfast. Open early April to late October. Moderate to expensive.

Orleans Holiday Motel, 44 Route 6A, 255-1514. *Motor inn.* Comfortable accommodations; large swimming pool; restaurant, lounge, and live entertainment. Open all year. Moderate.

The Cove, 13 Route 28, 255-1203. *Motor inn.* Excellent waterfront accommodations; some efficiency units; swimming pool. Open all year. Moderate to expensive.

The Barley Neck Inn Lodge, 5 Beach Road, 255-8484 or (800) 281-7505. *Inn.* Handy to Nauset Beach, eighteen rooms in center of town. Moderate to expensive.

Governor Prence Motor Inn, Routes 6A and 28, 255-1⸱
Excellent accommodations close to downtown Orle⸱
and Cape Cod National Seashore attractions. Swimmii⸱
whirlpool; coffee shop. Seasonal. Moderate.

Old Tavern Motel and Inn, 151 Route 6A, 255-1565. *Motor inn*. T⸱ ⸱gh-
teenth-century inn was visited by Henry David Thoreau when he
trekked across the Lower Cape. Modern units adjoin the old inn.
Swimming pool. Continental breakfast. Seasonal. Moderate.

Orleans Dining

Captain Linnell House, 137 Skaket Beach Road, 255-3400. One of the
best places on the Lower Cape for elegant dining. Continental cuisine featuring fresh, local seafood. Breads and pastries made on the
premises. Live entertainment and dancing. Open all year. Expensive.

Fog Cutter, Routes 6A and 28, 255-2270. A favorite family eatery where
the fish and ribs are the best. Open all year. Moderate.

Arbor Restaurant—Binnacle Tavern, 20 South Orleans Road, 255-4847 or
255-7901. Two restaurants at this location: Arbor serves continental dishes, such as sweetbreads, and the traditional lobster; Binnacle is a casual place for Cajun dishes, seafood, and fancy pizzas.
Open all year. Inexpensive to moderate.

Orleans Lobster Pound, 157 Cranberry Highway, Route 6A, 240-1234.
Casual atmosphere for lobster and seafood. Open for lunch and
dinner. Inexpensive.

Kadee's Lobster & Clam Bar, 212 Main Street, East Orleans, 255-6184.
Casual dining in open-air cafe. Inexpensive.

Yardarm, 48 South Orleans Road, 255-4840. Fresh fish, prime rib
Monday and Thursday. Inexpensive to moderate.

Double Dragon Inn, junction of Routes 6A and 28, 255-4100. Chinese
and Polynesian cuisine. Open all year. Inexpensive to moderate.

Hunan Gourmet III, 225 Cranberry Highway, 240-0888. Light Chinese
food. All-you-can-eat buffet nightly. Open all year. Inexpensive to
moderate.

The Beacon Room Restaurant, 23 West Road, 255-2211. Casual dining
featuring seafood and pasta, wines by the glass. Open year-round.
Moderate.

Cooke's Seafood, junction of Routes 28 and 6A, 255-5518. Fried and broiled seafood, hamburgers. Open seasonally for lunch and dinner. Inexpensive.

Joe's Beach Road Bar & Grill, Main Street at Beach Road, 255-0212. Specializing in good food and fun. Located in the Barley Neck Inn. Inexpensive to moderate.

Barley Neck Inn, 5 Beach Road, 255-0212. Fine wines and continental cuisine. Elegant sea captain's home. Live entertainment. Open all year. Moderate.

Land Ho, Route 6A and Cove Road, 255-5165. Popular place with locals and visitors alike. Chowders, kale soup, burgers, sandwiches, steaks, seafood, and Wellfleet oysters; luncheon and dinner specials. Open all year. Inexpensive to moderate.

The Lobster Claw, Route 6A, 255-1800. Got a craving for lobster? This is the place. Fresh seafood and lobsters served daily. Children's menu. Open April to November. Inexpensive to moderate.

Old Jailhouse Tavern, 28 West Road, 255-5245. Fine dining in what was once a lockup for pirates and other local troublemakers. Warm and inviting architecture today. Fine food and service. Lovely surrounding grounds. Open all year. Moderate.

Eastham

Town offices—County Road, Eastham, 240-5900; Eastham Information Booth, Route 6 near Cape Cod National Seashore entrance, 240-7211.

The following villages, with their postal zip codes, are within the town of Eastham: Eastham—02642; and North Eastham—02651.

Eastham, one of the first four towns established on Cape Cod, was founded in 1644 by English Pilgrims. Among the earliest settlers were the families of Thomas Prence, Edward Bangs, John Doane, John Smalley, Nicholas Snow, Richard Higgins, and Josias Cook. At that time, the Town of Plymouth was the center of government for the colony. Plymouth, though, was experiencing growing pains, and its residents were seeking a better life. A number of them looked to Cape Cod as the place where their dreams for good land and prosperity might be better achieved. Eastham was settled by just such a group. But settlement was limited by government decree to those who came to America on the first three ships—*Mayflower, Fortune,* and *Anne.* The territory that today includes the towns of Orleans, Eastham, Wellfleet, Truro, and Provincetown was purchased by Puritan men from local tribes for hatchets, some of which, no doubt, were used during King Philip's War.

In Thomas Prence, Eastham found an able leader. Through Prence the community prospered enough so as to be designated an official township in 1646. The community formally took the name Eastham in 1651. During the 1650s, Eastham lost territory to other burgeoning settlements such as Harwich and Chatham. Thomas Prence served as governor of Plymouth Colony but got fed up with the long commute to the mainland and decided to govern from Eastham instead. This desire to govern Plymouth Colony from home made Eastham one of the first colonial capitals in the English-speaking New World. In 1673 Prence died while still serving as governor; he was a great man, long gone but not forgotten.

Life for members of the Congregational Church improved, while local Quakers, Methodists, and Baptists faced persecution. Eastham-area Native Americans were converted by Reverend Samuel Treat, a preacher who dramatically mixed metaphors of fire and brimstone with salvation on strict Calvinist terms. During the eighteenth century Eastham parishes became the towns of Orleans, Truro, Provincetown, and Wellfleet. With this dismemberment, Eastham diminished in size from being one of the largest towns in the colony to one of its smallest; along with this diminution, its political status evaporated. Other changes took place in Eastham, such as the decline in power of the Congregational Church and the rise of the Methodists.

During the nineteenth century Eastham was home port for a number of adventurous sea captains such as Freeman Hatch, who, in 1852, sailed the clipper *Northern Light* from Boston to San Francisco in seventy-six days and six hours, a tremendous feat at that time. Today Eastham is a quiet town where tourism is one of the major industries. Eastham offers excellent beaches on both the Atlantic and Cape Cod Bay as well as fine accommodations and restaurants. Eastham's main attraction is Cape Cod National Seashore with its prominent Salt Pond Visitor Center, hiking and biking trails, Coast Guard Beach, and Nauset Light Beach. Other attractions include Doane Homestead, First Encounter Beach, the 1741 Swift-Daley House, Old Cove Cemetery, the 1876 Captain Penniman House, Schoolhouse Museum, and the 1680 Eastham Windmill.

CAPE COD PANCAKES

You won't find any better pancakes than the ones served at the Whalewalk Inn. The Inn in Eastham, one of the finest on the Cape, sits along a windy quiet road near the Orleans line.

To make the pancakes, take ½ cup yellow corneal, ½ cup flour, ½ teaspoon baking soda, ½ teaspoon baking powder, ⅛ teaspoon salt, 5 tablespoons sugar, grated rind of one orange, ¼ teaspoon nutmeg, ¾ cup buttermilk, ¼ cup orange juice, 2 eggs separated, 5 teaspoons vegetable oil, ½ cup frozen blueberries, ½ cup frozen cranberries sliced.

Sift the cornmeal, flour, baking soda and powder, salt, and sugar together in a large bowl. Stir in the grated orange rind and nutmeg. In a smaller bowl whisk the buttermilk, orange juice, egg yolks, and oil until combined.

Meanwhile, beat the egg whites in a clean, dry bowl until they form soft peaks. Add the liquid ingredients to the dry mixture and stir to just combine. Fold in the egg whites. Heat an electric griddle to 350° Fahrenheit, or set a large skillet on the stove over low heat. Lightly oil the pan and when hot, spoon about 2 tablespoons of batter onto the griddle. Spread the batter slightly, then sprinkle a few blueberries and cranberries on top. Repeat with the remaining batter and berries. Cook very slowly for about four minutes, or until you see tiny bubbles forming on the surface of the pancakes. Flip carefully and cook another minute or two. Top with confectioner's sugar and serve with hot maple syrup and whipped butter. Yield about twelve pancakes.

These and other breakfast treats are served on the outdoor patio of the inn, an 1830s Greek Revival manse. Carolyn Smith has delightfully decorated the inn, which now also includes a carriage house where rooms feature fireplaces and whirlpool baths. Husband Dick creates the breakfasts.

Eastham Accommodations

The Penny House, Route 6, North Eastham, 255–6632 or (800) 554–1751. *B&B.* A 1751 sea captain's house with a bow roof. Close to Salt Pond entrance to Cape Cod National Seashore. French spoken.

Homemade breads and muffins at breakfast. Open all year. Moderate to expensive.

The Over Look Inn, County Road at entrance to Cape Cod National Seashore, 255-1886. *B&B.* Operated by a Scottish couple who came to the Cape from Toronto. Queen Anne–style Victorian house furnished with antiques and Inuit art from Canada. Substantial Scottish breakfasts served. Open all year. Moderate to expensive.

Four Points by Sheraton, 3800 Route 6, 255-5000. *Motor inn/resort.* One of the best places on the Lower Cape. Two swimming pools, saunas, whirlpools, tennis courts, and bikes; restaurant, lounge, and live entertainment. Shuttle service to beach. Open all year. Moderate to expensive.

Whalewalk Inn, 200 Bridge Road, 255-0617. *B&B.* An 1830s estate offering fine accommodations and gourmet breakfasts. Open April to November. Expensive.

Captain's Quarters Motel, Route 6, North Eastham, 255-5686. *Motor inn.* Fine accommodations; swimming pool; continental breakfast. Seasonal. Moderate.

Viking Shores, Route 6, 255-3200 or (800) 242-2131. *Motor inn.* Fine accommodations; swimming pool, tennis courts, and bikes. Open early April to end of November. Moderate.

Mid-Cape American Youth Hostel, 75 Goody Hallet Drive, 255-2785. Facilities include common kitchen, fifty beds in eight cabins, recreation areas. Seasonal. Inexpensive.

Eastham Ocean View Motel, 2470 Route 6, 255-1600. *Motor inn.* Good value and many amenities—pool, bikes, in-room movies. Open from early April to end of October. Moderate.

Atlantic Oaks Campground, Route 6, ½-mile north of Cape Cod National Seashore entrance, 255-1437. *Campground.* Many modern conveniences, including cable television hookups. Near Cape Cod National Seashore attractions. Open May 1 to November 1; 100 sites.

Eastham Dining

Eastham Lobster Pool, Route 6, North Eastham, 255-9706. Shore-dinner specialties of lobster, clams, seafood, and such. Open April through November. Moderate.

Flipper's Family Restaurant, Route 6, across from the Wellfleet Drive-In, on the Eastham/Wellfleet town line, 255-1914. Seafood and meat dishes at reasonable prices near Cape Cod National Seashore, Massachusetts Audubon Sanctuary, and flea market. Seasonal. Inexpensive.

Blossoms, Sheraton Ocean Park Inn, Route 6, 255-5000. Fine traditional American and gourmet continental food. Dancing and entertainment on weekends. Open all year. Moderate to expensive.

Arnold's Lobster & Clam Bar, 3580 Route 6, 255-2575. Open lunch through dinner until 10:00 P.M. Known for seafood baskets, raw bar, and lunch specials. Seasonal. Inexpensive to moderate.

The Box Lunch, 4205 Route 6, 255-0799. Nice sandwiches. Open all year. Inexpensive.

Finely JP's, 19 Freedjum Road on Route 6, 349-7500. Somewhat rustic setting, but the food is great. Varied menu. Open all year. Moderate.

Wellfleet

Town offices—Main Street, Wellfleet, 349-0301; Wellfleet Information, 349-2510.

The following villages, with their postal zip codes, are within the town of Wellfleet: Wellfleet—02667; and South Wellfleet—02663.

Straddling the Cape from the bay to the Atlantic, Wellfleet is largely an unspoiled town with pockets of commercialization along Route 6. Despite its obvious Yankee demeanor, it has become a fashionable vacation place. Wellfleet is coming close to rivaling Provincetown as a center for art galleries.

Wellfleet is a favorite Cape town not because of its sophistication, but because of its splendid natural environment—high sand-and-clay cliffs overlooking the broad sweep of the Atlantic; extensive salt marshes, the mystical Atlantic White Cedar Trail at Marconi Station; warm-water beaches on Cape Cod Bay; the abundance of marine life and the satisfying hikes within the Massachusetts Audubon Sanctuary and on the Great Island Trail; the pleasing architecture of Wellfleet center; and meandering roads that take you through pristine areas of woods, sand, glacial kettle holes, and marshes. Some of the most glorious sunsets can be seen from the wharfs and beaches at Wellfleet Harbor. The air seems fresher and more relaxing on the Cape Cod Bay side of Wellfleet than at other places on the peninsula. Wellfleet also offers Cape Cod National Seashore; Marconi Wireless Station Site; First Congregational Church, with its clock that strikes ship's time; Wellfleet Historical Society Museum; and the circa 1700 Samuel Rider House.

In the seventeenth century Wellfleet was part of Eastham and known as Billingsgate. The community, incorporated as the Town of Wellfleet in 1763, was said to be named after the Wellfleet oyster beds of England. In fact, the oyster beds of Wellfleet still provide the town with a mainstay of its economy. Because of its excellent harbor on Cape Cod Bay, Wellfleet also became a major center for New England whaling and commercial fishing.

In the 1870s a Wellfleet captain, Lorenzo Dow Baker, first brought unspoiled, green bananas to the United States in his schooner, the *Telegraph*. From this beginning, and with financing from Elisha Hopkins, his brother-in-law and also a Wellfleet resident, the L. D. Baker Company was established in 1881. This enterprise became the Boston Fruit Company in 1885, then the United Fruit Company in 1899. United Fruit, a powerful corporation in its time, was synonymous with the best and the worst of American involvement with the countries of Central America. Baker was also a visionary entrepreneur in the tourist trade, which was booming in the late nineteenth century. In 1886 he opened the Chequesset Inn, which was considered the best place to stay in Wellfleet at that time.

A TIMELESS TREASURE

The town clock has long been a fixture of colonial New England villages. In Wellfleet, though, the town clock is unlike any other in New England or the world. It may look no different than any other town clock, but when it sounds, it does so on ship's time:

One, five, and nine o'clock are two bells.

Two, six, and ten o'clock are four bells.

Three, seven, and eleven o'clock are six bells.

Four, eight, and twelve o'clock are eight bells.

The half hours are struck by adding one stroke to the corresponding even hours.

Believe it or not, it works and is unique. It's even listed in *Ripley's Believe It or Not*. As in colonial times, the clock is located at the base of the steeple of the First Congregational Church.

One of Wellfleet's most momentous events occurred in 1903 on the cliffs overlooking the Atlantic. Here Guglielmo Marconi transmitted the first transatlantic message by wireless telegraph. Also in Wellfleet, the past and the present have converged with the ongoing salvage operation of the eighteenth-century pirate ship *Whidah*. Though lying deep in Atlantic waters, its broken hulk is surrendering to divers millions of dollars' worth of treasure.

Wellfleet Accommodations

The Inn at Duck Creek, 70 Main Street, 349-9333. *Inn*. Excellent accommodations in a fine country inn. Near center of village and Cape Cod Bay beaches. Acres of salt marsh and a duck pond near the inn. Continental breakfast served. Excellent dining at its restaurants, Sweet Seasons and the Tavern Room; lounge with live entertainment. Highly recommended. Seasonal. Moderate.

Eventide Motel and Cottages, Route 660, South Wellfleet, 349-3410. *Motor inn*. Good value. Indoor swimming pool. In quiet location and near Cape Cod National Seashore attractions. Cottages also available. Open all year. Moderate.

Southfleet Motor Inn, Route 6, South Wellfleet, 349-3580 or (800) 334-3715. *Motor inn*. Fine accommodations. Indoor and outdoor swimming pools, saunas, and playground. Open early March to end of October. Moderate.

Wellfleet Motel and Lodge, Route 6, 349-3535 or (800) 852-2900. *Motor inn*. Fine accommodations; swimming pool and whirlpool; coffee shop. Open all year. Expensive.

Paine's Campground, Route 6, South Wellfleet, 349-3007. *Campground*. Near Cape Cod Bay beaches and Cape Cod National Seashore attractions. Open mid-May to October; 150 sites.

Wellfleet Dining

Bayside Lobster Hut, Commercial Street, 349-6333. Terrific lobster, chowder, scallops, and shrimp; raw bar. Seasonal. Inexpensive to Moderate.

Van Rensselaer's, Route 6, South Wellfleet, opposite Marconi Station (Cape Cod National Seashore), 349-2127. Seafood and prime rib. Seasonal. Inexpensive to moderate.

Aesop's Tables, Main Street, in the center of town, 349-6450. Highly regarded Lower Cape dining place in a historic sea captain's home. Attractive interior decor with original art. Creative American and continental cuisine; innovative seafood dishes. Live entertainment in the lounge. Open May to October. Moderate to expensive.

Painter's, 50 Main Street, 349-3003. Features New American cuisine in a friendly atmosphere. Seasonal. Moderate.

Sweet Seasons Restaurant, 70 Main Street, 349-6535. At the Inn at Duck Creek. Continental handling of duck, seafood, veal, and beef. Vegetarian dishes. Delicious food, casual elegance. Seasonal. Moderate to expensive.

Moby Dick's, Route 6, 349-9795. A classically decorated Cape Cod seafood house. Casual. Also take-out. Inexpensive.

Duck Creek Tavern Room, 70 Main Street, 349-7369. Popular eating and drinking place in the Inn at Duck Creek. Lobster, seafood dishes, steaks, Cajun chicken, and great desserts. Live entertainment in the lounge. Seasonal. Moderate to expensive.

Serena's Restaurant, Route 6, South Wellfleet, 349-9370. Family restaurant serving seafood and Italian cuisine. Seasonal. Inexpensive to moderate.

Captain Higgins Seafood House, on the pier at Wellfleet Harbor, 349-6027. Delicious seafood, lobster, shrimp, steaks, and chicken. Terrific location overlooking beautiful Wellfleet Harbor. Children's menu. Open mid-June to mid-September. Inexpensive to moderate.

The Lighthouse, 3056 Main Street, 349-3681. Popular in-town dining place. Good homemade meals. Open all year. Inexpensive.

Cielo's, East Main Street, 349-2108. Superb gourmet fare. Casual and relaxing. Seasonal. Expensive.

Beachcomber of Wellfleet, Cahoon Hollow Road, 349-6055. Seasonal.

Truro

Town offices—Town Hall Road, Truro, 349-3635; Truro Chamber of Commerce, P.O. Box 26, Route 6 and Head of Meadow Road, North Truro, 487-1288.

The following villages, with their postal zip codes, are within the town of Truro: Truro—02666; and North Truro—02652.

When one thinks of Truro, the austere but compelling paintings of Edward Hopper come to mind—windswept sand dunes crested with stands of bent beach grass, solitary lighthouses, and beach cabins. Except for the strip of tourist cottages along Route 6A, Truro is one of Cape Cod's least commercial towns. It is a place of long, lonely beaches and sand dunes that seem to undulate in every direction. Some individuals who prize their solitude happily live in cabins tucked between sand dunes, far from the parade of tourists speeding back and forth along Route 6 between Wellfleet and Provincetown.

Truro's fine beaches on the Atlantic side and on Cape Cod Bay include Head of the Meadow Beach, which is part of Cape Cod National Seashore. It is in Truro that you best see the effects of the wind and sea on the Cape Cod landscape. In the Highland Light area, the cliffs are eroding; the high ground is pulling back from the edge of the sea. At Pamet River Harbor and along the beaches on Truro's Cape Cod Bay side, in contrast, land is building up and pushing out to sea. The strong northeast winds are the great transporters of soil from one side to the other. Among Truro's interesting attractions are the 1827 Bell Church, Truro Historical Museum at Highland Light, and the Jenny Lind Tower.

When the Pilgrims first came to America in 1620, they considered the possibility of establishing a settlement in the area of what is now the Town of Truro, called Pamet in its early days. The exhausted among them wanted to stay, but others felt it was more prudent to continue on with the hope that an even more commodious place would be found. While these Pilgrims were on land here, however, they found their first fresh water at what is now called Pilgrim Spring and a cache of corn at a place called Corn Hill; they used the corn for their first crop grown in America. Permanent settlers arrived at the close of the seventeenth century when a group of Pilgrims from Eastham known as the "Pamet Proprietors" negotiated a land deal with the local tribes. In 1705 the growing community was named Dangerfield because of the many ships that were wrecked in this area over the years. In 1709 it became a town in its own right and was renamed Truro after a town on the Cornish coast of England.

Farming, fishing, and whaling, along with the related industries, prospered here. After the wars with Great Britain, Pamet River Harbor flourished with activity—wharfs, shipbuilding, saltworks, chandleries, sail lofts, fish processing and packing plants, and financial institutions that provided capital and insurance for seafaring ventures. As Truro entered the second half of the nineteenth century, however, the town, a maker of substantial profits from the fisheries and maritime industries, began to decline, as was also the case with many other communities along the New England coast. In 1860 the Union Company of Truro, the commercial heart and soul of the town in which many of the locals had invested their capital, went bust. What was once a bustling, frenetic town brimming with optimism and generating substantial profits became a quiet place passed over by economic progress.

What is left is a very beautiful and tranquil place existing in close harmony with nature. The best way to experience its many-faceted beauty is to wander over back roads, beaches, and rough trails without a precise plan. Expect to see wonders at every turn.

Truro Accommodations

The majority of Truro accommodations are located in the North Truro and Beach Point areas. Most of them are cottage colonies either with their own private beaches on Cape Cod Bay or within easy access of beaches. The cottage colonies are on Route 6A close to Provincetown and to Cape Cod National Seashore attractions. Many cottage colonies rent their units by the week, and advance reservations are essential for the months of July and August. For more information on renting a cottage in Truro, contact the Chamber of Commerce at 487-1288.

Sea Surf Motel, 487-0343 or (800) 773-0343. *Motor inn.* Located on Cape Cod Bay, with private beach. Also has units with kitchenettes. Moderate.

Outer Reach Motel 535 Route 6, 487-9090 or (800) 942-5388. *Motor inn.* Near beach with great views of Provincetown. Moderate to expensive.

Truro Vineyards of Cape Cod, 11 Shore Road, 487-6200. *B&B.* An 1836 bed-and-breakfast with five rooms, set within five vineyard acres. The first wines were produced in 1996. Moderate to expensive.

Kalmar Village, 674 Shore Road, 487-0585. *Cottages.* A complex of cottages along a 400-foot beach. Also large pool. Moderate to expensive.

Top Mast Motel, 209 Shore Road, North Truro, on Cape Cod Bay, 487-1189. *Motor inn.* Has 650-foot private beach; all units face beach, some efficiencies with cooking facilities. Moderate to expensive.

Cape View Motel, routes 6 and 6A, 487-0363 or (800) 224-3232. *Motor inn.* Views of Provincetown and Cape Cod Bay from all rooms. Efficiencies available. Pool. Moderate.

Seascape Motor Inn, Route 6A, North Truro, 487-1225. *Motor inn.* Many rooms have water views. Moderate.

Sea Gull Motel, Shore Route 6A, North Truro, 487-9070. *Motor inn.* Good value. Cape Cod Bay location. Private beach. Seasonal. Moderate.

Crow's Nest Motel, Shore Route 6A, North Truro, 487-9031 or (800) 863-2549. *Motor inn.* Motel and efficiency units. Private beach on Cape Cod Bay; sun deck. Open April to November. Moderate.

Seaside Village Motel, Shore Route 6A, North Truro, 487-1215. *Motor inn and cottages.* Fine oceanfront accommodations; private beach and sun deck. Seasonal. Moderate.

Horton's Trailer Park & Camping Resort, Route 6A in North Truro to South Highland Road, 487-1220 or (800) 252-7705. *Campground.* Near Cape Cod Bay beaches, Provincetown, and Cape Cod National Seashore attractions. Open first week in April to mid-October; 216 sites.

North Truro Camping Area, Route 6 to Highland Road East, North Truro, 487-1847. *Campground.* Near Cape Cod Bay beaches, Provincetown, and Cape Cod National Seashore attractions. Seasonal; 350 sites.

North of Highland Camping Area, Route 6, to Head of Meadow Road, North Truro, 487-1191. *Campground.* Near Cape Cod Bay beaches, Provincetown, and Cape Cod National Seashore attractions. Open end of May to first week in September; 237 sites.

South Hollow Vineyards, 11 Shore Road, North Truro, 487-6200. A Federal-style farmhouse with five rooms, all with four-poster beds and private baths. The acreage is planted with grapes, and the first wines were produced in 1996. Seasonal. Moderate to expensive.

Truro Dining

Adrian's, 535 Route 6 North, 487-4360. Features inspired dishes, views from a bluff. Both outdoor and indoor dining. Has a loyal following. Seasonal. Inexpensive to moderate.

Terra Luna, 104 Shore Road, 487-1019. Nice mix of art and shellacked wooden tables. Features American and Italian dishes. Seasonal. Moderate.

Whitman House, County Road in North Truro, 487-1740. Fine restaurant serving beef and seafood selections. Old Cape Cod decor. Open first of April to mid-December. Moderate.

The Blacksmith Shop, Route 6A, Truro Center, 349-6554. Rustic environment and setting capturing some of the tranquil spirit of Truro. Excellent meat and seafood dishes. Open from Memorial Day through September; weekends the rest of the year. Moderate.

Provincetown

Town offices—260 Commercial Street, 487-7000; Provincetown Chamber of Commerce, P.O. Box 1017, 307 Commercial Street, Provincetown, 487-3424.

Provincetown's zip code is 02657.

Provincetown is Cape Cod's most colorful and fascinating town. It runs from the subdued to the outrageous, the tasteful to the gaudy. The irony is that it was founded by starchy Puritans, who may be spinning in their graves.

Provincetown today is an amalgamation of many different kinds of people. You have descendants of the early settlers, newcomer WASPs, fishermen, merchants, professionals, Portuguese-American families, artists, writers, and craftspersons. It's also a mecca for gays and lesbians, particularly in summer. Somehow this bouillabaisse of humanity lives in peace together, each faction respecting differences and each contributing to the richness that makes Provincetown a truly special place in America.

Provincetown is at the narrowest part of Cape Cod, at land's end. It is surrounded by sea on three sides. You can't go any farther unless you fly or sail away. In a world where just about everything is relative, the absolute of being at the end of something does have its appeal and no doubt contributes to the attractiveness of Provincetown.

The town has long been a favorite refuge for creative people, from Eugene O'Neill to Norman Mailer. It was also home to Admiral Donald B. MacMillan, the famous Arctic explorer.

Provincetown has the largest number of art galleries on Cape Cod, featuring contemporary paintings, prints, and sculpture by established and new artists. There is a large number of shops selling excellent crafts and jewelry, cheap souvenirs, unique fashions, and army and navy castoffs. Commercial Street, Provincetown's main street, is flanked on both sides by shops, restaurants, hotels, bars, and night spots. Commercial Street is usually packed thick with people during the summer, which makes it difficult to negotiate by car. There are, however, parking lots off Commercial Street, on adjacent streets, and next to MacMillan Wharf. The center of Provincetown is where Commercial Street, MacMillan Wharf (the waterfront area), and Town Hall converge. Bradford Street, which runs parallel to Commercial, also has many hotels, motels, and restaurants.

The highest point in town is the Pilgrim Monument, which, on a clear day, can be seen from the Massachusetts mainland. MacMillan Wharf has several operations providing whale-watching adventures, sightseeing cruises, and deep-sea fishing trips. Daily ferry boats from Boston and Plymouth also come into the dock area. Most of Provincetown is within Cape Cod National Seashore. Two excellent beaches are here, Herring Cove and Race Point, as well as a visitor center offering information on biking, hiking, and off-road vehicle and horseback-riding trails. Among Provincetown's many attractions are the oldest cemetery in Provincetown; Mayflower Compact Memorial (historic bas-relief plaque) at town hall; Heritage Museum, housed in what was an 1860 Methodist church; the Pilgrim Monument and Museum; and the Whydah Museum, which features treasures of the pirate ship *Whydah*. If you get bored in Provincetown, look into the mirror for the cause.

The historical importance of Provincetown should be known to every American. Here, in 1620, the *Mayflower* Pilgrims sailed into American waters after an arduous voyage across the Atlantic. During their brief stay here, the Pilgrims created and signed the Mayflower Compact, an agreement whereby a free people would govern themselves and from which the fullness of American liberty would eventually emerge.

During the early seventeenth century, when the Pilgrims were establishing towns along the south shore of Massachusetts and in areas on Cape Cod, Provincetown, because of its remoteness from governmental authority, became a place where traders, seamen, and fishermen plying the Atlantic would come ashore to drink themselves silly, gamble until anything of worth was won or lost, and revel in diverse entertainments. Law, order, and sobriety had to wait until 1727, when the righteous colonists took control of the community to create an official township.

In succeeding years Provincetown, with its excellent harbor on the open Atlantic, became a thriving center for the whaling industry, ranking behind only Nantucket and New Bedford in importance. It was through whaling that the first Portuguese settlers came to Provincetown. From the Azores, the Canaries, and the Cape Verdes, they volunteered as replacements for English crew members who were either lost at sea or who had jumped ship in foreign ports. Provincetown has long been as much a Portuguese town as it has been a Yankee one. During its days as a primary port for the fleets that fished the Grand Banks, Provincetown also attracted fishing families from Cape Breton Island, Nova Scotia. Some of their descendants also continue to live in this land's-end community. The last whaling vessel to operate out of Provincetown was the *Charles W. Morgan.* She completed her final voyage in 1921 and can today be seen lovingly restored as the "center piece" vessel at Mystic Seaport in Connecticut. Although whaling has disappeared, Provincetown continues to be a major fishing port, with most of the fleet owned and operated by Portuguese mariners. Today's Provincetown fishery accounts for approximately eleven million pounds, all of it landed at MacMillan Wharf.

The first art colony in America began in Provincetown. Its impetus came in 1899 from the portrait painter Charles W. Hawthorne, who established the Cape Cod School of Art. This locus of excellence attracted talented artists from throughout North America. A summer stint of painting in Provincetown became an important credential that helped to open many a gallery door to new talent. Today the Provincetown Art Association, located on Commercial Street, carries on this tradition with exhibitions and courses. The large concentration of art galleries in Provincetown is another result of what Hawthorne set in motion.

The cultural high point of Provincetown came in the twentieth century when the Provincetown Players, with their Playhouse on the Wharf, were established. Eugene O'Neill, Sinclair Lewis, and John Dos Passos, now considered immortals in American theater and literature, were among many individuals who contributed their talents and learned the intricacies of their crafts in Provincetown. Unfortunately, the Playhouse was destroyed in a fire in the late 1960s. The Provincetown Players are continuing the tradition and offer performances on a regular basis, but in the town hall.

Provincetown Accommodations

Provincetown Inn, 1 Commercial Street, 487-9500. *Motor inn.* Top-quality accommodation at land's end offering indoor pool and private beach; restaurant, lounge, and live entertainment. Open all year. Expensive.

Bradford Gardens Inn, 178 Bradford Street, 487-1616. *B&B*. Home built in 1820 and located at the center of everything in Provincetown. Ample breakfasts feature many gourmet specialties. Open April to October. Moderate to expensive.

The Masthead Motel & Cottages, 31-41 Commercial Street, 487-0523. *Motel and cottages*. Waterfront location with harbor views, private beach, luxury kitchens, and sun deck. Mooring and launch services. Open all year. Moderate to expensive.

Ship's Bell Inn, 586 Commercial Street, 487-1674. *Motor inn*. Private beach, secluded patio; some units with kitchens. Near all downtown attractions. Open May to November. Moderate to expensive.

Holiday Inn, Shore Route 6A and Snail Road, 487-1711. *Motor inn*. Fine accommodations; restaurant, lounge, and live entertainment; swimming pool. Near beaches. Open all year. Moderate to expensive.

Cape Colony Inn, Shore Route 6A, 487-1755. *Motor inn*. Fine accommodations near all attractions. Open early April to late October. Moderate.

The Breakwater, Shore Route 6A, 487-1134. *Motor inn and cottages*. Uncongested area overlooking Cape Cod Bay; sun deck. Open from May to October. Moderate.

Somerset House, 378 Commercial Street, 487-0383. *Inn*. Beautiful interior environment—classical music, fresh flowers, paintings, and modern guest rooms. Near all downtown attractions. Seasonal. Moderate.

Surfside Inn, 543 Commercial Street, 487-1726. *Motor inn*. Fine accommodations; private beach and swimming pool; within walking distance of all downtown attractions. Seasonal. Moderate to expensive.

Best Western—Chateau Motor Inn, Bradford Street West, 487-1286. *Motor inn*. Excellent accommodations; beautiful grounds and views of Cape Cod Bay and sand dunes; swimming pool. Near all attractions. Seasonal; opens in May. Moderate.

Elephant Walk Inn, 156 Bradford Street, 487-2543. *Inn*. Spacious rooms and sun deck; morning coffee. Open all year. Moderate.

Blue Sea, Route 6A, 487-1041. *Motor inn*. On the ocean. One- and two-story units. Has indoor pool, coin laundry. Seasonal. Moderate to expensive.

Watermark Inn, 603 Commercial Street, 487-0165. *Inn.* Two-story inn with ten suites. Units have private patios, balconies. On the beach. Open year-around. Expensive.

Best Western Tides Beachfront, 837 Commercial Street, 487-1045. *Motor inn.* On private beach, has forty-five rooms, some suites. Heated pool, restaurant. Seasonal. Expensive.

Land's End Inn, 22 Commercial Street, 487-0706 or (800) 276-7088. *Inn.* A Victorian inn with sixteen rooms, all with private bath, plus tower rooms and loft with spectacular views. Open all year. Expensive.

White Horse Inn, 500 Commercial Street, 487-1790. *Inn.* Although accommodations are basic and baths are shared, it has a nice feel. Lots of art. Open all year. Moderate.

Fairbanks, 90 Bradford Street, 487-0386 or (800) 324-7265. *Inn.* Built in 1776, the inn has fifteen rooms, eleven with bath. Some rooms with balconies. Open all year. Moderate to expensive.

Bradford House and Motel, 41 Bradford Street, 487-0173. *Motor inn.* Accommodations in motel and Victorian-style guest house; swimming pool; sun deck overlooking town and harbor. Open mid-May to late October. Moderate.

Coastal Acres Camping Court, Bradford Street, 487-1700. *Campground.* Near Cape Cod National Seashore, Cape Cod Bay beaches, and downtown attractions. Open April 1 to November 1; 180 sites.

Dune's Edge Campground, Route 6 to left on Road Marker 116, 487-9815. *Campground.* Near Cape Cod National Seashore, Cape Cod Bay beaches, and downtown attractions. Open May 1 to end of September; 100 sites.

Provincetown Dining

Napi's, 7 Freeman Street, 487-1145. Excellent cuisine—eclectic continental and American—in an elegant place. Open all year. Expensive.

The Red Inn, 15 Commercial Street, 487-0050. Good food three times a day. Superb views of Cape Cod Bay. Open all year. Inexpensive to moderate.

Cafe Heaven, 199 Commercial Street, 487-9639. A storefront eatery with an extensive selection. Lots of hamburger creations at dinner. Open year-around; weekends only in off-season. Moderate.

Fat Jack's, 335 Commercial Street, 487-4822. Storefront dining with a casual ambience. Open breakfast to dinner. Closed in December. Inexpensive.

Post Office Cafe, 303 Commercial Street, 487-3892. Casual dining from breakfast to dinner. Popular spot with sandwiches to full dinners. Closed mid-January to mid-February. Inexpensive.

Tip for Tops'n Restaurant, 31 Bradford Street, 487-1811. A family restaurant since 1967. Portugese specialties and seafood. Breakfast until 3:00 P.M. Seasonal. Inexpensive.

Bubala's by the Bay, 183 Commercial Street, 487-0773. Open for breakfast, lunch, and dinner. Eclectic menu. Has outdoor dining in season. Seasonal. Inexpensive to moderate.

The Moors, Bradford Street, West Provincetown, 487-0840. Portuguese specialties: Espada Cozida, a marinated, grilled swordfish; Galinha a moda da Madeira, chicken breast sautéed with herbs in a Madeira wine sauce; and Bife Portuguese, beef tournedos rubbed with garlic and spices, topped with smoked ham, then grilled. Live entertainment in the lounge. Seasonal. Moderate.

Dancing Lobster at Wharf, 371 Commercial Street, 487-0670. One of Provincetown's finest gourmet restaurants. Many unusual dishes such as zuppa di pesce and steak Budapest. Panoramic views of the harbor and Cape Cod Bay. Open May to October. Expensive.

The Lobster Pot, 321 Commercial Street, near the wharf, 487-0842. Great seafood, very casual. In summer, an outside deck overlooking the water. Open year-round. Moderate.

Martin House, 157 Commercial Street, 487-1327. The 1750 home of a sea captain, the restaurant features New England fare. Offers daily brunch. Open year-round. Moderate.

The Mews, 429 Commercial Street, 487-1500. Continental specialties— veal Pomidori and seafood Cataplana—served in a casual environment overlooking boats bobbing in the harbor. Open mid-February to mid-November. Expensive.

Sal's Place, 99 Commercial Street, 487-1279. Northern Italian cuisine served on the water. Open April to October. Moderate to expensive.

Cafe Blase, 328 Commercial Street, 487-9465. Gourmet pizza and burgers, quiche, seafood, fancy sandwiches, and Italian coffees. Sidewalk dining. Seasonal. Inexpensive to moderate.

I N D E X

craftspersons, 103
dining, 206–7
general information, 203–5
historic homes, 133
libraries, 93

U

U.S. Coast Guard, 39

W

Walks, best of Cape, 69–73
Wampanoags, 6–7
Weather information, 24
Web site, 27–28
Wellfleet
    accommodations, 202
    art galleries, 97
    beaches of, 50
    craftspersons, 103
    dining, 202–3
    general information, 200–202
    historic homes, 133
    libraries, 93
Wellfleet Bay Wildlife Sanctuary, 122
Whale-watching, listing of cruises for,
    84
Whales, 85
Whydah Museum, 208
Wildlife sanctuaries, 121

Windsurfing, 81
Wineries, 104
Woods Hole
    accommodations, 151–52
    dining, 152
Woods Hole Historical Museum, 116
Woods Hole Oceanographic Exhibit
    Center, 116

Y

Yarmouth
    accommodations
        South Yarmouth/Bass River,
            175–76
        West Yarmouth, 173–74
        Yarmouthport, 177
    beaches of, 48
    craftspersons, 98–100
        West Yarmouth, 100
        Yarmouthport, 100
    dining
        South Yarmouth/Bass River,
            176
        West Yarmouth, 174–75
        Yarmouthport, 177–78
    general information, 172–73
    historic homes, 128–29
    libraries, 92

About the Author

JERRY MORRIS writes and edits for the Sunday Travel section of the *Boston Globe*. A former resident of Cape Cod, he lives in Rhode Island.

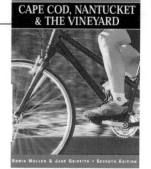